KU-141-765

University of Wales College, Newport
School of Social Studies
Allt-yr-yn Campus, P.O. Box 180
Newport, South Wales
NP20 5XR

Rethinking What Works with Offenders

Rethinking What Works with Offenders

Probation, Social Context and Desistance from Crime

Stephen Farrall

WILLAN
PUBLISHING

Published by

Willan Publishing
Culmcott House
Mill Street, Uffculme
Cullompton, Devon
EX15 3AT, UK
Tel: +44(0)1884 840337
Fax: +44(0)1884 840251
e-mail: info@willanpublishing.co.uk
Website: www.willanpublishing.co.uk

Published simultaneously in the USA and Canada by

Willan Publishing
c/o ISBS, 5824 N.E. Hassalo St,
Portland, Oregon 97213-3644, USA
Tel: +001(0)503 287 3093
Fax: +001(0)503 280 8832
e-mail: info@isbs.com
Website: www.isbs.com

© Stephen Farrall

The right of Stephen Farrall to be identified as the author of this book has been asserted by
him in accordance with the Copyright, Designs and Patents Act of 1988.

All rights reserved; no part of this publication may be reproduced, stored in a retrieval
system, or transmitted in any form or by any means, electronic, mechanical,
photocopying, recording or otherwise without the prior written permission of the
Publishers or a licence permitting copying in the UK issued by the Copyright Licensing
Agency Ltd, 90 Tottenham Court Road, London W1P 9HE.

First published 2002

ISBN 1-903240-95-6

British Library Cataloguing-in-Publication Data

A catalogue record for this book is available from the British Library

Typeset by TW Typesetting, Plymouth, Devon
Printed and bound by TJ International Ltd, Trecerus Industrial Estate, Padstow,
Cornwall, PL28 8RW

Contents

Tables and figures

Tables

Figures

Acknowledgements

Numerous people assisted in the lumbering development of both the fieldwork and the analysis. In helping to smooth the transition from 'research design' to a 'workable project', management staff in each of the probation services from which the cases were recruited played an essential part. I would like to express my immense thanks to all the following for their invaluable assistance in helping to set up the project: Mike Frost, Rachel Murphy and Ros Harper (Middlesex Probation Service); Chris Wheeler (Wiltshire Probation Service); Imogen Brown (West Yorkshire Probation Service); Gerry Marshall, Steve Stanley and Pauline Durrance (Inner London Probation Service); John Budd and Martin Wargeant (Essex Probation Service); and Christine Knott, Andrew Underdown and Linsey Poole (Greater Manchester Probation Service).

Senior and main-grade probation officers played an especially important part in enabling the research to be completed: not only were they interviewed themselves, but they recruited probationers into the study and often went to extraordinary lengths to assist the efforts made to trace and secure interviews with probationers. The fieldwork could not have been completed without the assistance of all those working in field offices and it is a testament to the work of probation services that, in addition to their already burdensome workload, staff found time to return calls, arrange interviews and deal with the day-to-day running of a project of this size and nature. Those working in other sectors of the criminal justice system – most notably in prisons and hostels – must also be thanked for their efforts in helping to secure interviews with probationers.

At the Probation Studies Unit (PSU) and the Centre for Criminological Research (CCR) at Oxford University, Ros Burnett and Roger Hood assisted greatly in the design of the project and very much influenced the 'tone' of the research. Roger also had the thankless task of supervising me – a task which he completed with both good grace and humour despite my tendency to focus on the wrong thing or to miss the point completely. If Roger can ever bring himself to read this book again – and it would be entirely understandable if he cannot – he will notice much which is in no small part due to his own insights and approach to the topic. Similarly, Ros Burnett, Colin Roberts and Richard Young were kind enough, or felt sorry enough, to read drafts of entire chapters along the way. The thesis upon which this book is based was examined by George Mair and Carolyn Hoyle, and I thank them both for the interest with which they discussed the work and their helpful and supportive comments.

Conversations with successive generations of PSU and CCR staff were also insightful, and accordingly I thank Gwen Robinson, Kerry Baker, Giok Ong, Ilona Haslewood-Pocsik, Louise Harsent, Colin Roberts and David Faulkner for their observations on probation supervision, and Richard Young, Carolyn Hoyle, Kimmett Edgar, Ian O'Donnell, Ben Goold, Catherine Appleton, Aidan Wilcox and Carol Martin for their observations on a number of topics ranging from current trends in penology to the latest developments in the football transfer market and the EU. Colleagues associated with the PSU, namely, Lady Stephanie North, Simon Merrington and Chris May, provided further comments and encouragement as a final draft was produced. Anne Worrall (at Keele University) also deserves a mention of thanks for taking the time to discuss the emergence of the National Probation Service with me. Thanks are also due to Michael Spence (at Saint Catherine's College) for arranging for the college to pay for my attendance at the British Criminology Conference in 1999 and a further conference on analysing reconviction data held at Cambridge University in the spring of 2000.

The project employed a large number of part-time research interviewers to assist with the fieldwork and I thank, in no particular order, all of the following for their efforts during the fieldwork: Jan Appleton, Tony Bullock, Angela Coster, Carol Dowling, Venetia Evergeti, Susan Hill, Amy Horwell, Jamie Kinniburgh, Stuart Lister, Sarah Maltby, Ilona Haslewood-Pocsik, Anne Reuss, Paul Andell, Ejaz Ahmed, Celia Witney, Krishna Kaur, Tom Letchner, Gareth Rees, Kathryn Smith, Rachel Condry, Dawn Gordon, Janet Lee, Lucy Spurling, Ros Harper, Pauline Durrance and Pauline Wilson.

The interviews were transcribed by a number of people. Margit Kail, Hannah Bichard and Christine Holder made excellent work of transcribing all those taped interviews I either could not find the time to do myself or simply could no longer face. Similarly, Sylvia Littlejohns and Steve Ballinger – as administrators at the Centre for Criminological Research – have provided fantastic support in dealing with the payment and travel claims generated by the fieldwork. Hannah Bichard deserves an additional special mention of thanks for getting me out of numerous computer-assisted disasters. Away from Oxford, conversations with Ben Bowling, Shadd Maruna, Sue Rex, Paul Crosland and Simon Merrington helped me to 'think about' desistance, probation supervision and – in the end – desistance *and* probation supervision.

My final thanks must naturally be to the two hundred men and women who took the time and effort to explain in detail how their time on probation and the changes in their lives had either helped or prevented them from staying out of trouble. Without their insights this book would not exist.

Stephen Farrall

Foreword

By Christine Knott
(Chief Officer, Greater Manchester Probation Area)

In this important new book Stephen Farrall explains the reasons why offenders desist from offending, using their own perspectives and accounts. In his own words, he aims to 'open probation's back box and to discover what it is about probation that works'. In its use of outcome measures, the book goes well beyond the 'blunt instrument' of reconviction and attempts to understand reoffending, rather than simply record whether it has occurred or not. Farrall contributes both to what we know about the outcomes of probation supervision and why people stop offending.

The book describes research that began in 1997 and which was jointly commissioned by six Probation Areas. The research was undertaken and published at a time of unprecedented change for the Probation Service both nationally and locally. It deals with offenders who live in some of the most deprived inner city areas in the country, to some of the more rural areas. The research identifies the common factors of poverty, unemployment, and unstable housing which are all too familiar to those of us who have spent our lives working with offenders to reduce their criminality.

Towards the end of the book, Stephen Farrall introduces the aim of 'increasing offenders' personal and social capital' as a measure of successful supervision, which in my view is exactly what cognitive behavioural programmes, basic skills courses, resolution of family conflict and improved social conditions – all of which are components of the modern community sentence – are seeking to achieve. The author's observation and description of the processes of desistance makes an important contribution to the current debates about reducing reoffending, with its heavy emphasis on targets and 'instant success'. It also emphasises the uniqueness of the contract between the probationer and the supervisor(s) in the drive to reduce and prevent reoffending.

Since the research began, inevitably, some practices have changed. There is far greater availability of groupwork programmes, now externally accredited, than when Stephen's field work commenced. However, the story behind the practice, in the way described in the book, has not changed. Note also the offenders' views that as the more involved they become in the criminal Justice system, the more pessimistic they are about their likelihood of reducing offending. It must be the aim of all of us who practice with the Criminal justice system to reverse these trends.

Practitioners will not be surprised by the findings of this research. I believe it will help all of us to improve our understanding of offenders and their interaction with probation supervision. The research highlights the importance of motivation in ensuring desistance and as such emphasises the need for Probation supervision to nurture this. There is also a coherent argument for the importance of dealing with community issues to prevent further offending – this must surely beg the question of the effectiveness of short prison sentences in reducing reoffending.

As a practitioner, rather than an academic, to me the true test of good research is its ability to inform the future as much as its ability to describe the past. In my view, Stephen Farrall has ably achieved both and the value of the findings seem even more relevant at the time of publication than when we originally identified the need for the research.

This book provides some interesting challenges to both practitioners and policy makers in the world of probation and community sentencing. I hope it serves to open up further research opportunities into some of these very important arenas. It certainly extends our evidence base, from which we draw, to make important decisions about the likes of offenders, and which could have an even greater impact on the lives of potential victims.

Christine Knott,
July 2002

Part 1
Introduction

Chapter 1

Probation, social context and desistance from crime: introducing the agenda

The purpose of this book is to explore and throw further light on the processes that occur during probation supervision which are either conducive to desistance or which contribute to further offending. Whilst it is true that the correlates of recidivism and desistance are well known, the mechanisms by which these correlates are produced and the role that criminal justice sanctions play in this remain less well understood. In order to understand better the role of probation supervision in encouraging the processes associated with desistance, the criminal careers and behaviour of 199 people made subject to probation and combination orders[1] were examined in detail. This book reports on that four-year examination.

Many of those who embark on offending careers would appear to stop at around the same time that they gain stable employment, embark upon stable life-partnerships and disengage from a delinquent peer group. On the other hand, for those convicted and sentenced, their age and gender are better predictors of their likelihood of a further conviction than the type of sentence they received. Indeed, no study has yet demonstrated conclusively that sentences have markedly different outcomes from one another in terms of rates of reconviction. There are, however, numerous disadvantages with the research methodologies employed to investigate desistance and recidivism. Studies of sentence outcomes have generally been based on official statistics, have not considered in depth the nature of the interventions undertaken, have tended to be retrospective and have not collected the views and experiences of those made subject to such disposals. Thus these studies suffer from what Shadd Maruna (2000a: 12, emphasis in original) has referred to as the 'black box' syndrome – the outcomes are known, but the precise sequence of events and processes involved in their production has been left largely unexamined: 'by concentrating

almost exclusively on the question of "what works", offender rehabilitation research has largely ignored questions of *how* rehabilitation
works, *why* it works with some clients or *why* it fails with others.'

This chapter provides the background to a project which has
attempted to open this 'black box' so as to investigate the role that
probation supervision, individual motivation and wider social and
personal circumstances play in helping some people to stop offending.
Unlike previous investigations of the impact of probation supervision,
it has aimed to bring to the evaluation some of the techniques and
styles of research developed by those investigating the progression of
criminal careers. Thus, the research has departed from the conven-
tional sources of data, types of variables collected and styles of
analyses. It has

- not therefore relied predominantly on data derived from official
  sources but has collected data directly from probationers and
  probation officers by way of face-to-face interviews;

- examined the impact of changes in the social and personal circumstances of the probationer on their offending career; and

- employed a prospective longitudinal methodology.

Its origins, therefore, lay in two key areas of criminological research:
the evaluation of criminal justice interventions and the study of the
course of criminal careers, their persistence and desistance. Both these
paradigms offer insights and set the agenda for many of the issues
investigated, but a review of each suggests that there are areas of both
where current knowledge is deficient. By addressing these deficiencies,
the project throws new light on the impact of probation supervision on
probationers' lives and on the factors conducive to their desistance
from crime.

The background

Some of the most commonly observed regularities in criminology
concern rates of offending over the course of a person's life. For
example, by the time that they had reached their thirtieth birthday,
approximately a third of the males in England and Wales born in 1953
had received a conviction for a non-motoring offence (Home Office
1995). However, only around 7 per cent had received six or more
convictions and most of those convicted had an officially recognised

criminal career which spanned no more than four years (Home Office 1995: Table 8). The peak age of conviction[2] for males in England and Wales is currently around 18 years of age (Barclay 1990; Newburn 1997; Flood-Page *et al.* 2000). This broad picture, based upon official statistics, has been supported by numerous other studies (e.g. Farrington 1992a) and by researchers collecting data in different countries (e.g. Blumstein *et al.* 1988) and during different historical eras (Gottfredson and Hirschi 1990). Taken together, the evidence suggests that whilst many people are caught offending at least once, few go on to become persistent offenders. Such is the uniformity of the relationship between age and crime that it has become one of the 'laws' of criminology, and is commonly referred to as the 'age–crime curve'. For males, the line which describes the 'age–crime curve' starts around 10 years of age (until that age, for UK males, those under 10 are below the age of criminal responsibility). The line then starts to climb rapidly until it reaches a peak around the ages of 17–19. The curve then starts to decline – steeply at first, but becoming less steep as the years progress. For females the 'curve' is different. First of all, far fewer females would appear to embark upon offending careers. However, following a climb almost as steep as the male curve, the female 'curve' quickly flattens to something approaching a plateau between 14 and 18, before declining gradually.

Given the salience of this issue for policy-makers and its role as a source of much debate in criminology, it is little wonder that the 1980s and 1990s have witnessed a continuation of the efforts of criminologists to chart the extent, contours and correlates of patterns of offending with greater sophistication and in greater detail. In particular, interest in the reasons why some people stop offending and others persist has increased rapidly since the early 1980s. This same period has also witnessed a renewed interest in the investigation of the outcomes of various court disposals – both community disposals and custodial sentences (see Lloyd *et al.* 1994; McGuire 1995). For example, Lloyd *et al.* (1994) reported that whilst 43 per cent of probationers were reconvicted within two years of the start of their orders, the proportion of those reconvicted after community service orders was even higher (49 per cent), and higher still for those given probation orders with conditions (63 per cent).

These two bodies of work represent closely related, but nevertheless subtly different paradigms. One – referred to here as the criminal career paradigm – has charted the incidence and patterns of offending across the life spans of numerous cohorts of members of the general population. Such cohorts are followed from a young age for several years, often decades, and the data collected are usually based on interviews with cohort members or others involved in their lives (such as parents, teachers, social workers or peers). Official data relating to offending are frequently used to supplement and validate such reports. Although this paradigm has relied on quantitative research methods, it has not precluded the use of qualitative data sets.

The second paradigm – measuring the effectiveness of attempts by the criminal justice system to reduce such behaviour – has followed up those persons found guilty and sentenced to some form of punishment. These follow-ups often last no longer than two years, although in some instances follow-up periods of five or seven years have been recorded. This paradigm has relied – to the virtual exclusion of all other methodologies – on official records which have been analysed quantitatively (e.g. Lloyd *et al.* 1994).

The criminal career paradigm

Research by criminologists such as Sheldon and Eleanor Glueck, Alfred Blumstein, Marvin Wolfgang and Thorsten Sellin in the USA and David Farrington in the UK has suggested that whether or not an individual participates in offending is closely associated with his or her age and a number of social and psychological variables. For example, Farrington (1992b: 129) listed some of the variables found to be most strongly related to offending in the Cambridge Study in Delinquent Development – a follow-up study of over four hundred boys originally living in London. Included were 'problematic' behaviours between 8 and 14-years-old (e.g. bullying, lying and aggressiveness), teenage anti-social behaviours (e.g. heavy alcohol, tobacco use, gambling and frequent sexual activity), impulsiveness, school problems (e.g. low school attainment, frequent truancy and failure to take examinations), family factors (e.g. poor child rearing and supervision, and poor relationship with parents), anti-social factors (e.g. convictions of other family members and friends) and socioeconomic factors (low family income, poor housing and poor employment record). Several of these influences have also been found by other researchers to be associated with the onset of offending behaviours (see, for example, Graham and Bowling 1995: 33–43; also Wolfgang *et al.* 1972; Sampson and Laub 1993; Elliott and Menard 1996). The data employed in studies of this nature have usually been derived from repeated interviews with members of cohorts, often followed from school age to adulthood. During these interviews, self-reported data on offending and various other topics have been collected from the cohort members. As noted, these data are often supplemented by official records and further interviews with partners, peers and teachers in order to gain these perspectives as well as to validate responses.[3]

A number of researchers have focused their attention specifically upon the later stages of offending careers, and in particular on the factors conducive to desistance from offending. Drawing on the insights of earlier work on criminal careers, they have pointed to a number of correlates of desistance. The literature on desistance is commonly based on criminal career data sets (e.g. Knight and West 1975; Loeber *et al.* 1991; Sampson and Laub 1993), or on one-off retrospective research (e.g. Shover 1983; Cusson and Pinsonneault 1986; Graham and Bowling 1995). In a few cases (e.g. Burnett 1992; Leibrich 1993) data have been collected by following the careers of persons after they have been made subject to criminal justice interventions.[4] The research undertaken so far has shed light on the role of social and personal factors in desistance (see Adams 1997; Farrall 2000; Laub and Sampson 2001, for outlines of this body of work).

The factors associated with desistance

A number of researchers (e.g. Uggen and Kruttschnitt 1998: 356) have provided evidence that desistance is associated with gaining employment, although the precise causal links between engaging in legitimate employment and desistance from offending have yet to be satisfactorily established. Mischkowitz (1994: 313) reported that 'erratic work patterns were substituted by more stable and reliable behaviour' amongst his sample of desisters. Meisenhelder (1977) noted that the acquisition of a good job provided the men in his sample with important social and economic resources, whilst Shover (1983: 214) reported how a job generated '. . . a pattern of routine activities – a daily agenda – which conflicted with and left little time for the daily activities associated with crime'.

Similar sentiments were expressed by Sampson and Laub (1993: 220–22) when they wrote that desisters were characterised as having '. . . good work habits and were frequently described as "hard workers" '. Farrington *et al.* (1986: 351), reporting on the Cambridge Study in Delinquent Development, wrote that 'proportionally more crimes were committed by . . . youths during periods of unemployment than during periods of employment', a finding supported by the later work of Horney *et al.* (1995). However, as researchers such as Ditton (1977) and Henry (1978) have shown, full-time employment does not preclude either the opportunities to offend nor actual offending.

Graham and Bowling (1995: 56, Table 5.2) found that for young males employment was not related to desistance, as did Rand (1987) when she investigated the impact of vocational training on criminal careers.

Another of the most common findings in the literature on desistance is that individuals cease to offend at about the same time that they start to form significant life-partnerships (e.g. Chylicki 1992). One of the clearest statements in support of this line of reasoning came from Shover (1983: 213), who wrote that 'The establishment of a mutually satisfying relationship with a woman was a common pattern [and] an important factor in the transformation of their career line'. Cusson and Pinsonneault (1986: 79–80) and Mischkowitz (1994: 319) followed West (1982: 101–104) in arguing that what was important (in terms of facilitating desistance) was not marriage *per se*, but rather the *quality* of the relationship and the offending career of the person whom the would-be desister married. The recent work of Laub *et al.* (1998) supports this contention – as marriages became stronger amongst the men in their sample, so these men's offending began to be curtailed. A number of studies have suggested that the experience of becoming a parent is also associated with desistance from offending (see, for example, Irwin 1970: 203; Parker 1976: 41; Trasler 1979: 315; Caddle 1991: 37; Leibrich 1993: 59; Sampson and Laub 1993: 218; Hughes 1997, 1998: 146; Uggen and Kruttschnitt 1998: 355; Jamieson *et al.* 1999: 130).

Despite the evidence suggesting that forming a life-partnership may result in desistance, some researchers have questioned this rather simple cause-and-effect model.[5] Rand (1987: 137) tested the hypothesis that '. . . young men who marry are less criminal than those who never marry' and found no support for this in her data. Knight *et al.* (1977: 359) found no significant differences (in terms of the number of subsequent convictions) between the married and unmarried groups from the Cambridge Study in Delinquent Development. Similarly, Mulvey and Aber (1988) reported finding no connection between partnership and desistance, nor were they able to find any firm link between parenthood and desistance. Rand (1987: 143) also found no support for the idea that men who became fathers were less criminal than those who did not.

However, at least some of these negative findings can be reassessed following the findings of Uggen (2000) and Ouimet and Le Blanc (1996), which suggest that the impact of various life events upon an individual's offending is age-graded. For example, Ouimet and Le Blanc (1996: 92) suggest that it is only from around the mid-20s that cohabitation with a woman was associated with desistance for the males in their sample. In a similar vein, Uggen (2000: 542) suggests that work appears to be a turning point in the criminal careers of those offenders aged over 26, whilst it has a marginal effect on the offending of younger offenders. When findings like these are taken into consideration, the importance of structuring the inquiry by age is made apparent. However, many of the earlier studies concerning the factors associated with desistance were unaware of this caveat and, as such, their findings that there was no impact of employment or partnership on desistance must be treated accordingly.[6]

Various other factors have been identified which appear to be related to desistance. Amongst members of the Cambridge Study in Delinquent Development cohort, Osborn (1980) found that leaving London (where they had grown up) was associated with reductions in subsequent offending (both self-reported and official). Similar findings using alternative data sets have been made by Sampson and Laub (1993: 217) and Jamieson *et al.* (1999: 133). The break-up of the peer group has been another, and more commonly, cited factor. Knight and West (1975: 49) and Cromwell *et al.* (1991: 83) both referred to cases in which peer group disintegration was related to subsequent desistance (as did Warr 1998). Experiencing a shift in identity (Meisenhelder 1982; Shover 1983: 210; Burnett 1992; Maruna 1997, 2000b) and feeling shame at one's past behaviours (Leibrich 1993: 204, 1996) have also been posited as processes associated with desistance.

An individual's motivation to avoid further offending is another key factor in accounting for desistance. West (1978), Shover (1983), Shover and Thompson (1992), Moffitt (1993), Sommers *et al.* (1994) and Pezzin (1995) have all pointed to a range of factors which motivated the desisters in their samples. Burnett (1992: 66, 1994: 55–56) has suggested that those ex-prisoners who reported that they wanted to stop offending and, importantly, felt they were able to stop offending, were more likely to desist than those who said they were unsure if they wanted to stop offending.

Others have pointed to the influence of the criminal justice system on those repeatedly incarcerated. Cusson and Pinsonneault (1986), employing data drawn from in-depth interviews with ex-robbers, identified the following as influential factors in desisting: shock (such as being wounded in a bank raid); growing tired of doing time in prison; becoming aware of the possibility of longer prison terms; and a reassessment of what was important to the individual. Similar findings have been made by other researchers. Shover (1983: 213), Cromwell *et al.* (1991: 83) and Leibrich (1993: 56–7) reported that desisters experienced a period of re-evaluation before coming to their decision to desist. Within a perspective heavily influenced by rational choice models, Shover and Thompson (1992: 97) wrote that '. . . the probability of desistance from criminal participation increases as expectations for achieving friends, money, autonomy and happiness via crime decrease'. Hughes' (1998) study of ethnic minority desisters living in the USA reported how fear of serious physical harm and/or death was cited by 16 of her 20 respondents. Similar fears were reported by those interviewed by Cusson and Pinsonneault (1986) and Sommers *et al.* (1994), and amongst Maruna's (1997) study of published autobiographies of desistance.

Work by Meisenhelder (1977: 323) and others (e.g. Shover 1983: 212; Burnett 1992; Hughes 1998: 147) has revealed that some of those repeatedly incarcerated say that they have become tired of prison and feel that they can no longer cope physically and emotionally with the experiences of prison life. In effect, some offenders reach a point in their lives when they can 'take no more' from the criminal justice system 'burn out'.

Very few of the investigations undertaken so far have considered female desisters. Graham and Bowling's (1995) was one study which did. They found that the processes leading to desistance for men and women appeared to be quite different. For women, becoming 'an adult' (e.g. leaving home, finishing schooling and starting a family) was related to desistance. Yet, the same was not true for men. As this study was not longitudinal and as all respondents were aged 15–25 years old, it is hard to assess the significance of this finding. It could be due to males needing longer to mature – so that if older males had been included in the sample, the gender differences in the processes of desistance may have been less pronounced – or it could be that the processes of desistance for males and females actually *are* quite different. A similar study by the Home Office which extended the upper age limit to 30 (Flood-Page *et al.* 2000) has since suggested that males *do* need longer to desist, but it did not comment on the processes of desistance for older males and females. However, the factors associated with female desistance from 'street crime' (as reported by Sommers *et al.* 1994) were very similar to those reported in studies of male 'street offenders' (e.g. Shover 1983; Cusson and Pinsonneault 1986; Cromwell *et al.* 1989). This could, however, be due to the similarities in desistance from such *crimes*, rather than *gender* similarities. Similarly, there are few studies which have sought to investigate the relationship between desistance and race (however, see Rand 1987; Elliott 1994; Hughes 1997, 1998).[7]

Whilst the effects of prison on the processes of desistance have been well documented, this body of literature has had little to say about the impact of probation on criminal careers and desistance. To this end, the role of probation supervision in helping probationers to desist has barely been touched upon by those interested in the development of criminal careers. This book now 'plugs' that gap.

In summary, the desistance literature has pointed to a range of factors associated with the ending of active involvement in offending. Most of these factors are related to acquiring 'something' (most commonly employment, a life partner or a family) which the desister values in some way and which initiates a re-evaluation of his or her life, and for some a sense of who they 'are'. Others have pointed to the criminal justice system (in most cases, imprisonment) as eventually exerting an influence on those repeatedly incarcerated. This body of work suggests that any attempts to investigate the impact of probation on offending careers needs also to consider the role of various social processes, namely, employment, marriage, ageing and so on. However, the literature on desistance has often not paid sufficient attention to criminal justice interventions, and in an attempt to redress this imbalance, this study has tried to chart the processes of desistance following one of the commonest criminal justice interventions – probation.[8]

The contribution of research concerning the outcomes of specific criminal justice interventions

The second research paradigm relates to the effects of specific criminal justice interventions on subsequent offending. Whilst the work of Cusson and Pinsonneault, Shover, Meisenhelder and Cromwell *et al.* has elucidated the phenomenon of 'burn out' following repeated incarceration, these investigations have relied upon small samples and have not been able to control for several key variables, such as previous criminal histories or age. The published literature on the outcomes of prison, probation, parole and so on is vast, and accordingly only the most salient findings will be reviewed here, in particular those which relate to probation.

Initial investigations were concerned chiefly with outlining the general patterns in the usage of probation, and devoted considerable attention to describing which offenders (in terms of their age, gender and criminal history) were made subject to probation supervision (e.g. Radzinowicz 1958: 12–13; Barr and O'Leary 1966: 9). As part of this initial period of investigation, trends in the rates of 'success' and 'failure' started to emerge. For example, Radzinowicz (1958:

2) reported that 79 per cent of adults, but slightly fewer juveniles (73 per cent), successfully completed their orders. As few of the studies during this initial period considered probationers outside the 17–21-year-old age range, the impact of age on rates of success and failure was rarely commented upon. However, later studies have found age to be one of the best predictors of reconviction, especially for males (Phillpotts and Lancucki 1979).

The gender of the probationer was, however, more commonly noted to be associated with probation outcomes. For example, Radzinowicz (1958: 23) reported that 19 per cent of males placed on probation, but only 8 per cent of women, had their orders terminated following a further offence whilst still on probation. This finding was supported by the work of Folkard *et al.* (1966: 56) and Barr and O'Leary (1966: 14) and remains as salient today (Lloyd *et al.* 1994: 26; Oldfield 1996: 41; May 1999). Another commonly observed factor associated with failure was the number of previous convictions. As early as Radzinowicz's pioneering study (1958: 7), the relationship between failure on probation and the number of previous convictions an individual had received had been observed. Like Radzinowicz, Phillpotts and Lancucki (1979: 18, Table 3.4) and later Lloyd *et al.* (1994: 27–32) found that those with more previous convictions, a higher number of previous guilty appearances at court, a faster rate of guilty court appearances and a higher number of previous custodial experiences were all more likely to be reconvicted regardless of the penalty imposed.

However, whilst the correlates of reconviction had been identified, there appeared to be little evidence that probation-based interventions could do very much to lower the possibility of offending once these variables had been taken into account. Folkard *et al.* (1974, 1976) reported on one of the most ambitious research projects on probation outcomes ever undertaken. Using experimental and control groups they attempted to study the relative effectiveness of different treatment methods (chiefly, 'control' or 'support') for different types of probationers (neurotics and extraverts) who were in different situations (delinquent or stressful). Despite the rigour with which the study was designed and the theoretical support for such an approach, they found no statistically significant differences between the experimental or control groups in terms of their rates of reconviction. This finding appeared to hold across different probation areas, over time, gender, officer assessments and probationer's degree of neuroticism (Folkard *et al.* 1976: 14–19).

Some indications of the processes involved in mediating probation outcomes were uncovered, however. For example, Folkard *et al.* (1966)

found statistically significant differences for the following variables when outcomes were compared: good rapport between officer and probationer and keeping the same officer were related to successful outcomes, whilst a high level of control exercised over the probationer was related to failure (ibid.: 56). Similarly, Davies (1969) found a number of variables, such as high job turnover, peer group influence and general hostility towards probation work, to be related to failure. More recently May (1999) investigated the role played by social factors in reconviction amongst a sample of probationers. He found that those living in unstable accommodation, without employment, with a drug problem, and with literacy and learning problems were more likely to be reconvicted (ibid.: 16–20). However, May could find no relationship between alcohol use or financial problems and reconviction (ibid.: 18–19). The number of problems experienced by probationers also increased their chances of reconviction (ibid.: 21). In more complex analyses, May reported that probationers who had experienced *all* the following problems – accommodation, alcohol, drugs and employment – were more likely to be reconvicted (ibid.: 32–34).

Two features distinguish the recent and ongoing work in this field from the earlier studies. First, there is a greater emphasis on assessing the outcome of cognitive-behavioural interventions. Secondly, the development of day centres, group work programmes and other specified activities has meant that research has focused upon assessing the outcomes of these particular probation interventions rather than 'generic' probation (for example, see Mair and Nee 1992 who studied day centre reconviction rates,[9] Brownlee 1995 on intensive probation[10] in Leeds, and Wilkinson 1997 on the Idlerton motor car project run by Inner London Probation Service). These interventions were 'time-limited' and often did not cover the whole period of probation and, as such, did not develop a picture of the *whole* probation order from beginning to end.

McGuire and Priestly (1995: 16) have argued that models of intervention based on cognitive and behavioural psychology have emerged as 'offering the most encouraging approaches'. They have suggested that teaching probationers new styles of thinking and acting will help them to avoid the situations and temptations which had previously led them to offend. These approaches include techniques such as reinforcement (Lawson 1983); covert punishment (Guidry 1975); mentoring (O'Donnell *et al.* 1979, see also Hughes 1997); behaviour modification (Bank *et al.* 1987); relaxation (Hazaleus and Deffenbacher 1986); social skills training (Priestly *et al.* 1984); and training in moral reasoning (McDougall *et al.* 1987).

Lipsey (1995), employing a meta-analysis of interventions aimed specifically at juvenile delinquents, suggested that treatments which focused on employment, behaviour modification, gaining skills or which were multi-modal (that is to say, interventions which attempt to address a range of issues) produced the greatest effects on the future conduct of juveniles (ibid.: 75). This line of thinking was echoed by Lsel (1995: 91) when he wrote that 'it is mostly cognitive-behavioural, skilled orientated and multi-modal programmes that yield the best effects'.

Palmer (1996: 139) concluded that vocational training and other interventions aimed at providing probationers with employment were found to have some impact on rates of recidivism. Educational training was also reported to have had positive effects (ibid.: 140), as were behavioural interventions; cognitive-behavioural approaches; life skills (which included outdoor activities as well as education and social skills development); and – again – multi-modal approaches (ibid.: 141–43).

Thus, to sum up: the investigation of the outcomes of criminal justice interventions has found that, in general, younger males have been the group most likely to be reconvicted. Their chances of reconviction are increased still further the greater their previous criminal history. Various other factors, such as poor employment history, being easily influenced by a peer group or being hostile to probation, serve only to increase reconviction and failure rates. The more recent literature – of which more presently – has repeatedly pointed to cognitive-behavioural techniques, skills training, moral reasoning, employment schemes and multi-modal interventions as being those methods of intervention that are most likely to be associated with reduced rates of reconviction.

Opening the 'black box' of probation supervision

However, few of the studies have attempted to unpack the 'black box' of criminal justice interventions. It is therefore very hard to say definitively *why* any of these observed relationships exist or *how* they operated. Notable exceptions exist, however. Burnett's (1992) study investigated the processes by which a group of property offenders recently released from prison managed either to desist or continued to offend. When compared to those who persisted, desisters in Burnett's study were found to have been more motivated to avoid further offending, to have secured better post-release employment careers, more of them were in stable accommodation and more of them rated their personal relationships as good (ibid.: 71–81). Leibrich (1993) undertook a follow-up of those sentenced to probation and not reconvicted within three years and found that responding to new family commitments, desires for a better future and the development of self-respect were cited as the reasons for wishing to desist (ibid.: 56–60). These studies have shown the important roles played by social and individual processes as former prisoners and probationers attempt to avoid further offending.

Summarising what is known about the correlates of crime cessation

From these two bodies of work it is possible to sketch an outline of what is known about the factors associated with the later stages of criminal careers. Despite differences in the data sets which they have employed and the variables on which they have focused, some uniform findings have emerged. For example, older people have been consistently found to be less likely to reoffend, as are those who start to offend later in life and those with less extensive criminal careers. Another commonly observed finding concerns employment. Gaining 'good' or stable employment has been found to be related to stopping offending. Similarly, unemployment, irregular employment or poor employment records are associated with higher rates of persistence. The break-up of the peer group has also been cited as being related to desistance by both those researching criminal careers and the outcomes of criminal justice interventions.

However, there remain some findings which are unique to each paradigm. For example, family formation, the break-up of the peer group and feeling 'worn out' by the criminal justice system have all been cited by criminal career researchers but have not been subject to thorough investigations by those studying the outcomes of criminal justice sentences (although see Burnett 1992). Similarly, as previously stated, criminal career research has yet fully to develop an understanding of the impact of community penalties on criminal careers.

Perhaps this lack of uniformity in findings is to be expected. Despite their very similar areas of concern (how and why people avoid further offending), the criminal career and intervention-outcome paradigms are very different in several respects. Criminal career research has employed a different methodology (relying in the main upon self-reported data rather than solely on data from official sources) and has focused upon a different set of variables (for example, those related to school leaving, marriage and child-rearing). Research on the outcomes of particular sentences has relied almost entirely on officially recorded convictions and focused upon a much narrower range of variables (such as age at first conviction, previous disposals and type of intervention by the criminal justice system).

These, then, are the two bodies of literature from which our knowledge in this field is derived. On one hand is the criminal career research and in particular, that which focuses upon the cessation of offending – a relatively small corpus of work and thus far with little to say on the topic of probation supervision. On the other hand is the much larger literature which deals with the outcomes of criminal sentences. This literature is hampered by its reliance upon official data and – not totally unrelated to this – its concentration upon criminal history variables. This reliance upon official data sources has prevented this body of work from unpacking the 'black box' of probation supervision.

A research agenda

What was required, therefore, was a project which would focus upon patterns of persistence and desistance and which would specifically take account of the impact on these of probation supervision and the role of social circumstances, attitudes, personal relationships and the motivation and behaviour of the probationer concerned. Such a research project would need to bring to probation research some of the methods of research, styles of analysis and theoretical perspectives employed by those interested in criminal careers. By seeking to locate probation supervision in the context of the probationer's own personal and social circumstances, such a research project would illuminate the extent to which the aims, work and practices of probation intervention were mediated, reinforced or negated by the wider lives of those on probation and their attitude to their supervision. It would also serve to introduce to criminal career research the role played by community penalties in shaping patterns of offending in the short term, a subject which has hitherto been rarely examined by criminal career researchers. Since the original inception of the project in 1996, others have echoed the need for research of this nature:

'The shortcomings of both [the criminal career and "what works"] research literatures might be addressed by combining the methodological and substantive insights of desistance research of those of the rehabilitation literature' (Maruna 2000a: 13).

By asking officers and probationers to discuss probation supervision in the context of the probationer's personal and social circumstances, and by tracking the progress of probationers over time through repeated interviews, such a project would illuminate how officers and probationers understand and perceive:

- probation supervision;

- the probationer's wider circumstances;

- the relationship between these two; and

- their combined impact on risk factors and subsequent offending behaviour.

More specifically, the aims of the research were to:

- Investigate the specific obstacles which officers and probationers perceived as standing in the way of the probationer desisting, and to track, over time, how both the officer and probationer responded to such obstacles.

- Identify those aspects of probation supervision and the probationers' own circumstances which officers and probationers perceived to be key factors in motivating and assisting the probationer to avoid further offending.

- Explore the role of events (such as changes in home life, employment situation and area of residence) and changes in beliefs and motivation amongst those under supervision, and the extent to which these were perceived as reinforcing, negating or mediating the impact of probation supervision and offending behaviour.

- Contrast the views of the officer and probationer with regards to the probation work undertaken during the order and the probationer's response to this work.

Whilst there have been numerous investigations which have relied upon accounts of probation practice from the perspectives of either officers or probationers[11] or which have relied upon recorded information pertaining to the work undertaken with probationers (e.g. Lloyd *et al.* 1994), what was required was a project which would compare officers' and probationers' accounts of their work together. Data were collected so as to enable the comparison of their accounts of the probationer's offending, the obstacles to desisting which he or she was believed to face, how these were addressed during the order, the extent to which supervision was believed to have helped the probationer overcome such obstacles and how this was related to desistance or persistence in offending careers. The extent to which officers and probationers agreed over these matters was also investigated. By incorporating a longitudinal element into the project, shifts over time in perceptions and awareness were recorded and, in this respect, the project represented another departure from the probation studies referred to – most of which were 'static' investigations of probation supervision.[12]

'Tracking progress on probation'

In order to understand the role of probation supervision in helping people to stop offending and to locate these efforts within wider social and personal contexts, an innovative project, aimed at tracking changes in probationers' social circumstances, motivation to desist, and experience of supervision over the period of their probation order, was undertaken. The project recruited 199 probationers in six different probation services and followed them and their supervising officers through the course of their probation orders.[13] The remainder of this chapter outlines the way in which the project, which became known as 'Tracking Progress on Probation', sought to achieve these objectives. The rationale behind the data collection process, the manner and style of analysis, and general tenor of the research are outlined and discussed. This, then, was the 'mind-set' with which the project was approached.

A critique of current data sources

Officially collected data sets have formed a very large part of the materials used to evaluate probation outcomes (e.g. Barr and O'Leary 1966; Simon 1971; Oldfield 1996). These records have usually been based on officers' case notes or other official records of reconviction (such as the Home Office's Offenders Index). As such, these data tend to be concerned chiefly with the sorts of information that large administrative bodies routinely collate. For example, Radzinowicz (1958) related outcomes to the age and gender of the probationer, previous court disposals, requirements of the current probation order and the reasons for the termination of the order. Reliance upon official data sources has dominated probation research ever since. For example, in 1994 Lloyd *et al.* published their critical analysis which compared the officially recorded convictions of over 18,000 people sentenced to probation or prison. Following the Lloyd *et al.* study and in part inspired by it, Oldfield published his analysis of probation in Kent (1996). Like the study he wished to emulate, Oldfield relied exclusively upon official data sources (in his case local probation records).

However, official data sources severely limit the nature of the analyses undertaken. Although data relating to the courses completed by the probationer during the probation order and the eventual outcome of the order (completed successfully, terminated early for good progress or breached) are available, it cannot be guaranteed that all information relevant to assessing the impact of the order will have been recorded. For example, how did the probationer respond to the order? Did the probationer actually employ any new techniques for avoiding offending which were learnt during the order? Did the probationer really stop offending or just avoid detection? What were the probationer's views on the input he or she received from the probation service? Without examining individual case records, questions of this nature are very hard to answer using official data sources, and yet absolutely essential to a full evaluation of the impact of a probation order.

In addition, reliance upon official data sources can lead to a rather uncritical approach to case files. The case file, into which officers write notes of contacts with a probationer, the topics they discussed together and other relevant matters, is a record of the interactions between the officer and the probationer. However, the case file records the perspective of only the officer. The probationer's experiences and interpretation of probation may not have been recorded in sufficient detail to allow for meaningful research into this matter to be based on such records. Furthermore, probationers can play a crucial role in terms of what is recorded – for example, by concealing things which are not in their interests for the officer to know. One probationer interviewed as part of the 'Tracking' project said of his own case file:

> If I tell [my officer] that I'm likely to offend, he'll note it in his files. If I then *do* offend and go back to court, they'll see that high risk assessment and give me prison. So, I'm not worried about getting caught, I'm worried about what is written in the file (PR094).

Thus the reliance on official records limits the analyses undertaken solely to those topics about which information is routinely collected.[14]

Furthermore, this reliance ignores the fact that official probation records are based upon a complex series of interactions between the officer and probationer, which may conceal issues relevant to the eventual outcome of the order.

On the occasions when data have been collected from probationers themselves, the data have usually been elicited by officers during their routine interviews with probationers rather than by independent researchers (e.g. Davies 1969) or via restrictive 'tick box' question-naires, which do not always allow for expansions or explanations on the answers given. Indeed, data collected in these ways have rarely shed much light on the processes involved in the probation interven-tion, or upon how this intervention has impacted upon the probationer. There remains, of course, the real possibility that probationers for various reasons conceal certain aspects of their lives or offending from their officer, which in turn raises the issue of the validity of the material collated in official records (see, for example, the quote from the probationer above).

What was required, then, was data collected via an alternative method, or series of methods. The research sought to assess the impact of probation supervision by asking probationers in detail about the extent to which they found probation had made a useful contribution to their lives. Further light would be shed upon the processes and outcomes of probation supervision by asking probationers what they had learnt whilst on probation, whether they felt it had helped them to avoid further trouble or alleviated particular problems which they had faced. The project therefore collected data from both those on proba-tion and the probation officer supervising them. This strategy enabled reports of actual behaviours by both the probationer and officer to be recorded and ensured that both the professional judgement of the officer and the views and opinions of the probationer were collected.

Self-reported data

Of course, the reliance upon official data sources has meant that the measurement of offending behaviours is limited to *recorded* offending, rather than *actual* offending. The use of reconviction as a measure of outcome has been debated on numerous occasions over the years (see, in particular, Hood and Sparks 1970; Lloyd *et al.* 1994; Mair *et al.* 1997).[15] Generally, the outcome of the probation intervention is measured by how many people are reconvicted of a further offence within a set period of time (usually two years after the start of the order).

There have been several attempts to add variety to the nature of this outcome measure. Some have used length of time to reconviction instead of the simple reconvicted/not reconvicted dichotomy (e.g. Mair and Nee 1992; Lloyd *et al.* 1994, Brownlee 1995; Oldfield 1996). Others have attempted to measure the seriousness of reconviction by either assessing whether the offence for which the person was reconvicted was more or less serious than previous convictions, or by considering the severity of the disposal at reconviction, the assumption being that more serious offences receive more severe sentences (e.g. Mair and Nee 1992; Lloyd *et al.* 1994; Raynor and Vanstone 1997). How frequently a person is subsequently reconvicted is a further variation on the theme, but this is seriously complicated by the fact that further convictions may result in custodial sentences and thus take the person 'off the street' and reduce the time 'at risk' of offending (Brownlee 1995).[16] And, in any case, all these attempts to add 'subtlety' to the matter are limited by their being based on officially recorded convictions.

Reconviction is a relatively easy variable to collect (especially as all but the most trivial convictions and sentences are recorded by the Home Office). However, since several studies have suggested that (on average) only about 2 per cent of the offences actually committed result in a conviction; this means that the data employed to measure reoffending are severely biased (see, for example, Hood and Sparks 1970: 36; Figure 1.6, Home Office 1999: 28). There is no getting away from the fact that official data on offending are a poor substitute for well validated self-reported data on reoffending. Furthermore, conviction data alone reveal virtually nothing about the probationer's motivation for offending, the sequence of events which led up to the offence, the extent to which the offence was premeditated or indeed a range of other important contextual information.

The continued use of reconviction in place of reoffending is a pragmatic rather than an ideal choice. The issue is still further complicated by the fact that not all offences are equally likely to be reported, recorded, detected, proceeded against or result in a conviction. Securing convictions for some forms of sexual offending, for example, is particularly difficult, especially so if the victim is a minor.

Self-report studies, it must be said, have their own limitations. Graham and Bowling (1995) outlined some of the most serious of these, including: respondents concealing or exaggerating their offending; biases resulting from the reliance upon household or school-based samples (which could under-sample 'serious' offenders); memory and 'telescoping' problems;[17] the finding that those who refuse to partake in such studies are more likely to be offenders; and the inclusion of 'trivial' offences which may not be appropriate for the age of the respondents.

Nevertheless, several prominent researchers (Graham and Bowling amongst them) have argued that the investigation of offending by way of self-report methodologies remains a valid technique. For example, Farrington (1989: 406) found a high degree of agreement when self-reports of offending amongst the Cambridge Study in Delinquent Development cohort were checked with official convictions and concluded that 'none of the tests of the validity ... indicated that [self-reports] were seriously invalid or that there was any serious problem of deliberate distortion or concealment' (ibid.: 409). Barnea *et al.* (1987) and Ross *et al.* (1995) have claimed that self-reported data gained from drug users are valid, although they suggest that the intervals between interviews are kept as short as possible. Weis (1986: 44), in his gargantuan review of the literature pertaining to the measurement of criminal careers, concluded that 'there is much more convergence than discrepancy in [self-report and official] representations of the phenomena'. Additionally, Sampson and Laub (1993: 52) report high levels of agreement between self, parent and teacher assessments of offending. It would appear, then, that self-reports reveal more offences than official records, and that whilst there are some problems with the methodology, these are not so great as to suggest that the method is seriously flawed. When checks of self-reports have been made, these appear to have been favourable and as such support the continued use of this approach.

However, despite these generally positive assessments of the validity of the self-report methodology, the 'Tracking' project sought to address possible biases in a number of ways. It must be said that several of the criticisms levelled at self-report methods did not, in fact, apply to the project in any case: sampling would not be undertaken at the household or school level, and as all respondents would have been convicted at least once, 'serious' offenders were more likely to have been included in the sampling frame.[18] Additionally, 'telescoping' and memory problems were reduced by seeing respondents frequently (Barnea *et al.* 1987), and non-response biases were reduced (but never fully overcome, of course) by also collecting officers' accounts of the probationer's offending. Concealment and exaggeration of offending, always hard to assess in any study, can be assessed by making checks against the officer's accounts of offending and criminal records.[19]

In addition to this, the study incorporated Elliott's (1989: 181) suggestion that detailed follow-up probes be employed to distinguish between trivial and non-trivial offences. The use of detailed follow-up probes in the current study also ensured that data pertaining to the reasons behind the probationer's offending, the events preceding the offence and other relevant material were also collected.

This study therefore collected self-reported data on offending, first hand from the probationers themselves. By recording in greater detail the nature of the offence (e.g. the background to the offence and the social context within which it occurred, the nature of the harm done to others and the extent to which the offence was planned), it was possible to assess more thoroughly the seriousness of the offending and, hence, to reduce the reliance upon disposal at reconviction as a proxy of the severity of recidivism.

Reconceptualising outcomes

The outcome of probation supervision has generally been concep-tualised as a binary variable ('success'/'failure') rather than *degrees* of success or failure. This is due, perhaps, to the reliance upon officially recorded offending, whereby people are classified as either having been reconvicted or not. This conceptualisation of outcomes has severely curtailed the work on probation outcomes, both theoretically and in terms of substantive findings. Virtually all the evaluations of probation which have been reviewed treat other outcome variables (be it officers' assessments or the nature of the termination of the order) as a dichotomy – that is to say, an outcome which is 'a success' or 'a failure' (Barr and O'Leary 1966; Phillpotts and Lancucki 1979; Lloyd *et al.* 1994). However, any reasoned consideration of the outcome of *anything*, whether it be probation or some other pursuit, leads one to realise that very few things are likely to be *either* a complete success *or* a complete failure. It is more usually the case that the outcome of a venture is a certain *degree* of success.

By conceptualising probation outcomes in this way, more accurate and subtle measurements may enable us to identify the salient factors associated with successful outcomes. Despite a further offence being committed, the probationer *may* have gained something from the order – a reduction in a harmful habit or better employment prospects. These real, beneficial, changes are 'lost' when outcomes are considered as being solely about offending and solely as a binary measure. In order to tease out these gradations of impact, rather than approaching 'success' as being the total absence of offending, the extent to which an individual was showing signs of desisting was measured. This allowed for an individual to have

23

offended during the order without immediately declaring him or her to have 'failed probation'. Success was also assessed in terms of the eradication of specific obstacles to desistance faced by the probationers.

Describing probation supervision

Very few of the studies reviewed have gone much beyond the most basic descriptions of the work undertaken by the probation officer, a point made by Hedderman (1998: 1) when she wrote 'we know little about the content of one-to-one supervision'. The character of the intervention, the sorts of topics discussed and how key problem areas in the probationer's life were tackled have not been made the subject of exhaustive research. Yet one-to-one work remains the mainstay of probation supervision. Despite the increase in the use of group-work programmes, reporting schemes and partnerships, very few (if any) probationers will complete their supervision without having been subject at some point to one-to-one supervision. Some research studies have described various projects (e.g. Wilkinson 1997) or particular court requirements (e.g. Mair and Nee 1992). Wilkinson (1997: 569) for example, described the Ilderton motoring project run by ILPS thus:

> it gives young people who have become involved in car crime a chance to pursue an enthusiasm for cars in a constructive and responsible fashion. The aim is [that] this should take place in a disciplined environment which challenges their offending. Ilderton is effectively a large garage and workshop where young people can work on cars and learn about how they function and are maintained, most of the work is done in the project where young people may work on their own cars, or restore old cars for use in 'banger' racing . . .

Whilst Wilkinson's description gives one a flavour of the programme, it remains unclear exactly which of these features of the programme are intended to be of help to those involved, were actually of help or in what ways they helped.

Mair and Nee (1992: 330) considered the impact of day centres: 'Day Centres vary from place to place in terms of the number and types of staff, the kinds of offenders accepted, the programme and courses on offer, the length of order and the opening times of centres.' The most detailed description of the sorts of activities provided is '. . . social/life skills . . . health/welfare activities, art/craft work and sport . . .' (ibid.).

As such, the descriptions of the work undertaken and the impact that this has had on probationers, their lives and patterns of offending have never been fully spelt out. Without a full appreciation of what a *particular* officer did with a *particular* probationer at a *particular* time during their supervision with regards to a *particular* problem it is hard to understand fully the processes by which officers successfully intervene in the lives of those whom they supervise. The project therefore collected data about the specific obstacles to desistance faced by each probationer, how these were dealt with and the eventual outcome(s) of these efforts.

Exploring the role of social and personal factors

If the desistance literature demonstrates anything, it is this: that people can, and regularly do, stop offending without the assistance of any of the branches of the criminal justice system. This raises the question: to what extent is desistance after intervention the result of that intervention, or the result of other social or individual processes at work?[20] Because so much of the probation literature ignores the social and personal circumstances which might influence an individual, it also ignores the possibility that it may not be probation that induced change, but rather the influence of other factor(s) – or a combination of probation and other factors. There is a certain sense of irony haunting the literature with regards to this issue. Probation is a *community* penalty, but many have neglected to include the role of 'the community' in their investigations of probation supervision. The solution to this conundrum is to locate and understand probation interventions and changes in the life of the probationer in the social and personal milieus in which they live.

Although May's study (1999) went some way towards addressing this deficiency, most studies of probation supervision have been limited to those topics about which probation services routinely collect data, namely: age; gender; attendance; length of the order; reasons for termination; and previous disposals. One of the earliest attempts to locate probation work in a wider social context was that undertaken by Davies (1969), who addressed a range of probationers' circumstances (employment, health, peer groups, home life and partnerships). Davies found that a number of these variables were related to subsequent failure on probation. For example, it was found that those with poor mental health, who lived in 'dirty' homes, had disliked their previous two jobs, were hostile or were generally 'unfriendly' towards their officer were more likely to fail their probation order. However, since then, there has been little further work in this vein. Indeed one of the most important investigations of probation supervision in the UK

(Folkard *et al.* 1974, 1976) barely referred to social and personal variables at all.

This general neglect of social and personal factors is extraordinary in view of the well established fact that there is a strong link between some forms of offending and some social and personal circumstances (see, for example, the reviews of this literature in Johnson 1979; Tarling 1993; Adams 1997; Farrington, 1997). Thus, the 'Tracking' project collected data concerning the probationer's social and personal life in order to assess the impact of such variables on the work undertaken as part of the probation order.

Research design, data collection and analysis

Very few research projects conducted into probation outcomes have employed prospective longitudinal designs; most have been retrospective, and most have been concerned with comparing the reconviction rates of probation-based disposals with, most commonly, prison and community service (e.g. Phillpotts and Lancucki 1979). Many researchers have therefore not considered changes in variables over time. For example, Radzinowicz (1958) and Davies (1969) related probation outcomes to features of the probationers' lives when they *started* probation. As such, the sorts of variables which dominated these studies include age at the start of the order, previous convictions and disposals. These variables were all 'static' – that is to say, variables that could never change during the course of a probation order. However, there is good reason to hypothesise that 'dynamic variables' relating to the probationer, such as changes in employment, marital status or drug dependency, may be related to probation outcomes (Andrews 1989).

In recent years there has been an increasing interest in the role that dynamic variables can play in explaining successful probation outcomes. Dynamic variables, by their very nature, require time in which to change. Only a longitudinal research design, which at each interview asks probationers about the sorts of problems they face, how these have changed from the time when previous interviews were conducted, how the probationer anticipates them to change in the future, and locates these in both the context of the probation order and the wider social context, can measure the effects of change in these variables and their impact on offending.

One of the results of the reliance upon official records is that most of the data available for analysis have been numerical. Indeed, it must be said that the probation research reviewed earlier relied almost exclusively upon quantitative data sets. Whilst such data sets are essential for the production of rates of reconviction, quantitative data analyses miss the *nuances* of probation work. These criticisms are part of a wider critique of quantitative research methods as they are used in generic social investigation and criminology (see, for example, Bowling 1993: 241–43). Quantitative data sets convert social processes into 'events' and ignore subtle changes in experiences or feelings (Bryman 1984).

The 'Tracking' project therefore collected data in such a way that the nuances of probation work and their relationship to outcomes could be more readily understood. This has been achieved by the use of 'open-ended' questions and the tape recording of some interviews. In addition to overcoming the deficiencies noted above, the project also employed an innovative approach to longitudinal research based on the earlier work of Burnett (1992, 2000). Most longitudinal research involves returning to respondents in order to bombard them repeatedly with similar questions about the same topics. Results over time are then compared, the aim being to draw conclusions about the causal ordering and timing of key events. Does, for example, unemployment precede offending, or offending precede unemployment? Whilst analyses of this nature have driven forward the understanding of patterns of offending over the life-course, such a style of analysis does not fully establish why, how or in what ways variables may be related to one another over time. Whilst unemployment may precede offending, it does not follow that it caused it.

Similar issues are raised when one considers the impact of probation supervision. Whilst being on probation may precede the probationer gaining full-time employment, it does not follow that it was probation supervision which directly led to the probationer gaining employment. Thus in order to establish the ways in which probation supervision impacted upon the lives of those on probation, officers and probationers were prompted to discuss specific issues which they raised at previous interviews and how and why these had changed. Through this technique, the project had the measurement of *change* built into its very heart.

Notes

1 Probation orders are now known as community rehabilitation orders, and combination orders as community punishment and rehabilitation orders.
2 The peak age of conviction is the age at which the proportion of convictions per 100,000 of the population is highest.
3 See Farrington (1997) for a more thorough summary of the literature and Blumstein *et al.* (1986) for discussions of the methodological sophistication of this field, its policy uses and other substantive issues.

4 The studies undertaken by Burnett and by Leibrich could arguably be included with the research which has attempted to measure the effectiveness of the criminal justice system. However, their reliance on self-reported data, extensive use of qualitative interviews and exploration of the social and personal factors associated with persistence/desistance means that they have more in common with the criminal career paradigm.

5 There is also, of course, the issue of domestic violence, which clearly calls into to question the observed association between partnership and desistance. For a discussion of findings relating to desistance from domestic violence, see Fagan (1989), Feld and Straus (1989, 1990), Quigley and Leonard (1996) and Tolman *et al.* (1996).

6 For example, some of the earliest investigations of the relationship between employment and desistance relied upon relatively young populations. For example, Rand's (1987) sample was under 26 years old, the members of Mulvey and La Rosa's (1986) sample were all between 15 and 20 years old with an average age of 18 and, more recently, Graham and Bowling's (1995) sample were aged 17–25. Similarly, early investigations of the relationship between marriage and desistance were also based on relatively young populations: Mulvey and Aber's (1988) sample were aged between 16 and 19 years old; Pezzin's (1995) were between 14 and 22; Rand's (1987) were under 26; Knight *et al.*'s (1977) sample were all under 21, and the later extension of Knight *et al.*'s analyses (Osborn and West 1979) followed these men until they were 22–23.

7 See Chapter 10 on the relationship between desistance and gender and race in the current study.

8 Like any body of literature, the published studies of desistance suffer from certain biases and omissions, not least of all their geographical concentration. Virtually all the studies on desistance have been conducted in either the UK or North American (in particular the USA). There have been some studies conducted outside these areas – Mischkowitz's (1994) study was based in Germany, Leibrich's (1993) study in New Zealand and Chylicki's (1992) in Sweden – but it remains the case that the bedrock of our knowledge about desistance has come from two geographical regions. This is not to say that these findings would not hold in other regions (Mischkowitz, Leibrich and Chylicki did not suggest anything remarkably different from the main literature), but rather that findings have to be 'translated' with care. Societies which place less emphasis on employment or family relationships as indicators of 'success' may accordingly have different processes of desistance.

White-collar offenders are another neglected topic in the desistance literature. Most, if not all, of the research conducted so far has focused upon desistance from street crimes (robbery, violence, drug dealing), acquisitive crimes (burglary, theft and handling stolen property) or petty crimes (under-age drinking, cannabis use or fighting). The crimes of the powerful, once again, appear to have been omitted from the research agenda. Another group of offenders which have not been the subject of exhaustive investigation are sex offenders. Possibly the closest we get to a study of the processes of desistance by sex offenders is that by Acklerley *et al.* (1998), and even this is based entirely upon officially recorded data (which fails to tap undetected offending). Most of the literature on sex offenders details the various intervention programmes run by probation services and prisons.

9 Day centres were introduced as part of the Criminal Justice Act 1982 and were generally a condition made as part of a probation order for young people (17–25-year-olds) with several previous convictions and custodial experiences.

10 Intensive probation was a short-lived programme which was aimed at 17–20-year-olds and run as a series of pilot studies in the early 1990s (see Mair *et al.* 1994 for an outline of some of the schemes).

11 For example, see Stewart *et al.* (1994), which reports officers' accounts of the lives of their probationers, or Mair and May (1997), which reports probationer's accounts of the supervision they were receiving.

12 The distinction between 'static' and 'dynamic' investigations is discussed in greater detail presently.

13 The methodology, sample characteristics and research tools are dealt with in Chapter 3.

14 There is also the possibility that, knowing these records may be reviewed by probation management, probation officers use these records to 'construct' defendable accounts of their work. Similar processes have been observed in other branches of the legal and criminal apparatus (McConville *et al.* 1991).

15 Hood (1963: 90–92) was an early advocate of using additional criteria to judge outcomes, yet few have taken up his suggestion to measure the extent to which probation helps people build constructive usage of leisure time, improves attitudes, educates them and makes the '. . . inadequate more adequate'.

16 Although prisons, of course, should not be thought of as 'crime-free zones'; see O'Donnell and Edgar (1996).

17 'Telescoping' refers to respondents reporting offending which falls outside the time-frame of the study. For example, reports of offending which should have been limited to the year 1985 including offences committed prior to 1985 ('forward telescoping') or offences committed after 1985 ('backward telescoping').

18 See Chapter 3 for an outline of the probationers who were recruited into the study and the offences of which they had been found guilty.

19 The extent to which respondents exaggerate the frequency of their offending or the seriousness of their offending, may itself have been the subject of some exaggeration. Writing in the 1960s, Hood and Sparks (1970: 67) concluded that whilst there may be a problem amongst 'a few isolated individuals' there was 'no evidence of consistent exaggeration', and several

test-retest studies and other exercises to assess the honesty of reportings have confirmed this.

20 A point which few studying probation outcomes appear to have recognised (or been willing to admit to having recognised). Worrall (1997: 13) has been one of the few to have recognised the possibility that the sentence may have been irrelevant to an individual's desistance. She writes (ibid.): '[people] stop committing crimes for many reasons and the sentence they receive may be only one (and possibly the least significant) of several influential factors.'

Chapter 2

Realism, criminal careers and complexity

Being able to measure change is one thing, being able to account for it is quite another. Three bodies of literature informed the data analyses and, in particular, helped to make sense of change: 'realistic evaluation', as most notably outlined in Pawson and Tilley (1997); developmental and interactionist approaches to criminal careers (see, for example, Sampson and Laub 1993; Thornberry 1997; Ulmer and Spencer 1999); and David Byrne's work on complexity (1998). Pawson and Tilley placed social contexts centre-stage in their manifesto of how evaluation research should be improved and, as such, their work resonates with the intention of exploring in greater detail the role of social and personal circumstances in fostering or preventing desistance. The interest in developmental processes has been one of the most exciting growth areas in criminology in recent years, and has been important in shaping both conceptions and knowledge concerning criminal careers (see, for example, Moffitt 1997). Ulmer and Spencer's (1990: 107) critique of 'criminal careers' from an interactionist perspective formalised a set of assumptions which were useful when exploring probationers' responses to probation supervision. Finally, Byrne's (1998) work has introduced to social research an agenda and a set of ideas aimed at exploring the relationships between three or more variables, especially when these relationships are non-linear.

These ideas have been employed as 'sensitising devices'. Thus they are not referred to *continually* throughout this book. Rather they have been used selectively in analysing and 'thinking about' some of the issues to be dealt with. These ideas alerted the author to some of the issues and processes involved in the outcomes of probation supervision and the influence of such supervision on criminal careers, and suggested ways in which the analysis of these phenomena should be approached. Thus the manner of their usage is akin to Sparks *et al.*'s

(1996: 70) use of Anthony Gidden's structuration theory in their investigation of order in prisons – that is to say, these ideas are 'good to think with'.

Realistic evaluation

In a number of publications, Pawson and Tilley have argued that too little attention has been paid to the methodologies used to evaluate criminal justice interventions (Pawson 1997; Pawson and Tilley, 1994, 1996, 1997; Tilley 2000). They criticised the research community for having reached a state in which knowledge suggests that *'some things ... work'*, but '... in which *inconsistent results, non-replicability, partisan disagreement* and above all, *lack of cumulation* remain to dash the hopes of evaluators seeking to establish clear ... guidelines to policy making' (Pawson and Tilley 1994: 291–92, emphases in original). Whilst they did not deny that implementation failures, poorly designed policies and political processes have also contributed to this state of affairs, Pawson and Tilley (ibid.: 292) found fault with the research community, who, they said, should face the real possibility that '... research sloth rather than political blight is responsible for us being unable to speak with confidence about "what works in programming"'.

When the literature on probation outcomes is examined, it becomes clear that even those projects with similar styles of intervention, similar target populations and similar research methodologies have *not* produced a set of *consistent* results about which programmes 'work'. Ted Palmer (1996: 136–40), in reviewing the aspects of successful intervention with probationers, wrote that '... evaluations of physical challenge ... have been mixed and wide ranging ...', 'group counselling or therapy approach presents an especially mixed ... picture', 'individual counselling or therapy had similarly mixed results ...', 'work experience programs were associated with positive outcomes in about one in every three operations ...' and so on. The upshot from this rather confusing situation is that whilst some 'successful' aspects of interventions *have* been identified (e.g. 'multi-modal' programmes – Palmer 1996: 143 – or, in some reviews, employment schemes – Lösel 1995), generalised statements about 'what works' are hard to make with any level of certainty. This uncertainty poses a problem for those designing intervention strategies and for those working with probationers.

Pawson and Tilley's critique accordingly demands an answer to the question: 'What works in evaluation research?' The answer which Pawson and Tilley offer is that the 'traditional', quasi-experimental methodologies used to establish causality are the root cause of this gap in our knowledge base. Their solution is to incorporate what they refer to as 'scientific realistic methodologies' into criminal justice research.

Realist philosophy has attempted to avoid both positivist and relativist theorising in its explanations of social events. Some have characterised realist philosophy as being 'commonsensical' (Williams and May 1996: 81). Realists argue that the world has an existence independent of our experiences and perceptions of it, and view concepts such as 'causality', 'explanation', 'prediction' as valid. As such they argue that causal mechanisms can be discovered, understood and described.

Many realist philosophers take as the starting point for their conceptualisation of realism the activities of laboratory-based scientific investigations. Such investigations only make sense as explanations of 'the way the world operates' if one believes that the objects or people under investigation in the laboratory continue to behave in the same ways when they are not in these laboratories. However, social realism (and therefore realistic research) is committed to a number of principles which suggest that people will *not* act in the same way inside a laboratory as they would outside a laboratory. Laboratory settings are essentially 'closed' – that is to say, extraneous variables are controlled for and/or removed. In contrast, non-laboratory settings are essentially 'open' systems. Any number of factors may be introduced at various times, for various reasons and with various outcomes. In short, in non-laboratory settings it is virtually impossible to control for *all* possible influencing variables. This critique led Pawson and Tilley (1997: 38) to conclude that:

> . . . corrections evaluation needs to develop a much more comprehensive model of the way that different subjects make choices in response to the range of opportunities offered in the course of a programme. Experimental evaluation is simply not attuned to grasping this challenge. The volition of the subject [in laboratories] has to be treated in the same way as any other threat to the integrity of the basic [laboratory] design. That is to say, it is to be regarded as 'noise', as a 'confounding variable' which has to be controlled . . . in order to allow the real experimental apparatus to get rolled into place.

Working on the assumption that 'communities clearly differ' (1994: 298) – a point that can easily be extended to individuals – Pawson and Tilley attempt to take account of specific contexts and individual

33

motivations. They view communities as having different cultures (e.g. religious beliefs, pro-offending); different structures (e.g. rates and nature of employment, long or short term); and different relationships (e.g. the amount and nature of contacts between various groups in the community). The same can be said of individuals – for example, a probationer will have a set of cultural beliefs (e.g. 'stealing from private companies is acceptable, but stealing from private individuals is wrong'); will be located in a series of structures (past and ongoing employment histories and peer groups); and will have a number of relationships with other people and organisations (e.g. employer, friends, the benefit office and so on). A particular form of intervention will only 'work' if the circumstances in which it is enacted enable it to operate in the manner intended. If, for example, a probationer with a 'quick temper' is unable successfully to reduce or control her alcohol intake, is unwilling to accept that she has 'a problem' or believes that probation is 'a waste of time', then the intended purposes of an anger management programme will be affected accordingly.

Five 'component parts' ('embeddedness' – the relationship between a 'thing' and the wider social context in which it is to be found; 'mechanisms' – the processes through which a form of intervention achieves an outcome; 'contexts' – the wider social, temporal, geo-graphical 'backgrounds' which impinge upon the intervention; 'regu-larities' – the relationship between two or more variables; and 'change' – making the regularity between the chosen variables different) characterise realistic evaluation (Pawson and Tilley 1997: 63–78). To say that something is 'embedded' into a wider range of social processes is to say that it only 'makes sense' because it contains assumptions about the norms, rules and procedures which govern other social institutions. For example, breaching a probationer for the non-attend-ance of the Community Service element of his probation order, the completion of all the attending paperwork and the imposition of a new disposal only 'makes sense' in the wider organisation known as the criminal justice system. Translating this into the language of social causality produces a statement something like this: *causal powers lie not with particular objects (such as the paperwork), nor with individuals who process this paperwork (the court clerks), but in the social relationships, organisations, rules and procedures to which they belong and of which they form a part.* As such, one particular action (for example, a court's request for a pre-sentence report), leads to another action (a PSR meeting and the eventual writing of the report) because of the accepted relationship of these actions both to one another and to a completion of a wider task (in this case appropriate sentencing).

This relatively simple principle is the starting point for understanding how programmes can be evaluated along realistic principles. The 'delivery' of, for example, an employment training course, involves a complex series of events and actions. It is (often) made up of a curriculum of activities which are attempts to impart a set of ideas and skills to the probationer. Such ideas include (for example) understanding how to organise a job search, how to present oneself at interview and so on. These actions and events take place (in the main) in probation offices and, as such, will be bound by expectations of how probationers should behave, both in the office and away from it, and about how the probationer should be treated. Similar expectations govern the activities of officers. The officer will have one set of priorities in terms of the work that needs to be addressed during a probation order, and the probationer may (or may not) share this agenda. The employment and training course is also about the people involved in its delivery – the probationer, the officer leading the course, partnership staff, secretarial staff and perhaps others still. All these people will bring with them their own set of backgrounds, ideas, assumptions and prejudices – which may influence a particular probation order or group programme in numerous ways.

In addition to this, a programme of intervention takes place in a particular place, at a particular time. That is to say, not just in a particular country but a particular region, and even then not just a particular city, but a particular suburb of that city. Different locales will experience a variety of structural conditions (such as chronic unemployment or a vast housing shortage). These conditions will in turn affect the services that are available in that locale and the amount that can reasonably be done to help a probationer; thus less should be expected from seeing an employment training officer when local unemployment rates are running at 20–25 per cent than if they were at 2–3 per cent. A programme must also be understood to be temporally located. Not only is probation supervision in the late 1990s different from probation supervision in the 1960s or 1970s, new social and economic factors have also emerged. Heroin, video-players and credit cards – common features of the 1990s – were either less widespread or non-existent in the 1960s.

Employment training courses, probationers, probation officers and probation services are embedded in wider social contexts. These range from the truly macro (global economic down-turns) to the micro (the office may be a long way from where many of its probationers live). Probation is '... its personnel, its place, its past and its prospects' (Pawson and Tilley 1997: 65). To ignore such aspects of a programme of intervention is perhaps to ignore the very elements which ensure its success or contribute to its failure.

Mechanisms are the processes through which a form of intervention achieves its aims (or fails to achieve its ends). Understanding a mechanism means coming to understand the choices people are presented with and the capacities which they possess via the membership of various social groups. For example, understanding why a probationer failed to attend a group programme being run for unemployed probationers in a town 20 minutes by bus from where he lives means understanding his choices (to go or to not go) and the capacities he possesses as a result of being unemployed (the time, but neither the money nor car). Similarly to understand why the same programme worked for another probationer (this time, say, an educated female white-collar probationer), one needs again to consider her choices and capacities: money left from having worked recently, motivation to gain employment, good presentational skills, availability of suitable jobs in that area, similarity to programme staff in terms of goals and educational qualifications and so on. Having identified the programme mechanisms, one is able to start to move to a position in which one is able to identify what it is about the programme which makes it work – or not work.

How would evaluating such mechanisms work in practice? Consider again the group programme for unemployed probationers. One could start by thinking about the mechanisms that may be involved in its operation. The programme may work via a process of empowerment – for example, putting probationers in touch with services that improve their interview skills. Alternatively, it may work by increasing the probationers' motivation to work by coercing them into demonstrating each week that they have applied for jobs, which they then find they want. Such schemes may also work by getting probationers to think about their own resources, through making probationers list those they know who may be able to get them work, or who may know of job vacancies elsewhere. The mechanisms by which a group programme may work are numerous, and may not be easy to tease out.

Clearly, whichever of the mechanisms is found to be operating, there will be elements of both individual actions and the wider social context at work in producing the outcome. A programme may have numerous contacts and ways of getting people to think about their opportunities for finding employment, but in the end it is the individual who completes the application form, goes for the interview and decides to take the job if offered it. As such, in explaining an outcome in this manner, one is not simply producing a list of correlates which associate actions with outcomes – rather one is attempting to explain how this outcome is *produced*. The mechanism is therefore an account of the '. . . make up, behaviour and inter-relationships of those processes which are responsible . . .' (Pawson and Tilley 1997: 68) for producing that particular outcome.

Pawson and Tilley (ibid.) portray 'contexts' as being the 'partner concept' to mechanisms. They argue (ibid.: 69) that '. . . the relationship between causal mechanisms and their effects is not fixed, but contingent', meaning that such relationships rely upon the context being one which encourages (or at least does not discourage too greatly) the relationship between mechanisms and outcomes. To return to the example of the group programme for unemployed probationers, in a context of high unemployment and very little opportunities for work, most programmes of this nature would fare poorly. This may lead some to conclude that such programmes 'don't work', but rather the more accurate conclusion should be that the programme did not work in *those conditions*.

A 'regularity' is the relationship between two or more variables which can be translated into a general rule, for example, the age–crime curve discussed in Chapter 1. Explaining such 'regularities', 'rates', 'patterns' and 'associations' is the very task of research. This takes the form of positing a mechanism which is key to the production of the regularity. This is understood further (e.g. in terms of why a mechanism operated, or failed to operate) by reference to the various contexts upon which the success of the mechanism is contingent. Pawson and Tilley (1997: 72) claim that 'when an evaluator tells us that a programme is a success (the regularity), s/he should demonstrate what it is (the mechanism) about the programme which works for whom in what conditions (the contexts)'. In other words, if an evaluator reports that the employment training course is a 'success' he or she has to demonstrate that the regularity changed in the desired direction (i.e. that rates of offending for those who were enrolled on the course were reduced), that this could be attributed to some particular aspects of the course (e.g. it was being taught how to write speculative letters asking about vacancies), and the groups and contexts (e.g. middle-aged men with recent experience of semi-skilled employment) to which this applied.

Social systems such as probation are 'open' – which is to say that they are open to influence from a number of sources. This includes the very people running the programme and those undertaking the programme. Aware of the regularities and mechanisms which help to shape their lives and the lives of others, these actors will be aware of the wider social forces which limit their own options. Whilst some people may wish to change the regularities which pervade their lives, these changes may or may not occur as they may or may not – for a number of reasons – be able to alter these regularities. For example they may not have sufficient capacities to produce the desired changes, others may be able to counteract their actions or they may be unaware of exactly how the mechanisms operate and, therefore, be unable to produce the exact changes desired. These insights bring to the investigation of the outcomes of criminal justice interventions a concern with documenting the social and personal contexts within which such interventions occur, the responses of those engaged in these interventions and an emphasis on understanding and accounting for the mechanisms of change.

Approaching criminal careers

The emphasis on employing insights gained from individual histories and contexts as suggested by realistic research methodologies, and the earlier call for a greater degree of specificity in understanding the role of probation supervision, resonates with some of the approaches adopted by developmental criminologists (e.g. Moffitt 1993; Sampson and Laub 1993; Warr 1998), and the interactionist perspective on the development of criminal careers as summarised by Ulmer and Spencer (1999).

The criminal career literature has become heavily influenced by a set of ideas commonly referred to as the developmental (or life-course) perspective.[1] The life-course perspective is concerned with 'pathways through the age differentiated life span' and 'expectations and options that impinge on decision processes and the course of events that give shape to life stages, transitions and turning points' (Elder 1985: 17, quoted in Sampson and Laub 1993: 8). Two concepts central to this perspective are the notions of 'trajectory' and 'transitions'. The first refers to a line of development over the life-course (such as, for example, an employment career), and the second refers to events (e.g. first job, promotion and so on) which may alter in some way a trajectory. Sampson and Laub (1993: 8) summarise the perspective as focusing upon '. . . the duration, timing and ordering of major social events and their consequences for later social development'.

As well as being the source of several debates (see Hirschi and Gottfredson 1995; Sampson and Laub 1995), the life-course perspective has contributed greatly to the insights generated by criminal career research and the ways in which these have been interpreted. For example, Sampson and Laub (1993) relied heavily on life-course perspectives in developing a theory of age-graded informal social control. The aim of those who have employed insights gained from the life-course perspective in the study of crime has, essentially, been to understand involvement in crime as a developmental process. To this end, researchers who have relied upon this perspective have aimed to identify features of an individual's life, or behavioural patterns, which increase their likelihood of offending. These features and behavioural patterns may start in the very early years. For example, Farrington (1997: 383) has shown how persistent offending between the ages of 21 and 32 was best predicted by variables associated with life-styles between 8 and 18 years. This approach to explaining offending often emphasises the outcomes of offending as much as the precursors. Thus, offending at an early age may create problems at school for an individual, resulting in him or her leaving school with few or no qualifications, making secure employment harder to gain, and which may in turn make for a life in which offending is more likely than if employment had been gained (Farrington 1977; Farrington *et al.* 1978, 1986).

Thornberry (1997: 1–10), in his introduction to a volume devoted to the application of the life-course perspective to criminological theorising, outlined a number of advantages of developmental approaches in criminology over non-developmental approaches. Developmental theories have been able to identify and offer explanations for important variations in rates of offending over the life-course. As such, this perspective has introduced a new vocabulary to research on offending behaviours. Onset, escalation, persistence, deceleration, specialisation, desistance (to name a few of the terms currently employed) are now all aspects of offending about which more is now known than was the case even ten years ago.

Secondly, when the developmental aspects of offending are taken into consideration, two 'ideal types' of offender emerge. The first type (often referred to as persisters or early starters), start their offending at a young age (pre-teens in some cases), and continue to offend for long periods of their lives. The second type start their offending at an older age (often during adolescence) and have usually ceased to offend by the time they have reached their mid to late 20s (Moffitt 1997). The observation that these two types of offending careers differ has implications for both policy and theory and has been validated by further research (Kratzer and Hodgins 1999). In theoretical terms it suggests that different explanations of engagement and desistance may be required for each of these groups. In policy terms it suggests that those who can be identified as likely to have lengthy offending careers ahead of them may be candidates for selective incapacitation (Farrington 1992a). However, there are persuasive ethical arguments against such a policy.[2]

The third way in which developmental theories improve upon non-developmental explanations is that they have been more directly concerned with the wider contexts of offending behaviour. The roots of offending behaviours have been shown to be related to early experiences, often in childhood. By understanding the role of these correlates (such as poor housing, poor parental supervision, low family income), the ability to explain the onset and persistence of offending is enhanced. Similarly, involvement in offending is likely to have a profound effect upon the rest of an individual's life; indeed, 'Serious and prolonged involvement in delinquent behaviour is likely to adversely influence social relations with family and peers, belief systems, and the success and timing of transitions to adult roles and the life course' (Thornberry 1997: 4).

Finally, developmental theories of offending highlight the role of particular events in shaping offending trajectories. Engagement in offending has been observed to alter as people's lives undergo various transitions, such as changes in marital status, employment status, place of residence and so on. Thus a person's engagement in offending behaviours can be described in part by the trajectories along which his or her life unfolds and the occurrence (or lack of, in some cases) of certain transitions which alter the course of his or her trajectory.

Despite its utility in accounting for offending amongst the general population, the developmental perspective has yet to be widely adopted by those researching the impact of specific criminal justice interventions. Burnett (1992) has been one of the few to adopt a developmental approach. In her study of those released from prison, Burnett found that changes in family and employment circumstances were cited by desisters as the reasons for their wishing to avoid further trouble.

Related to these issues, Ulmer and Spencer (1999) argue convincingly that the term 'criminal career' has been used in different ways by two contrasting approaches to understanding offending over the life-course. The positivist tradition, which has dominated recent research (especially as it relates to policy concerns), has viewed a criminal career as a sequence of offences committed by an individual who for any period of time has a detectable rate of offending. That is, for each individual for any given period of time, the rate at which he or she was offending is calculable (known as 'lambda' – see Blumstein *et al.* Volume One, 1986: 19–20). These studies are overwhelmingly quantitative and characterised by Ulmer and Spencer (1999: 97) as being concerned with 'how offender characteristics, social environmental factors and ... criminal justice interventions can predict onset, frequency, persistence, and exit from criminal activity from crime'. However, this body of work has experienced two theoretical difficulties: accounting for why some offenders' careers exhibit stability, whilst others with similar offending histories experience changes in their offending career, and why some of those predicted to offend do not in fact offend (the problem of individual-level indeterminacy). Ulmer and Spencer argue that positivist work on criminal careers would benefit from the incorporation of insights gained from an interactionist perspective of criminal careers. They suggest that by incorporating some of the insights from interactionsts, positivist approaches would be better able to meet the challenge posed by stability and change in offending careers, and also be in a better position to account for some of the indeterminacy observed in such careers.

The merits of their argument, their portrayal of both the 'positivistic' approach to criminal careers and their proposed solution are outside the remits of this discussion. Of more immediate importance is their summary of the assumptions interactionists make about crime and deviancy (ibid.: 107), and the extent to which these can aid understanding of probation outcomes. They argue that four key principles emerge from the interactionist position. These are (ibid.) that:

1. People confront situations and act on the basis of their definitions of those situations.

2. Different probabilities of action are conditioned by the constraints and opportunities presented by situational contexts, and definitions of situations are influenced by an actor's biography and prior repertoires of action. Further, situational and biographical constraints can influence individuals' definitions and actions both with and without their awareness of those constraints.

3. However, behaviour involves a dialectic of choice and constraint – the potential for novel choices and emergent lines of action is always present.

4. Situational contexts are set by, and actors' biographies are located within, larger arrangements of institutional organisation and social structure.

Regardless of the extent to which these four principles accurately summarise *all* the principles inherent in interactionism, they immediately resonate with both the approach to realistic research as outlined above, and with the emphasis of the current project on *specificity* of actions, actors and contexts.

These principles offer fruitful ways of approaching not just criminal careers, but the impact of attempts to *alter* those careers. The work of a probation officer, for example, may be deemed 'useless' by a particular probationer even *before* he or she has commenced an order. Previous experiences of probation supervision, attempts to stop offending, find employment and so on will permeate the approach of each probationer to his or her period of supervision and the problems which he or she faces in desisting. Experiences of past failures will not suggest to individuals that success is likely – a source perhaps of much of the continuity associated with offending careers. However, change, no matter how unlikely, is always a *possibility*; hence some of the indeterminacy also observed in criminal careers.

Complexity

The third 'sensitising device' employed during the analyses, Byrne's (1998: 2–28) understanding and use of the term 'complexity', can similarly be reduced to a set of core statements. These are:

1. That complex social processes have *multiple* causes;

2. That these causes are not necessarily additive, in other words, the outcome is not *simply* the sum of the separate effects;

3. That *small* differences in initial conditions may, over time, produce big differences in eventual outcomes; and

4. That many outcomes, nevertheless, fall within a range of known or calculable outcomes.

Two examples – one drawn from Byrne and the other a hypothetical criminological example – illustrate these assertions. Byrne (1998: 38–39) cites the example of an eminent inter-war physician called Bradbury. Bradbury was interested in what caused tuberculosis (TB) on Tyneside. The answer, as both Bradbury and Byrne point out, is (initially) very simple: tuberculosis bacteria cause TB. The problem, however, was that not everyone exposed to the TB bacteria developed TB. Bradbury's investigations suggested that three factors were important in understanding who developed TB and who did not. These were poor housing, poor diet and being Irish. The first two are fairly easily understood: the worse the conditions of one's housing and the worse one's diet, the more likely one was to develop TB. However, the third was less straightforward. Irish migrants had, at that time, not been living on Tyneside for very long, and had less experience than the rest of the Tyneside population of urbanisation. TB, like many other bacteria, bred for resistance. Hence at that time Irish migrants were particularly susceptible to developing TB as they had had less exposure to the TB bacteria and the conditions in which it thrived. Thus the causal mechanisms for TB on Tyneside during the 1930s were complex and contingent. Good housing and good diets prevented infection, being Irish made it more likely.

The second example (this time hypothetical) concerns sentencing in criminal courts. Imagine a study designed to explain the sentences which were imposed on all of those found guilty in a magistrates' court. A number of factors can be identified which might be of use in accounting for variations in sentences: previous criminal history (chiefly previous convictions and outcomes of previous disposals); current offence (intentions to harm and actual harm to victim, the efforts made by the guilty party to repair the harm he or she caused, the tariff and so on); the pre-sentence report and the recommendations made in it; the plea entered; the characteristics of the guilty party (demeanour, signs of distress, age, gender and so on); the public's attitude towards crimes of that nature at the time; and probably several other factors. In coming to their decision, magistrates may take into account any number of these factors. Some will make custody more likely, others will make probation seem appropriate and still others may make community service or a suspended sentence appear to be a sensible disposal.

These two examples illustrate the sorts of issues with which Byrne attempts to deal. In both, there can be found a conglomeration of factors which influence the outcomes. In the TB example these were housing conditions, diet and ethnicity (or rather, ethnicity in particular time and space dimensions). In the sentencing example, these were hypothesised to be criminal history, offence, etc. However, as shown in the TB example, these causes are non-additive. Similarly, sentencing decisions can also be hypothesised to be non-additive: unique factors, variations and contingencies may influence the outcomes of sentencing decisions in various ways, some aggravating and some mitigating. Despite this, the range of outcomes in both cases is known with some degree of certainty: people either will or will not get TB. The range of sentencing options can often be estimated both in terms of the type of sentence (custodial or non-custodial) and the severity of the sentence (length of custody or numbers of hours community sentence, for example).

Byrne places a heavy emphasis on the fact that small differences in initial conditions can result, over time, in disproportionate outcomes. However, this assumption is based on the (almost exclusively) quantitative framework within which Byrne locates his own attempts to explore complexity. When one considers the concept of 'smallness' in qualitative investigations, the concept of 'small' loses some of its (already vague) definition. Because the current project deals with people's assumptions and understandings about how the world around them operates and their place in this world, the word 'subtle' is preferred to 'small'. Subtle implies discerning, discriminating or slight. As such 'subtle' does not invoke a *quantitative* assessment in the same way which the word 'small' does. Therefore it was felt to be a more appropriate term to employ when seeking an understanding of complex outcomes involving variations between individuals, their perceptions of the world and their social circumstances.

Realism, contexts and complexity

These, then, were the ideas which informed portions of the analyses undertaken and which were borne in mind when 'thinking about' the outcomes of probation supervision and how these were generated. Although, as stated before, these ideas are not explicitly referred to throughout the text, they 'percolate' through much of the analyses presented. Used selectively, these ideas influenced the approaches adopted during the efforts to open probation's 'black box' and to discover what it is about probation that 'works'.

Notes

1 See Elder (1985) and Giele and Elder (1998) on the life-course perspective and Loeber and LeBlanc (1990) and Sampson and Laub (1993) for examples of its use in criminology.
2 See Tarling (1993: 156) for a review of these arguments.

Chapter 3

The study

This chapter outlines the methodology of the study. The characteristics of those people interviewed, issues relating to the sampling, the representativeness of the sample, sample attrition and the honesty of the responses gathered are discussed.

In all, 199 probationers and their supervising officers were recruited into the sample. The methodology builds upon that employed in an earlier study of recidivism among prison inmates who had recently returned to the community (Burnett 1992, 2000). Due to the high number of cases required for reliable analysis, the geographical distribution of cases and the need to keep to a tight timetable of fieldwork, a number of part-time interviewers were recruited to assist with the fieldwork.[1]

The data collected for this study come from six English probation areas: Middlesex, Greater Manchester, West Yorkshire, Essex, Inner London and Wiltshire. All the people interviewed for the study were either employed as probation officers (or, in a very few cases, senior probation officers or probation service officers), or were probationers who were being supervised by these probation services. Some probationers moved home and were transferred to other probation areas. Follow-up data were therefore also collected in the following probation areas: Berkshire, Hampshire, Hertfordshire, Lincolnshire, Liverpool, Mid-Glamorgan, Norfolk, South Yorkshire, and in various prisons.

The socioeconomic contexts

The six probation services from which cases were taken were spread widely across England. From Manchester and West Yorkshire in the north, to Essex, Middlesex and Inner London in the south-east and

Table 3.1:   Problematic circumstances at the time of the offence: probationers' reports

Social circumstance	Percentage reporting it as 'a problem'
Accommodation	37
Employment	55
Finances	53
Partner	32
Family	39
Alcohol	23
Drugs	34
Feeling down/depressed	63
Other	31
Three or more problems	47
Total	199

Wiltshire in the south-west. Despite this range of locations (north-south, east-west, urban-rural and metropolitan-town), similarly high rates of social and economic deprivation were observed. These rates of economic and social deprivation, which were mirrored in the probationers' reports of the social circumstances at the time which they offended (see Table 3.1), were hardly surprising given the social and economic profiles of the areas served by probation offices.

Local social and economic contexts: an example from Manchester

Greater Manchester is a large metropolitan area. Six of the seven offices from which data were collected were within the main area of the city, the seventh being in Stockport – a town adjacent and to the south of Manchester. The six offices in the city centre serve, to all intents and purposes, some of the most run-down inner-city areas of England. Indeed some parts of Manchester (such as Moss Side, where one of the study offices was located) have gained a rather unenviable national profile as being 'crime ridden'. The socioeconomic profile of each area is outlined below and is based on 1991 census data.

The Beswick and Clayton area (in which one office was located and another, on Varley Street, adjacent) had experienced a decrease in its population since 1981 of 5 per cent. Almost a fifth of the residents reported having a limiting long-term illness (the city averaged was 17 per cent), and of the 16–64-year-old males who were economically active living in Beswick and Clayton, 29 per cent were unemployed (the city average was 23 per cent). Rates of unemployment for local females were also higher than the city average (18 per cent compared with 14 per cent). About half of the local housing stock was local authority owned. Car ownership (taken as an indication of wealth) was lower than the city average too, with 68 per cent of households not owning a car. Only 2 per cent of the population of Beswick and Clayton had a degree or diploma. One of the police beats in this ward was cited as being a 'hotspot' for criminal damage to dwellings by Manchester City Council (1998: 17), with 68 offences of this nature in the area between April and August 1998. Certainly when the author visited the Beswick and Varley Street offices the levels of deprivation were clear to see. The Varley Street office was surrounded by high wire fences and other security measures to deter break-ins. Houses in the local area had numerous broken windows and graffiti, and generally appeared to be in a state of decay. The Beswick office was located above a parade of shops (many of which had closed).

The Cheetham Hill office (to which cases from the Varley Street and Beswick offices were transferred when those offices closed during the course of the fieldwork) was similarly located in an area which could be described as 'impoverished'. Rates of unemployment for males in the Cheetham area were 38 per cent, and for females 25 per cent. Like Beswick and Clayton, a high number of households did not own cars (67 per cent) and about 16 per cent of the local population had a limiting long-term illness. The population had decreased between 1981 and 1991 by 12 per cent. However, the office was set in what appeared to be an reasonably 'well-off' part of Cheetham and the visible signs of decay observed on the visits to Beswick and Varley Street were less apparent in Cheetham.

Regardless of probation area, many of the offices, all of which would have taken their cases from the local population, were to be found in some of the worst urban conditions in England. Whilst some of the offices were located in affluent areas such as Stockport in Manchester or Finchley in Middlesex, these were the minority. Most offices took their case loads from those people living in poor housing, with high rates of unemployment, few indicators of wealth (such as cars), high rates of illness, deprivation and crime. Even when probationers in the sample moved – which they did frequently – they often moved to areas which were no better than those they had left behind. Drug and alcohol problems served only to compound the problems experienced in these areas. It is hardly surprising, then, to find that many of the probationers interviewed as part of this study reported experiencing a range of problems. Not only were the probationers likely to be unemployed, so, too, were many of the people within the areas in which they lived.

The processes of selecting and interviewing probationers

Probation areas were recruited into the study in a number of ways. Some probation services had existing contracts with the Probation Studies Unit at Oxford University's Centre for Criminological Research and were asked if they would be prepared to become involved in the 'Tracking' project. Others asked the PSU if it 'would like to undertake research in their area' and access to others was secured on the basis of personal contact.

Once it had been established in which services the fieldwork would take place, the offices from which the cases were to be recruited were selected. This was a process driven by pragmatic concerns. In some areas offices were chosen randomly, whilst in others the choice was limited to those offices which were not too heavily swamped by other research studies or by operational concerns. Once the offices had been chosen all staff working in each office were briefed about the study: its purpose, methodology, impact on routine work and ethical consider-ations. Each officer was asked to invite probationers to take part in the study and to be interviewed themselves. In order that officers did not invite only 'interesting' or willing subjects, each officer was required to invite *all* probationers meeting the criteria (the details of which are discussed below) until two had agreed and been interviewed.[2]

Probationers aged 17–35 years old and who were commencing probation or combination orders of 6–24 months duration between the start of October 1997 and the end of March 1998 were eligible for inclusion in the study. This age range, it was anticipated, would produce a high number of probationers who were experiencing a number of salient life changes, such as marriage, entry to the labour market and moving away from the parental home, which were expected to be related to whether or not they desisted from further offending.

It was suggested to officers that they wait until the third or fourth meeting with the probationer before they raise the issue of taking part in the study. This was because it was felt that to raise such an issue too early on in the order might be counterproductive, and in any case there was a conscious desire not to affect the officer–probationer relationship in a way that may harm their future work together. Officers called the research office to register cases who had agreed to be interviewed, at which point brief details about the probationer were collected and an interview arranged. Interviews were then conducted when the probationer next attended the probation office.

The first sweep of interviewing

The first sweep of interviewing took place from mid-October 1997 to April 1998, and the majority of interviews were completed seven weeks after the commencement of each of the orders. The longitudinal nature of the project and the desire to record both officers' and probationers' opinions meant that it was not feasible to recruit a large sample of cases. If both officer and probationer were seen at all three sweeps, each case could generate six interviews. It was important, therefore, to strike the correct balance between having sufficient cases to enable meaningful analyses to be undertaken without recruiting so many cases that the management of the project became too burdensome. In all, counting the 15 or so pilot interviews and the 999 interviews conducted as part of the main fieldwork, there were over 1,000 one-to-one interviews completed during the study. The achieved sample of probationers had the socio-demographic characteristics as shown in Tables 3.2–3.5.

Table 3.2: Sample characteristics: gender

	n	%
Males	173	87
Females	26	13
Total	199	100

Table 3.3: Sample characteristics: age

	n	%
17–23	88	44
24–29	62	31
30–35	49	25
Total	199	100

Table 3.4: Sample characteristics: ethnicity

	n	%
White	164	82
Asian	13	7
Afro-Caribbean	10	5
Mixed	4	2
Other	7	5
Unknown	1	—
Total	199	100

Table 3.5: Sample characteristics: length of order

	n	%
6 months	10	5
9 months	3	2
12 months	98	49
15 months	2	1
18 months	24	13
24 months	62	31
Total	199	100

Table 3.6:   Sample characteristics: main offence

| | Achieved sample | | National data |
	(n)	(%)	(%)
Violence	20	10	9
Sexual	2	1	2
Burglary	22	11	10
Robbery	4	2	1
Theft/handling	64	32	28
Fraud/forgery	11	6	5
Criminal damage	7	4	2
Drugs	17	9	—[4]
Other indictable	19	10	12
Summary offences	33	17	33
Total	199	100	100

Some 47 (24 per cent) of the orders were combination orders.[3] Table 3.6 reports the main convicting offence which resulted in the order, and shows the comparable national statistics for persons commencing a probation order in 1996, the most recent year for which data are available.

The single largest offence type was crimes of dishonesty – with burglary, theft/handling and fraud/forgery accounting for some 49 per cent of cases. The average Offender Group Reconviction Scale (OGRS) for the sample was 58 per cent, just above the national average of 55 per cent (Home Office 1996: Annex 1). Probationers were grouped into four types of previous conviction experience: 'no previous', '1–3 previous', '4 or more' and 'unknown'. They were similarly grouped into four types of previous custodial experience (the right-hand side of Table 3.7).

Table 3.7:   Sample characteristics: previous convictions and custody

Convictions	(n)	(%)	Custody	(n)	(%)
No previous	43	22	No previous	121	61
1–3 previous	51	26	1–3 previous	50	25
4 or more	98	49	4 or more	22	11
Unknown	7	3	Unknown	6	3
Total	199	100		199	100

Table 3.8: Sample characteristics: age and gender

	Age	Achieved sample	National (%)*
Males	17–23	40	40
	24–29	26	25
	30–35	17	21
All males		83	86
Females	17–23	8	5
	24–29	6	5
	30–35	5	4
All Females		19	14

*The national data kindly provided by the Home Office. Due to rounding, the figures do not always sum to 100.

Sample representativeness

Because of the desire to interview both officers and probationers, consent was required from all probationers involved in the research. Like any other research which relies upon consent, this meant that certain unavoidable biases were built into the research. However, as a check against biases, the achieved sample was compared against national statistics in relation to age, gender, commencement offence, OGRS and previous convictions. These suggested a sample that was not too greatly different from the national statistics and therefore that the findings may have some general relevance. In terms of the age composition, the sample is very similar to the national picture, as Table 3.8 demonstrates, although the achieved sample is slightly skewed towards females. Furthermore, in terms of the offences committed for which probation was imposed, the sample closely mirrors the national picture (see Table 3.6).

The impact of second and third sweep attrition

The reporting of attrition rates is somewhat complicated by the fact that probationers were serving orders of varying lengths, and therefore not all needed to be interviewed during the final sweep of interviewing. During the second sweep of interviewing, some 156 probationers were relocated, and of these 137 interviewed (190; 96 per cent of officers were also re-interviewed during the second sweep). During the third and final sweep 135 (68 per cent) of the 199 probationers were located and 120 of these (89 per cent; 60 per cent of the whole sample)

Table 3.9:   Attrition rates: offence type (%)

Offence type	Sweep one	Sweep two	Sweep three	Seen at all sweeps	National
Burglary	11	10	8	9	10
Violence	10	10	8	9	9
Sexual	1	2	1	1	2
Robbery	2	2	3	3	1
Theft and handling	32	34	33	34	28
Fraud and forgery	6	4	7	5	5
Criminal damage	4	4	3	4	2
Drug offences	9	8	10	9	—[5]
Other indictable	10	11	9	9	12
Summary	17	16	18	17	33
Total (n of sample)	199	137	120	100	—

Table 3.10:   Attrition rates: age and gender

Age and gender group		Sweep one (%)	Sweep two (%)	Sweep three (%)	Seen at all sweeps (%)	National (%)
Males:	17–23	40	37	40	38	40
	24–29	26	27	28	29	25
	30–35	21	23	18	20	21
Females:	17–23	5	4	4	3	5
	24–29	5	5	4	4	5
	30–35	4	4	6	6	4
Total (n of sample)		199	137	120	100	—

interviewed. Of all the officers required for interview ($n=172$), 90 per cent ($n=154$) were successfully re-interviewed for a third time.

In all, 141 (71 per cent of the original 199 probationers) were seen either towards the end of their orders, or shortly after they had completed their orders. The same figure for officers was 182 (91 per cent). One hundred and fifty-seven of the probationers were interviewed for a second time (during either the second or third sweep; 79 per cent), although, of course, obviously not all these follow-up interviews coincided with the end of the order.

Tables 3.9 and 3.10 show the impact of attrition on the sample of probationers across all three sweeps. As can be seen (from Table 3.9), the attrition rate had little effect on the sample in terms of the distribution of offences for which they received probation. The impact of attrition on the age and gender breakdown of the sample was also minimal (see Table 3.10). Thus, the sample remained reasonably representative of the national picture.

As mentioned above, not all probationers were seen three times. Of the 120 seen during the third sweep, 20 were amongst those who had not been interviewed at the second sweep. Thus there were 100 probationers who were seen at all three sweeps. The age, gender and offence characteristics of these 100 probationers is presented in the fourth column of Tables 3.9 and 3.10. Again it can be seen that this group of probationers very closely resembles the national caseloads. In the light of these analyses, it was decided that there was no need to weight the sample in order to achieve a better approximation with the national rates.

Individual sweeps never achieved less than a 60 per cent response rate. These rates, taken in the light of the fact that many of the respondents were highly mobile, often with no fixed abode, urban-living, with drug and alcohol problems and with good reason to conceal themselves (i.e. their past criminal record), can be regarded as very good. Osborn (1980: 60) reported that delinquents in the Cambridge Study in Delinquent Development were more likely to move than non-delinquents (a finding supported by Gottfredson and Taylor 1988: 79). Attempts to follow up similar groups of people have often yielded low response rates. For example, Cordray and Polk (1983) reported that attrition rates in surveys of crime were anywhere between 5 and 60 per cent. Capaldi and Patterson (1987) reported that average attrition rates in surveys with 4–10-year follow-up periods was 47 per cent. Wolfgang et al. (1972) were only able to trace 58 per cent of their sample after three years of searching. In addition, recent data suggest that there is a tendency for respondents in more deprived areas to be most likely to refuse to be interviewed (Thorogood et al. forthcoming).

Interview measures

Two forms of information were collected as part of the study. Initially a small amount of data were compiled when the case was registered with the research office (this is referred to as registration data). However, the data which the study relies upon most heavily were collected through a series of face-to-face interviews with probationers and officers.

The interviews were very much focused on the work undertaken with the probationer and his or her response to this work and social and personal circumstances. Extensive data relating to the probation officers, the extent and level of their training and experience of probation work were not collected. Whilst it remains possible that this information would have helped to account for some of the observed variations in the interactions between officers and probationers, there were a number of reasons why such data were not collected. The interview schedule was extensive, and it was felt that a further section on the officer would have made the interview too long. In addition, in a world in which their work is already frequently scrutinised, this element might have felt threatening to many officers. During the fieldwork it also emerged that several officers only saw their proba-tioners briefly (especially towards the end of their orders), and in any case some probationers had several officers during the course of their supervision.

Registration data

Basic information about the probationer was collected over the telephone when the case was registered with the research office. This included personal details (age, date of birth, gender, ethnic group), information about *previous* involvement with the criminal justice system (number of previous convictions, offences convicted of, previ-ous probation history and previous custodial history) and *current* offence details (length of order, additional requirements, offence(s) convicted of and name of supervising officer). In addition, where possible, Criminal Record Office and Police National Computer numb-ers were recorded. Other relevant information was often relayed informally by officers. For example, some female probationers reques-ted to be interviewed by a female interviewer. One or two probationers had to be interviewed at home as they were agoraphobic. All such requests were met as far as was possible and appropriate. As well as providing information which would be employed in the analysis, this summary data were used as a way of 'vetting' cases so as to reduce any risks to the interviewers' safety.

Interview data

The main source of data came directly from the probationers and the officers supervising them. The schedules used to interview officers very closely mirrored those used to interview probationers.[6] The inter-viewers were trained to use the schedules in a very open-ended fashion and to be flexible in their wording of questions. This decision, which departs considerably from mainstream thinking on questionnaire design and delivery, was partly driven by a desire to make the interviews as 'respondent friendly' and as enjoyable as was possible, and partly by two pragmatic concerns. First, the delivery of the interview schedule had to be versatile enough to accommodate a wide range of offences – issues that were sensible to ask a burglar may not be relevant to someone convicted of unlawful sexual intercourse. Similarly, issues of concern at the time of the offence for drink drivers may not be the same for those convicted of possession of heroin. The second pragmatic concern related to the range of educational qualifications and levels of literacy which could be expected from a diverse group of probationers. It was anticipated that some probationers may have required questions to be re-expressed in simpler terms whilst others would find 'dumbed down' questions boring and 'switch off'. With this in mind, interviewers were encouraged to approach the questions contained in the interview schedules as being the questions *to which they sought the answer* rather than questions which they asked *verbatim*.

The potential drawbacks of allowing the interviewers this freedom were that some may have inadvertently led respondents, or that the data collected may have become contaminated in some way through the discursive nature of the interviews. However, a number of observations suggested that these were not serious problems. The interviewers received two day's training prior to the commencement of the fieldwork and a further day's training which introduced them to the follow-up interviews. During these training days the importance of ensuring that they did not lead respondents was impressed upon interviewers and they were coached in the best techniques of asking questions and receiving answers. In addition to this, the author was in frequent contact with each of the interviews and proved further guidance as and when required. The tape-recorded interviews (see below) also suggested that interviewers adhered to good interviewing techniques and that they did not stray unduly from the interview guides.

A general problem with relying on interviews is that self-report data can 'only report what people say they do and feel and not what the researcher has seen them say, do and feel' (Herbert Gans, quoted in Bryman 1984: 81). One technique to ensure that erroneous conclusions are not drawn from an over-reliance upon interview data has been to triangulate self-reports with others' reports of the same event or processes. Where convergence between accounts is found, it is assumed that the accounts are 'trustworthy'. In the current study there were, of course, examples of both agreement and disagreement between officers and probationers. On some issues an officer and the probationer he or she was supervising would disagree over the problem faced by the probationer or the best solution to this. This is entirely naturally – people with different backgrounds and with different points of view can reasonably be expected not to agree on every issue. As such disagreements over the minutiae of any one probationer's life were not felt to represent a threat to the validity of the study. Dissimilarities – at the aggregate level – between the officers and the probationers over the processes which led to desistance or continued offending, however, *could* be seen as a threat to the validity of the study. If the processes which officers pointed to as leading to desistance were remarkably different from those identified by probationers, then the data set as a whole would have to be viewed with caution. However, from the data analyses which were undertaken and which are reported herein, there is a high degree of agreement in the types of processes which officers and probationers identified as being related to the latter's subsequent offending careers. Thus, whilst the study relies upon interview data, corroboration between officers and probationers in individual cases and parallel findings between the officers' and probationers' data sets in aggregate analyses would suggest that the data are robust.

The interviews covered the following issues:

- Details of the offence which had resulted in the conviction subsequent to offending, and occasions when the probationer came close to offending.

- Information about the probationer's social circumstances at the time of the offence and at the time of each of the interviews (accommodation, employment, finances, life-partner, family, drug use, alcohol use, gambling, friends and feelings of depression or anxiety).

- The probationer's desire and abilities to stop offending.

- Specific people or 'things' which might help the probationer stop offending.

- The obstacles which might stand in the way of the probationer stopping offending, and what could be done (or, in later interviews, what *had* been done) to address each of these.

- What the probationer had learnt on probation, and whether it had helped him or her stay out of trouble.

- The 'biggest single' change in the probationer's life, what had 'caused' this, how it had impacted upon the probationer and whether he or she had sought advice from his or her officer.

- Future ambitions (not asked of officers).

The follow-up interviews (at both second and third sweeps) with probationers and officers were designed to assess how things had progressed since the previous interview. With this in mind, each interviewer was therefore provided with a summary of the previous interview(s) tailored to provoke respondents into discussing changes in particular facets of their lives. The summary, which was referred to during the follow-up interview at various points when appropriate, was used to ask officers and probationers in detail about how each obstacle had been tackled; the current status of that obstacle; and the extent to which changes in the nature of the obstacle were the result of the advice given to them by their officer. In addition both parties were reminded of their previous responses to questions concerning the probationer's social circumstances and were asked whether each had changed, why and with what outcome. After they had been asked whether the probationer wanted to stop offending and if they were able to stop, they were reminded of their previous answers and, if their answers differed from the previous interview, to reflect on why this was the case. The only major changes for the subsequent interviews were that:

- If the probationer had completed the order, the officer was asked what he or she thought the purposes of the order had been, and to what extent these had been met; and, during the second sweep.

- Probationers were asked a short series of questions about victimisation in the previous year.

Tape-recorded interviews

As a way of capturing in greater details the subtleties of the work undertaken on probation, a small subsample of second and third sweep interviews were tape recorded.[7] Both Officers and probationers were asked if they would consent to having their interviews recorded, and very few declined. As well as providing a source for capturing in greater detail the nuances of probation work and the factors which facilitated or prevented desistance, the tape recording of interviews allowed for an assessment of how the questions and the interview schedule were delivered 'in the field'. No major instances of inconsistency or poor question delivery were encountered.

The validity of the data collected

Any research which asks people directly about sensitive topics, such as criminal behaviour, must take steps to ensure that the data collected are as reliable and truthful as possible. Despite our assurances that anything said during the interview was confidential (a common practice intended to increase truthful responses), it could be that probationers still concealed some things from us. It is assumed that any concealment, if it existed at all, was *most* likely when probationers were asked about their offending. Some respondents may have suspected, despite our assurances of confidentiality, that any admissions of undetected offending made during an interview would be relayed to their supervising officers or the police. In order to check the extent to which previous offences were concealed by the probationers in the sample, the following analyses were undertaken.

During the course of the first sweep interviews, probationers were asked if they had ever before committed an offence. From these responses it was possible to create two groups – those who admitted to having committed any crime before, and those who did not admit to having committed a crime before. These responses were then compared against previous convictions (undertaken for all cases where previous offending was known; $n = 192$). If a respondent claimed not to have committed a crime before, but was found to have a previous conviction, his or her answers would have to be regarded with some suspicion. Of the 21 cases who *claimed not* to have committed a crime before, only three had previous convictions. Of these three, one had two previous convictions (for violent and indictable offences); another also had two previous convictions (theft and handling, and an indictable offence); and the third had two previous convictions, both for motoring offences. It is conceivable that the last of these three (who had motoring convictions) may not have realised that these constituted criminal offences. Of those that *did not* have any previous convictions ($n = 43$), 25 admitted that they had committed some sort of crime previously – suggesting an openness to admit to undetected offending on their part. This comparison of self-reported previous offending and officially recorded previous offending suggested that levels of honesty were good – only three people with convictions did not admit to previous offending, and 25 probationers admitted to undetected offending. Further analyses (Farrall n.d.) suggest that of the 137 probationers who could be traced through the Home Office's Offenders Index, only 14 per cent of those who claimed not to have offended were recorded as having been convicted during this period, suggesting that the honesty of the probationers had been consistently high.

Notes

1 The research interviewers received a minimum of three days training, and some received four days. These training days introduced the interviewers to the research project and its aims, the arrangements for completing the interviews, the research instruments and other administrative issues. These days also placed a heavy emphasis on developing the interviewers' familiarity with the research instruments and their appropriate usage, and the confidential nature of the materials which would be gathered.
2 Alternative techniques for recruiting probationers into the study were considered, but were felt to be impractical. For example, if an interviewer had been based in the office he or she could have invited probationers to take part in the study. However, this option was not pursued for two main reasons: first, it would have been costly to do this (there were 22 offices which would have had to have been permanently 'staffed' during the recruitment phase); and, secondly, the probationers would be more familiar with their officer than the interviewer (who they would never have met before) and therefore were considered more likely to respond positively to a request from their officer. Repeated telephone calls were made to officers to ensure that all members of their caseload were being given the opportunity to become involved in the study.
3 These cases were included in the sample because of their probation element. The community service element of these orders is not subject to exhaustive investigation.
4 The Home Office include drug offences in summary offences, hence the discrepancy.
5 The Home Office include drug offences in summary offences, hence the discrepancy.
6 Copies of the interview schedules are available upon request from the author.
7 Interviews were not tape recorded during the first sweep as it was felt that respondents may be reticent about being taped (they would not have met the interviewer until immediately prior to the interview) and perhaps refused to be taped, or gone ahead with the taping of the interview but concealed or altered some responses (chiefly those concerning offending it was suspected). At the second interview, respondents 'knew' the

interviewer and were more likely to feel that the research team could be 'trusted' (indeed only one probationer of the 24 approached at the second sweep declined to be taped at this stage). Not all interviews were tape recorded as time and monetary costs would have made this prohibitive. Rather than select 'interesting' cases, it was decided to tape record the author's own interviews and those undertaken by two of the research interviewers. The interviewers were chosen because of their prior experience of taped interviewing and were given addition training in the exact requirements for this project (in addition to the three days they had already received). In all, there were 111 tape-recorded interviews completed at either sweep two or three, many of which consisted of pairs of officers and probationers whose interviews were taped recorded at both these sweeps. All taped interviews were transcribed in full (totalling over 150 hours of taped interviews).

Part 2
Probation, Motivation and Social Contexts

Chapter 4

Defining 'success'

What is 'success'?

Most research which has investigated the outcome of probation has assessed the outcome of the order in terms of reconviction rates. For the reasons outlined in Chapter 1, this project employed alternative measures of success and failure. The extent to which orders were considered to have been 'successful' or 'unsuccessful' was assessed by a variety of criteria. These were:

- whether there had been any continuation in offending (as reported by the probationers themselves and their supervising officers);

- regardless of whether an individual had offended, the extent to which the probationers appeared to be desisting; and

- the extent to which impediments to desistance had been removed.

Leaving to one side for the moment the last of these, which we shall return to in subsequent chapters, let us concentrate on offending behaviours. As noted in Chapter 3, 141 of the probationers and 182 of the officers were followed to either shortly before the very end or to shortly after the end of their orders. Table 4.1 reports the extent to which probationers reported that they had offended and officers *believed* that they had offended during the course of their orders (offending, and the variables associated with it, are discussed in greater detail in Chapter 11). Officers reported that fewer probationers had offended (by 12 percentage points). Of course, officers also sometimes *suspected* that an individual had offended and when *suspected* offending was included, 50 per cent of officers reported that their probationer had

Table 4.1: Offending whilst on probation (those seen to the end of their orders)

	Not offended		Offended		Total	
	(n)	(%)	(n)	(%)	(n)	(%)
Probationer-reported	59	42	82	58	141	100
Officer-reported	98	54	84	46	182	100

Table 4.2: Amount of offending whilst on probation (those seen to the end of their orders)

	Did not offend		One to four offences		More than four offences		Total	
	(n)	(%)	(n)	(%)	(n)	(%)	(n)	(%)
Probationer-report	59	42	31	22	49	35	139	99
Officer-report	98	54	51	28	33	18	182	100

Note: There were two probationers who reported having offended, but who gave no indication of the number of offences they had committed. These cases have been excluded from these analyses.

either offended or that they suspected he or she had offended – a rise of 4 percentage points (eight cases).[2]

The number of offences which probationers were reported to have committed whilst on probation is shown in Table 4.2. Again, the focus is upon those for whom complete reports of behaviour during the order exist. It is clear from the probationers' accounts that about a third of them had offended quite often (more than four offences during the course of the order). Whilst about a third of the probationers seen to the end of their orders admitted to having committed more than four offences during the order, the same figure for the officers' reports was naturally lower. Indeed, only 18 per cent of officers reported that their probationer had committed four or more offences.[3]

Because the investigation of offending was longitudinal, it was possible to chart the progression of each probationer's involvement in offending. In other words, it was possible to assess the extent to which each individual probationer appeared to be desisting. Whilst relatively straightforward to define, desistance is harder to operationalise. Operationalising desistance poses particular problems as it is essentially an issue of 'absence' rather than of 'presence'. That is to say, that an individual is classified as a desister not on the basis of *having* a particular characteristic, but rather because of the *continued absence* of this characteristic over a period of time. This peculiarity has already been discussed by Shadd Maruna (1998: 10–11, emphasis added) who likens these problems to what he describes as 'billiard-ball causality':

> Desistance is an unusual dependent variable for criminologists because it is *not an event that happens*, but rather the sustained absence of a certain type of event occurring. As such, desistance does not fit neatly into the linear, billiard-ball models of causality found most acceptable to criminologists.

Maruna has not been alone in his recognition that desistance is not usually 'an event' but more akin to a 'process'. Chief amongst the theorists of desistance are Robert Sampson and John Laub who, in a recent article (Laub *et al.* 1998), provided convincing evidence that desistance was not abrupt but rather a 'gradual movement away from criminal offending' (ibid.: 226). Laub *et al.* theorised that when men married into what became 'good' relationships they were *increasingly less likely* to engage in offending. Thus 'good' marriages will, over time, produce (first) de-escalators, 'near-desisters' and (eventually) desisters.[4]

Initial operationalisations of desistance were based on assumptions which are now felt to have been rather crude approaches to the topic at hand (Bushway *et al.* 2001). For example, Bushway *et al.* (2001) accused Farrington and Hawkins (1991) of having defined desisters in their study as those who had been convicted before the age of 21, but were not convicted thereafter. Bushway *et al.* argued that the age of 21 was derived from a desire to split the available data set into roughly two equal halves, rather than for any theoretical reason, and that this approach to operationalising desistance resulted in some people being classified as a persister for being convicted once at the age of 21, when in fact they may have had more in common with non-offenders or desisters. Such an approach, Bushway *et al.* argued, did not adequately capture the *processes* associated with desistance.[5]

Regardless of these definitional 'skirmishes', desistance is probably best approached as experienced by many as a process.[6] With this in mind, the operationalisation of desistance employed in the current study has placed an emphasis on *gradual processes*. Such an operationalisation both better captures the true nature of desisting from offending – in which 'lulls' in offending, temporary resumption of offending and the such like are common – and provides a schema in which *reductions* in offence severity or the frequency with which offences were admitted to could be interpreted as indications of the *emergence* of desistance.

Table 4.3: Desistance (those seen to the end of their orders)

| | Probationers' reports | | Officers' reports | |
	(n)	(%)	(n)	(%)
No offending	59	42	98	54
Showing signs of desisting	28	19	32	17
Continued offending (trivial)	17	13	14	7
Continued offending (non-trivial)	15	11	11	6
Continued offending (escalating)	22	16	27	15
Total	141	100	182	100

An important feature of this schema was that it allowed for changes in offending *trajectories* which indicated a shift in patterns of offending *towards desistance* to be charted. This entailed careful examinations of each probationer's reports of all his or her offending at each sweep – the outline of the offence(s) committed, the amount of offences reported and the nature and severity of the offences. On this basis each probationer was classified into one of five groups: no offending; an offending trajectory which suggested he or she was desisting; continued trivial offending; continued non-trivial offending; and offending which was escalating. The extent to which those probationers seen to the ends of their order were judged to be in the process of desisting is reported in Table 4.3. Whilst around a half the probationers *did* offend – according to themselves (58 per cent; Table 4.1) or their officers (46 per cent; Table 4.1) – about half these either showed signs of starting to desist, or engagement in fairly trivial offending (Table 4.4). So, despite the fact that about half the probationers were reported to have

Table 4.4: Desistance (all)

| | Probationers' reports | | Officers' reports | |
	(n)	(%)	(n)	(%)
No offending	64	32	105	53
Showing signs of desisting	28	14	33	17
Continued offending (trivial)	20	10	15	8
Continued offending (non-trivial)	18	9	15	8
Continued offending (escalating)	27	14	30	15
Impossible to code	42	21	1	—
Total	199	100	199	100

offended, in all, seven out of ten officers reported either no offending or offending trajectories which were becoming less serious, as did six out of ten of the probationers followed to the end of their orders[7] (Table 4.4). Table 4.4 reports the assessment of the entire sample's offending trajectories.[8]

Examples of offending trajectories

Those probationers who were seen only once formed the entirety of those cases deemed 'impossible to code'. Those probationers who 'showed signs of desisting' reported a decline in the frequency or offending which became distinctly less serious over time. For example, case 099 – originally convicted of going equipped to steal car radios – admitted at the first sweep to having been in possession of cannabis and amphetamines. At the second sweep he reported buying and selling stolen electrical goods – to 'help out a mate who was selling the stuff' – and to having considered stealing car radios, but said that he had not gone through with this as it was 'not worth it – too much trouble'. At the third interview he said that he had not committed any further offences, but had been asked by a friend to help with some 'credit card frauds', but had again decided that 'it was not worth it' and declined. On the basis that he had not offended since the second interview, and had even turned down the opportunity to 'help with some credit cards' 099 was classified as showing signs of desisting.

Around 10 per cent of probationers were classified as having committed trivial offences. For example, case 114 was a student at university when he was convicted of possession with intent to supply cannabis (he was in the habit of buying extra amounts of cannabis for his friends). At the first interview he said that he was continuing to smoke cannabis, but admitted no other offences. At the second sweep he admitted to continuing to smoke cannabis and to having driven over the speed limit (for which he received three points on his driving licence). At the third interview he again reported that he had smoked cannabis, but said that he had committed no further offences.

Those cases classified as non-trivial offenders reported frequent, serious offending, such as 'hard' drug use, violence or burglary. Case 022 was given his probation order after becoming involved in a fight with the police, who were trying to arrest him for being drunk and disorderly. The probationer claimed that they had been 'heavy-handed' when arresting him, and in response he had bitten the arresting officer and spat in his face. When seen for the first time he said that he had not committed any offences since the start of the order, but at the second interview said that he had again assaulted someone and 'given him a good hiding' and that same night he had again tried to assault the officer trying to arrest him. He also said he had considered stealing cigarettes when in a shop, but decided against it as he was 'in too much shit already'. At the third interview the probationer had gained employment working at an amusement park, where he said he had 'two or three times' taken people round the back of the shed to 'beat them up – but not bad enough to put them in hospital'. He also said he had shoplifted.

Amongst the escalators were those probationers who reported increases in both the severity of their offending and the frequency with which they offended. Case 083 was given his probation order after being found guilty of robbery. At the time of the first interview he said that he had not offended since the start of the order. At the second interview he said that he had been arrested for fighting. At the third interview he reported how, angry at seeing heroin being sold to kids in a local playing park, he had twice beaten up these 'dealers', on each occasion taking between £300 and £500 from them. He had also been charged with using threatening words and behaviour against his partner and admitted to having shoplifted and handled stolen goods.

The schema described above captures the desistance *process* in that it is the nature of an individual's offending career (recorded at up to three points in time) upon which the classification is based. Thus the desistance process is captured as it extends through time, rather than as a state which is reached by some arbitrary point in time (such as by a certain age).

This chapter has outlined the chief outcome measures used to assess probation supervision. Chapter 5 considers the aims and purposes of probation supervision and explores the impediments to desistance faced by the probationers in 'going straight'. The extent to which officers and probationers shared these beliefs and their proposed solutions to these is also examined.

Notes

1 Further analyses, which examined just those cases for whom *both* officer and probationers were seen to the end of the order ($n = 137$), suggested no variation from those rates reported in Tables 4.1 and 4.2.

2 Of the 58 probationers who were not seen to the end of their orders, some 25 (43 per cent) admitted that they had offended on the occasion(s) when they had been interviewed and their officers reported that 30 (52 per cent)

had offended and a further four were suspected to have offended (bringing the total percentage of known or *suspected* offenders to 59 per cent). Of the 17 officers who were not seen to the end of their probationer's orders, 9 reported that their probationer had offended and another 2 that they suspected that the probationer had offended. In other words, fewer of these 58 probationers *themselves* reported offending, although when compared to those seen to the end of their orders, more were reported by their officers to have offended.

3 Of the 58 probationers who were not seen to the end of their orders, 33 (59 per cent) did not report offending on the occasion(s) when they were interviewed. Six probationers (10 per cent) reported having committed between one and four offences, and 16 (28 per cent) that they had committed more than four offences. There were another two probationers who reported offending, but for whom it was impossible to assess the extent of their offending. Their officers reported that 29 (50 per cent) of them had not offended, that 16 had committed between one and four offences (28 per cent) and that 13 (22 per cent) had committed more than four offences. Of the 17 officers who were not followed until the end of their probationer's orders, 8 reported no offending on the part of their probationers, 5 between one and four offences and 4 reported more than four offences. So, in terms of the *number* of offences this group was *reported* to have committed, they were committing marginally fewer offences than the 'completers'. Bear in mind, however, that reports are incomplete and the officers might not have known the full extent of this group's offending.

4 Mark Warr (1998) has questioned the causal mechanism proposed by Laub *et al.* Warr suggests that marriage reduces the amount of time spent with peers, and that it is the reduction in time with peers that eventually leads to desistance, not marriage *per se*.

5 However, whilst their assertion that desistance is a process rather than an event is correct, Bushway *et al.*'s critique may be mistaken. The operationalisation used by Farrington and Hawkins does not automatically mean that desistance was assumed to be 'an event' – rather it was assumed to be either an event or a process that by the age of 21 would have been completed. In short, Bushway *et al.* would appear to have mistaken Farrington and Hawkins' operationalisation for a conceptualisation.

6 Of course, there will be some people for whom desistance is more like an event – see Cusson and Pinsonneault (1986) for examples of 'shocking events' which led some in their sample to the decision to desist.

7 It was possible to assess the offending trajectories for only 16 of the 58 probationers not seen to the end of their orders. Quite simply the remaining 42 had not been seen enough times for sufficient information about their offending to have been collected to enable an assessment of this sort to be made. Of the 16 for whom it was possible to make an assessment, 5 appeared to be desisting, 3 reported continued low-rate offending, 1 continued high-rate offending and 7 had offending trajectories which

appeared to be getting worse. Of the 42 probationers who were not seen enough times for assessments of their offending trajectories to be made, officers' reports for these cases suggested that 25 (59 per cent) of this group were desisting, 13 (31 per cent) were getting worse, 2 had continued high-rate offending and 1 had continued low-rate offending (there was one case in which the officer had only been seen once too, so again no assessment could be made). These 'surrogate' rates suggest that the 42 probationers for whom assessments could not be made were dissimilar from those for whom assessments could be made. Fewer of them were assessed as desisting (59 per cent compared to 71 per cent; officers' reports), and more were rated as having offending careers which were 'getting worse' (31 per cent compared to 15 per cent).

8 The officers' and probationers' classifications showed quite a high degree of agreement. Of the 154 probationers for whom sufficient data existed for a classification to be made by *both* officer and probationer, reports of offending trajectories for 95 cases suggested that the probationer was a desister (i.e. he or she had either not offended since the start of their order, was showing the signs of desisting or had committed only trivial offences) whilst for a further 14 cases both reported that the probationer was a persister (i.e. he or she had either committed non-trivial offences or had offending trajectories which were escalating). Thus some 71 per cent of cases were placed in the same classification group by officers and probationers. Of the 'disagreeing' cases, the majority (31 of 45) were probationers who reported persistence and whose officer had reported desistance. This was to be expected, as officers would not have known about all the offences which probationers had committed.

Chapter 5

The focus of probation

What does probation seek to do?

It is surprising how few studies of probation define what probation 'is', what it consists of, what its purposes are or how it could be expected to achieve these purposes. One of the most succinct definitions was provided by the United Nations half a century ago (1951: 4): 'probation is a method of dealing with specially selected offenders and . . . consists of the conditional suspension of punishment while the offender is placed under personal supervision and is given individual guidance or "treatment".' Of course, this definition is now somewhat past its 'best before date'. Amongst other changes during the period since the UN document was written, probation in England and Wales has, since 1991, been a sentence of the court in its own right, rather than a 'suspension of punishment', and there has, of course, been a gradual move away from individualised treatment towards group-based interventions.

The purposes of probation supervision, as outlined in *National Standards* (1995: 17), are: 'securing the rehabilitation of the offender; protecting the public from harm from the offender' and 'preventing the offender from committing further offences'. The same document lays down the following objectives designed to achieve these purposes: 'confronting offending behaviour'; 'making offenders aware of the impact of the crimes . . . on their victims, the community and themselves'; encouraging the probationer into taking responsibility for his or her actions; and remedying the practical impediments to the probationer's rehabilitation.[1]

When asked to outline the purposes of supervision, the officers interviewed for the current research project suggested similar 'goals' and means for achieving them. For example, 59 per cent said the purpose was to 'help the probationer stop offending', 38 per cent to 'advise the probationer', 28 per cent to address a specific alcohol or drug problem and 27 per cent to help the probationer 'understand why he or she had offended'. One officer said:

> The purposes that we agreed between us were to look at the offending – why he had committed it, what his beliefs were about it, what the impact of the offending on the victims was, what led to the offending and the connection between offending and drug use, and also one of the major factors was to look at his drug use [PO 042].

Thus the core aims of probation supervision are identifiable. Officers and probationers 'work together' (Osler 1995: 75; Boswell 1996: 37; Whitfield 1998: 55) in order to stop or reduce the probationer's offending; to help the probationer with an addiction or habit; to assist with practical impediments to 'rehabilitation'; to increase victim awareness; and to ensure the protection of the public. What the UN definition also does not mention explicitly is that probation is a *community sentence* and that, if revoked, can be replaced with an alternative, sometimes more severe punishment. Indeed Stone (1998: 8) reports that around a third of probation and combination orders which were revoked in 1996 resulted in immediate custody. With these points in mind, it is possible to sketch what probation 'is':

- A sentence which takes place in the community (rather than in prison).
- A form of help (in that guidance or 'treatment' is available).
- A form of punishment (in that the offender has to comply with various conditions).
- A deterrent to further offending (in that further offending could result in additional or harsher forms of punishment).

Through these processes, probation is intended to rehabilitate the probationer (United Nations 1951: 15; National Standards 1995: 17; Brown 1998: 58–59). But how might these processes actually operate to produce desistance? The following are arguably the most immediately obvious ways in which they could, as a result of:

- The direct help of the probation officer (including referrals to special programmes or partnerships);

- Some of the social and individual processes associated with desistance (as outlined in Chapter 1) and which occur as the result of the probationer being in the community rather than in prison; and

- Threats of further punishment, which deters the probationer from further offending.

Data collected from the probationers during the course of this investigation suggested that the third of these, the 'deterrence model', was spurious. Although 59 per cent of probationers said that they wanted to stop offending because they were concerned by the thought of further sanctions, logistic regression analyses suggested that they were in fact no more likely to have avoided offending (or to have desisted) by the end of the order than the 41 per cent who had *not* said they were worried about the consequences. Therefore, the present investigation has focused on the impact of the direct interventions of probation staff and those to whom they refer the probationer, and the role of social and individual processes in securing successful outcomes.

Regardless of whether or not one accepts the aims of probation as outlined above as legitimate, the underlying premise of probation work is that the officer and probationer should *share* a set of common goals – or, at the very least, that the officer will try to encourage the probationer to adopt some of these goals. The opposite of this – the officer and probationer having a totally different set of 'goals' – would lead to a situation in which 'working together' would become impossible or, at the least, severely hampered.

The aim of this chapter, therefore, is to explore the extent to which officers and probationers shared a common set of relevant 'goals' and beliefs as they commenced probation and were therefore in a position to 'work together'. This commences with an examination of the officers' and probationers' understanding of the aspects of the probationer's life which were felt to be obstacles to desistance – that is to say, aspects of their lives represented impediments and obstacles to desistance.

Looking to the future: obstacles to desistance

Several previous studies of the processes associated with desistance from offending have established that many would-be desisters – be they eventually desisters or recidivists – faced obstacles to desisting.[2]

A shared understanding of the obstacles probationers faced is, arguably, essential for a productive working relationship between officer and probationer. Without a clear understanding of why an individual might reoffend it is hard to know which aspects of his or her life should be prioritised for intervention. The following analyses are therefore based on the 'concordance' between the assessments of obstacles made by each probationer and his or her officer. Few studies have considered probation from the perspectives of *both* officers and probationers. Although Willis' investigation (1986: 170–75) found generally high levels of agreement on the purposes and aims of probation between officers and those they were supervising, his work, like that of Bailey (1995), Brown (1998) and Rex (1999), was a qualitative investigation with a modestly sized sample. Rex (1999) had a sample of 60 officer–probationer pairs, Willis had 30 pairs and Brown 16. Such sample sizes (whilst entirely appropriate and defensible for the investigations at hand in each study) render generalisations about *rates* of agreement between officers and probationers somewhat limited.

When asked about the obstacles which the probationers faced, probationers and officers held quite different views (Table 5.1). Half ($n = 98$) the probationers said that they did not face *any* obstacles in desisting, but only one out of ten officers (18 of 199) believed that the probationers they were supervising faced no obstacles to desisting.

Of the 101 probationers who said that they faced one or more obstacles, their own use of substances (drugs and alcohol, 19 per cent) was the most commonly cited, closely followed by their friends and family (15 per cent). Other obstacles were even less frequently mentioned. Overall (Table 5.1), few probationers cited social problems (such as their employment and housing situations) as obstacles to desistance, despite the well documented evidence that social factors

Table 5.1: Obstacles to desistance[3]

Category	Probationers		Officers	
	(n)	(%)	(n)	(%)
No obstacles expected	98	49	18	9
Friends and family	29	15	74	37
Financial reasons	17	9	13	7
Drugs and alcohol	37	19	74	37
Social problems	13	6	54	27
Personal characteristics	18	10	60	30
Other responses	8	4	32	16
Total obstacles	122	100	307	100

play a large part in offending careers (e.g. Smith *et al.* 1991; Farrington 1997: 390–92), and only one in ten probationers regarded any of their own personal attributes as obstacles.

Unlike those whom they supervised, nine out of ten officers said that the probationer faced at least one obstacle. Several officers thought that friends and/or family along with drugs and alcohol were likely to be obstacles (37 per cent). Officers also reported more obstacles relating to social problems, in particular the probationer's employment situation, than did probationers. Interestingly, there were few citations of cognitive-behavioural obstacles (such as poor thinking skills or anger management), suggesting that these were either not features of the current sample's problems, or that they were not features which were readily identified by officers.[4]

Agreement between officers and probationers concerning the obstacles faced

Of crucial importance, of course, is the extent to which the officer and the probationer he or she was supervising agreed with one another about the obstacles which the probationer faced. As can be seen from Table 5.2, very few ($n=12$; 6 per cent) officers and probationers *both* felt that the probationer faced no obstacles in stopping offending.

Almost all probationers who said that they faced at least one obstacle in stopping offending ($n=101$) were being supervised by officers who agreed with this assessment ($n=95$). However, almost half the officers (86 of 181) who felt that the probationer they were supervising faced an obstacle were supervising probationers who felt that they faced no obstacles at all. When obstacles which were specifically related to friends and family were considered, only around one quarter (19 out

Table 5.2: Officer–probationer pairs: obstacles to desistance

Obstacle type	Officer and probationer 'yes'	Officer and probationer 'no'	Officer 'yes' and probationer 'no'	Officer 'no' and probationer 'yes'	Total
Any obstacles	95 (48%)	12 (6%)	86 (43%)	6 (3%)	199
Friends/family	19 (10%)	115 (58%)	55 (28%)	10 (8%)	199
Finances	4 (2%)	173 (87%)	9 (5%)	13 (7%)	199
Drugs/alcohol	27 (14%)	115 (58%)	47 (24%)	10 (5%)	199
Social problems	5 (3%)	138 (69%)	49 (25%)	8 (4%)	199
Personal characteristics	8 (4%)	128 (64%)	52 (26%)	10 (5%)	199

of 74) of officers who thought that the probationer faced such an obstacle were supported in this assessment by the probationer themselves. On the other hand, of the 29 probationers who reported an obstacle relating to their friends and/or family, 19 (two thirds) were being supervised by officers who supported this assessment.

Drug and alcohol usage was the obstacle which officers and probationers most frequently cited as a problem in avoiding future offending. For 27 (14 per cent) of the cases in the sample, *both* the officer and the probationer reported substance use as an obstacle. However, there was again a tendency for officers to report it more frequently than probationers. Of the 74 officers who cited drugs or alcohol as an obstacle, only one third ($n=27$) were supervising probationers who agreed with this assessment. The obstacles grouped together as 'social problems' also followed this pattern: officers reported obstacles with far greater frequency than did probationers. The same can also be said of the citations of the probationer's personal characteristics as an obstacle to desistance.

Thus, even at the very outset of the order – following the often intense pre-sentence report writing sessions and the high contact demanded by *National Standards* in the first months of supervision – there were few officers and probationers working 'in tandem'. Almost half (43 per cent) the officers were supervising probationers whom they believed faced at least one obstacle, but whose supervisees felt that they faced no obstacles (Table 5.2). These differential levels of agreement suggest that officers were much more likely to support probationers' assessments than vice versa. Assuming that the officers *were* correct in their understanding of each probationer's situation and their diagnoses, this suggests that some probationers were only partially aware of the issues which needed to be addressed during the order. This could, of course, be seen as a 'good sign' – obstacles which the probationers were unaware of had been spotted by the officers. Thus there exists an 'awareness gap' which officers could fill. However, as the first research interviews were undertaken – on average – some seven weeks into the order, one might have expected that the probationers would have started to show some recognition of the obstacles they faced.

Overcoming obstacles – anticipated solutions

Officers and probationers were asked, in relation to each obstacle identified, how they expected to overcome it. The solution most commonly proposed by probationers (and some probationers proposed more than one solution) involved what could be described as 'home-grown' techniques, such as 'just learning to cope with it' or unaided attempts to reduce drug intake (33 per cent of the 122 proposed solutions). Another group of responses focused upon direct action, such as 'finding work' or 'getting new friends' (28 per cent). The third most common response was to 'seek professional help'. This included strategies such as enrolling on rehabilitation schemes (usually associated with drugs) and seeking counselling (23 per cent). It is especially noteworthy that only *one* probationer said that he would ask his officer for advice. Another small group of respondents denied that anything needed be done – usually as it was felt that the problem would not materialise, or need not be addressed anyway (6 per cent).

Thus even when obstacles *were* recognised by probationers, their proposed solutions more often suggested 'the *ad hoc*' (learning to cope with the obstacle or unaided drug reduction) rather than 'the focused'. Many probationers would appear to have failed to grasp the task confronting them in dealing with these obstacles. They either thought that there would be no impediments to their 'going straight' – although only 12 of the 98 probationers who claimed they faced no obstacles were supervised by officers who supported this assessment – or if they did recognise the existence of obstacles, appeared to suggest 'homespun' solutions.

Officers were also asked to discuss the interventions which they proposed to employ in tackling the obstacles they had identified. Their responses were coded using the schema developed by Colin Roberts and his colleagues at the Probation Studies Unit, Centre for Criminological Research, Oxford for classifying modes of intervention (see Appleton and Roberts 1999; Haslewood-Pocsik and Roberts 1999a, 1999b, 1999c), and are summarised in Table 5.3.

Nearly three quarters of the officers (72 per cent; see the emboldened row in Table 5.3) said that they would rely on open-ended discussions with the probationer. After this, referrals to other agencies and practical help were the next most frequently cited methods of work (35 per cent).

In order to explore in greater depth officers' and probationers' proposed solutions to the obstacles identified, case studies of those officers and probationers who had *both* identified each of the same three most commonly cited obstacles (friends, drugs and alcohol) were undertaken. Despite the small numbers, the data suggest some variation between officers and probationers in their plans for tackling each of these obstacles and in their views of the problems associated with tackling such obstacles.[6]

Table 5.3: *Proposed methods for tackling the obstacle: officers' reports*[5]

Proposed method	(n)	(%)
Reporting only	3	2
Practical help	59	33
Talk – open ended	**131**	**72**
Talk – about past	32	17
Talk – about present	42	22
Activity – written	20	11
Activity – visual	3	2
Activity – role play	22	12
Activity – task	8	4
Family work	22	12
Referral – group programme	37	21
Referral – other in-house	36	21
Referral – partnership	41	23
Referral – other agency	63	35
Other	46	26

Friends

Thirteen officers agreed with their probationer that their friends posed an obstacle to them desisting. When asked how she would help the probationer cope with his offending friends, one officer said: 'Seeing him regularly, monitoring what he is doing and pointing out the risks of custody. Encouraging him to get training and employment so he has a reasonable income and does not need to think about offending' [212]. Her probationer (who was on probation after getting involved in a fight whilst out with some friends of his) said: 'I have moved out of the area where these friends were. [My] new friends are more interested in getting jobs than getting into trouble.' He went on to add that probation supervision acted as 'a weekly reminder of what I need to do to keep out of trouble [and] what I should be doing with my life'.

Another officer said: '[I will] try to remind him how he has felt about them [his friends] in the past – how he has got into trouble with them' [091]. The probationer in question, a 21-year-old male on probation for 24 months after being found guilty for driving whilst disqualified, said: 'It is not that I want to [drive whilst disqualified], but I get caught doing it. My friends can't drive . . . I can't tell them to "get stuffed" – they're okay really.' In other words, he proposed to do little directly about his peers. When asked if being on probation would help him deal with his friends, he said:

It does help, but when you go from here [the probation office], your mind is not there and when you are with mates they get you out of your head and it is not that you look for it, it is just ... I cannot tell them to 'get stuffed' they would bang me on the head. It is okay when I leave here but that is just until I am with my mates.

So probation supervision, whilst acknowledged as being helpful, had, in this probationer's opinion, a potentially limited impact which was partly contingent upon the behaviour of his friends: if they enticed him sufficiently he might offend. Likewise, the following officer also lamented the fact that the input she would eventually have would be minimal:

I can only work on what he tells me. He doesn't want to upset me and therefore he would rather tell a lie than the truth if it results in conflict ... He wants to be liked – so it's difficult to follow through a challenge without destroying him again. My contribution is about laying the foundations. My influence will be a drop in the ocean. It'll take far more time than what I'll spend with him [165].

Her probationer said that whom he 'hung around with' had 'nothing to do with probation'. Another officer suggested that her probationer's friendships with other drug users were exacerbated as a result of contact with the probation service:

I think we make [heroin user networks] worse here because of our waiting room. That inevitably reinforces the network connections. I don't know what we can do about that – beyond not making people wait long. I am a bit cautious about heroin users' group-work programmes. She doesn't go to one, but it is our policy that one goes unless there is a good reason not to refer. I know there are positive sides to it, what we don't know is how much harm it does by reinforcing old networks [060].

This same officer, when asked how much she felt she would be able to help the probationer overcome this obstacle said 'not at all – we just make it worse'. The probationer in question – a 23-year-old female who said she had been using heroin since she was 16 – also appeared to place little emphasis on probation interventions:

I've just got to stay away [from heroin users]. I stay at home most of the time. My mum – who lives with me at my Gran's – and my Gran are very supportive. I can talk to them whenever I'm feeling down and that helps. I can't think of doing much else at the moment – 'cause of this methadone treatment. I'm struggling not to take drugs.

Two of the probationers were already in prison at the time of the first interview. Both had received probation orders, agreed to be interviewed and subsequently been remanded in custody. The officer of one of these probationers said that she would employ the following techniques in combating the influence of his peer group: 'Trying to look at long term strengths. He can make use of his time in prison by fulfilling his education and gaining work skills. He attended several college courses before, but these fell through' [084]. The probationer, for his part, when asked how he expected to deal with his friends, said: 'I don't know. Move out of the area when I get out [of prison]. Move away from [here] – maybe even . . . isn't far enough away! Need to go even further – as far as possible'.

Peer groups, of course, present a particularly tricky obstacle for officers. Whilst they are often cited as the source of much offending – especially amongst young males (see Farrington 1997: 381–82) the actual mechanics of intervening in this aspect of the probationer's life are extremely difficult – not to mention felt to be ethically dubious by some officers. As shown above, although probation supervision was felt to be helpful by some, its impact was also acknowledged by both officers and probationers to be 'under threat' by these same friends.

Drugs and alcohol

Potentially at least, drug and alcohol obstacles offered more tangible challenges for officers to work with. Sixteen officers and probationers both cited drug use (in effect, heroin use) and 13 cited alcohol use as an obstacle for the probationer in avoiding future offending (two cited both as obstacles). The following quotations concern a 23-year-old female probationer who had started to use methadone since the offence for which she had been given her 12-month order:

She is doing a programme of preventing drug relapse on a one-to-one basis with me, which heightens her awareness of relapse [and] addresses the four stages of relapse . . . She has been encouraged to go to [a local drug help centre] where she gets acupuncture for withdrawal [PO 058].

I stay in to baby-sit, avoid users and use methadone. My officer is directing me on a drugs education programme and I visit an acupuncture centre to relieve the symptoms of withdrawal [PR 058].

As one would expect, partnership agencies and group-work programmes dominated both officers' and probationers' planned responses to drug and alcohol obstacles. In some instances, as with the case below, the probationer was already known to local drug agencies, and so the officer's role was confined to one of monitoring the probationer's progress:

He has actually referred himself back to [a local drug centre] and we're waiting for him to be accepted again. I'm trying to keep his motivation up, but it's quite difficult – knowing that he is using – so we're talking about harm reduction [PO 008].

When I'm on my de-tox programme, they're going to put me on tablets so if I purchase a £10 wrap,[7] it won't have any effect 'cause of the tablets – so it would be a waste [to use]. Also, group sessions – ex-addicts talking about how they have coped. There is a de-tox programme where I can go away from home for three to four months, but I wouldn't want to do that 'cause of my family [PR 008].

Another officer outlined her thinking behind sending her client to a local group programme:

He will attend drug groups ... these include drug education, information on safe drug use and managing drug use. I'll try to get him funding for rehabilitation – I think that this would be more effective than the groups, although the drug groups might help his motivation and put him in contact with [a specialist worker] who would assess him for residential rehabilitation. He needs the funding to go to rehab, which comes from the probation service and [a local partnership]. The groups are part of his order, so he has to do them, but I don't think they will be that useful to him – apart from the motivational side. I think if he gets funding and goes to rehab it will help him a lot. It depends on the probation service and social services having the money available to finance this [PO 086].

Her probationer said that he was relying on methadone, reduced over time, as his main technique for dealing with his addiction. Such schemes, however, offered the probationer a chance to 'play off' one agency against another, as illustrated by the following quotation from an officer [198] who was supervising a 23-year-old male on a two-year order made for possession of heroin: 'Consultation with his prescriber and counsellor to stop him playing each other off with us. I'm going to see if I can get access to his urine tests to find out if he is still using heroin – then I'll be able to challenge him on this.'[8] Other officers preferred more overt liaisons with medical staff: 'I went with him to his GP and supported him in getting a methadone script with the aim of reducing criminal behaviour' [PO 013]. The probationer concerned noted that: 'I am getting medication, I need to stick with it and try to stop using on top of it. If I could find work, that would keep me away [from using]' [PR 013]. In other words, the intervention itself was not enough – other distractions from heroin were required. 'Staying busy' was also referred to by another probationer [105], who described her own response to her drug use as being: 'One step at a time, thinking positive, changing the people that I associate with and seeing it as a wrong thing to do. Get some work'.

Officers' responses to drug-related obstacles suggested a reliance on referrals. The solutions proposed by officers to alcohol-related obstacles, whilst again showing a willingness to refer, suggested that discussions with the probationer were the preferred technique for intervening with alcohol problems. In some cases an eclectic approach was employed:

Drink diaries, mood diaries, anger management ... He also attends a substance misuse programme. Essentially a behavioural approach with a strong cognitive element. A re-examination of his personal construct – examining his self-perception in a social context, extracting the positives and reinforcing these and building a new positive self-construct leaving behind negatives [PO 171].

The probationer in question said he would 'take every day as it came', cut himself off from drinking buddies and attend Alcoholic Anonymous (to which he had been introduced via the probation service). However, even in the cases discussed herein – where alcohol-related obstacles were identified by both probationers and officers – the proposed solutions were sometimes admitted to be precarious at best:

The only thing I can do is to isolate myself from people who are a bad influence. I'll have to work on that. But this is not easy because you can't cut [yourself] off completely – its unrespectful. Because it is like I was explaining before – it's a community thing, a sense of belonging.[9] You have to look after them and they look after you when there's a need. I'm working on it. It would be an offence to be with them and not drink. It would mean you are not one of them [PR 076].

His officer said that he would refer him to a specialist social worker who worked with those who had alcohol problems and try to encourage him to enrol on a de-tox programme whilst supporting him on a one-to-one basis.

The analysis of officers' and probationers' beliefs has suggested some important differences in opinions. Officers' and probationers' assessments of the obstacles facing probationers suggested that few agreed over the obstacles faced. Probationers who reported a particular obstacle to desistance were likely to be supported in this assessment by their officers – but the reverse was not true: probationers less frequently supported their officer's assessments. Thus it would appear that there were few officers and probationers who had identified the same obstacle, or – when they did agree over the obstacles faced – were approaching its resolution in the same way. In short, there were few officers and probationers who were 'working together'. As such, the principles of 'guidance' and 'treatment' (as enshrined in the UN definition), the officers' reports of their work (see above) and the wider literature (e.g. Rex 1999: 373), whilst worthy values, would *not* appear to be typically part of the actual 'business' of probation. Some of the quotations above hint at explanations for this sorry state of affairs. The next task, however, is to explore the extent to which this effected the rates with which the probationers overcame the obstacles they faced. Chapter 6 examines this matter and considers the efforts of both the officers and the probationers to resolve these obstacles – including the extent to which they 'worked together' – and the impact of these efforts on resolving obstacles.

Notes

1 Imogen Brown (1998: 58–59) listed a similar range of 'goals' reported to her by the probation officers she interviewed in her sample. Officers reported 'stopping offending' to be the 'ultimate goal'. They stated that dealing with alcohol problems, immaturity, instability, drug use, low self-control and irresponsibility as amongst the steps needed to achieve the cessation of offending.

2 It should be noted that the studies concerned employed various sampling frames and methodologies. Therefore the finding that desisters have faced problems in stopping offending is probably not a function of inadequate or biased research. For example, Rex (1999) relied upon a probation-based sample, Burnett (1992) on a sample drawn from those recently released from prison, Cusson and Pinsonneault (1983) and Dale (1976) on samples drawn from outside the criminal justice system and Maruna (1997) on published autobiographies of desistance.

3 Multiple responses possible.

4 For example, of the 60 obstacles relating to personal problems identified by the officers, 28 related to the probationer's 'state of mind', depression or stress whilst only 7 officers referred to their probationer as having 'poor temper control'. Of the 18 probationers who reported that they faced personal characteristics which would make desistance hard, only 6 were related to poor temper control – the rest being problems associated with changing ones lifestyle, boredom, finding crime exciting or being depressed.

5 Multiple responses possible, n of Officers = 181.

6 It is, of course, impossible to compare how those officers and probationers who did *not* agree about the problems faced by the probationer proposed to tackle these problems because these problems were not probed during both interviews.

7 A 'wrap' is a common expression used to refer to small amounts of, in this case, heroin which are measured out by dealers prior to the sale into amounts of sufficient dosage to allow the purchaser to use all the 'wrap' in one go.

8 Interestingly, the probationer in question said that he had already solved his drug use problem by 'moving off the estate' and 'trying to keep away from druggies'. He also said that he 'didn't talk to his officer much about drugs'.

9 The probationer was a 'born alcoholic' who periodically lived on the streets.

Chapter 6

Resolving obstacles: the role of probation supervision

One of the key criterion of successful probation supervision is the overcoming or negation of obstacles which would otherwise have led to further offending. As one of the principal aims of probation supervision is to prevent further offending, tackling an obstacle in such a way that it is no longer felt to represent a risk factor is used as the measure of success. As can be seen by examining the emboldened row in Table 6.1, around a half the obstacles identified at the beginning of the orders were felt to have been successfully resolved.

Because the outcome of probation supervision was assessed by rates of offending and desistance, it was important to design a measure of successful obstacle resolution which was sufficiently different from these measures to avoid a tautology. By asking whether each specific obstacle had made it hard for the probationer to stop offending, the focus is on the outcome of the work undertaken to resolve *that* obstacle, as opposed to the probationer's offending in *general*. Of course, it was anticipated that those who had not offended or who showed signs of desisting would be drawn heavily from those who either faced no obstacles or had resolved those which they had faced.

Table 6.1: The extent to which obstacles were successfully resolved

	Probationers		Officers	
	(n)	(%)	(n)	(%)
Total obstacles identified at start	122	100	307	100
... of which followed up by research team	101	83	307	100
... of which resolved	**53**	**52**	**147**	**48**
... of which not resolved	48	48	160	52

What was the relationship between facing obstacles, resolving obstacles and desisting? Those probationers who said that they faced no obstacles when first interviewed were less likely to have reported having offended at the subsequent interview ($p = .001$). There was also a strong relationship between reports of successfully overcoming an obstacle and the avoidance of offending. When successfully overcome obstacles were cross-tabulated with the reports of *actual* offending – gained in a separate section of the interview – a clear trend could be observed. Obstacles which were felt to have been overcome were strongly associated with reports of non-offending. For example, of the 80 probationers who reported facing at least one obstacle when first interviewed and who were followed up, 40 said that at least one of the obstacles had made it hard for them to stop offending. Of these 40, 28 (70 per cent) also reported having offended since starting probation as a result of the obstacle(s). Of the 40 probationers who said that the obstacle(s) had not made it hard for them to stop offending, only 17 (42 per cent) reported having offended during the same period ($p = < .000$) – furthermore, an analysis of their descriptions of the events leading up to their offending suggested that these episodes were unrelated to the obstacles they said they faced. Similarly, the 12 probationers who said that the obstacle which they had identified had made avoiding offending hard, but who had not offended, reported that they had been tempted or come close to offending, but had (so far) managed to avoid this.[1] In order to check the validity of these results, officers' assessments of whether the obstacles had led to further offending or not were also compared with probationers' self-reports of offending – again the results were statistically significant: officers who reported that obstacles had been resolved were supervising more probationers who did indeed report having avoided offending than those for whom the obstacles had not been resolved ($p = < .000$).

There was a similarly strong relationship between resolving obstacles and desisting (Table 6.2). Of the 76 probationers who reported facing no obstacles and whom it was possible to classify as either a desister or a persister, 62 (82 per cent) were rated as desisters. Those who reported having overcome the obstacles they faced were slightly less likely to have desisted, but still almost seven out of ten had done so. Finally, those who did not resolve their obstacles were even less likely to have desisted (although 51 per cent still managed to do so).

What were the 'motors' which drove obstacle resolution? Was this the result of the good work of probation officers? Was it due to the motivation of some probationers to avoid further trouble? Or was it due to some other factors, or combination of factors? It was these sorts

Table 6.2: Desistance by obstacles: probationers' reports[2]

	Faced no obstacles		Obstacles were resolved		Obstacles not resolved		Total	
	(n)	(%)	(n)	(%)	(n)	(%)	(n)	(%)
Desisters	62	(82)	27	(69)	20	(51)	109	(71)
Persisters	14	(18)	12	(31)	19	(49)	45	(29)
Total	76	(100)	39	(100)	39	(100)	154	(100)

of questions to which the project sought answers. Because the aim of the project was to develop the understanding of the processes involved in influencing these outcomes rather than just the correlates of these outcomes (Pawson and Tilley 1997), it was not enough to employ 'black box' approaches to these sorts of outcomes. The keys used to 'open' the 'black box' of probation required a reliance upon both quantitative and qualitative data sources, and an emphasis on locating probation supervision in wider social and personal contexts. To this end it was assumed that, to varying degrees, all the following would influence the outcome of probation supervision:

- The work of the supervising probation officer;
- The motivation of the individual probationer; and
- The individual probationer's social and personal circumstances.

It was further assumed, in line with Byrne (1998), that these influences would (1) interact with one another (sometimes working to support one another and sometimes working to 'cancel each other out'); and (2) would be dynamic, changing both their nature and the extent to which they influenced one another and, ultimately, the outcome of supervision.

The role of supervision

The remainder of this chapter explores the attempts to resolve the obstacles identified by officers and probationers and it focuses on the extent to which probation supervision helped to resolve obstacles. Because so few officer–probationer pairs agreed about the obstacles faced by the probationer (see Chapter 5), this chapter proceeds with separate analyses of officers' and probationers' accounts of their efforts. The officers' accounts are dealt with first.

Officers' responses

When followed up,[3] officers' reports of the work which they had undertaken suggested that they had employed practical help, written work, role playing, family work and referrals less frequently than they had anticipated – general discussions dominated their work (Table 6.3). It is interesting to note the limited use of group-work programmes – less than half the proposed uses of such programmes actually came to fruition. One fifth of the officers said that, in their opinion, the probationer had resolved the obstacle themselves, and just over a quarter said that the obstacle had not been addressed at all.

Officers' answers regarding the extent to which the obstacles they had identified had been resolved are summarised in Table 6.4. As can be seen, around 40–50 per cent of each type of obstacle were felt to have been resolved. Officers were asked to describe not only their own efforts to tackle the obstacle which they had identified, but also their assessment of the efforts of the probationer to tackle the same obstacle. The officers' descriptions of their own efforts[6] and their reports of the

Table 6.3: Methods used to tackle sweep-one obstacles: officers' reports[4]

Category	Sweep one: proposed		Follow-up: employed	
	(n)	(%)	(n)	(%)
Reporting only	3	2	1	—
Practical help	59	33	24	13
Talk – open ended	**131**	**72**	**129**	**71**
Talk – about past	**32**	**17**	**22**	**12**
Talk – about present	**42**	**22**	**34**	**19**
Activity – written	20	11	2	1
Activity – visual	3	2	3	1
Activity – role play	22	12	3	1
Activity – task	8	4	4	2
Family work	22	12	6	3
Referral – group programme	37	21	15	8
Referral – other in-house	36	21	17	9
Referral – partnership	41	23	33	18
Referral – other agency	63	35	39	22
Other	46	26	17	9
Nothing – probationer did it all	—	—	34	19
Nothing – not addressed at all	—	—	50	28
Missing	—	—	5	3
Total (officers)	181		176	

Table 6.4:   Resolving obstacles: officers' reports[5]

Obstacle type	Identified at start (n)	Percentage which were resolved by next interview (%)
Drugs/alcohol	74	51
Friends/family	74	38
Personal characteristics	60	52
Social problems	54	52
Finances	13	38
Other	32	50
Total (obstacles)	307	48

probationers' efforts[7] to overcome the obstacles were similarly re-coded into a number of variables.

For *all* obstacles types taken together and *each* individual obstacle type, analyses were undertaken to assess whether any specific types of intervention employed by officers or types of responses taken by probationers were more frequently associated with the successful resolution of obstacles. For example, did officers who referred proba-tioners have a higher proportion who had successfully resolved the obstacle they faced, than, say, officers who gave practical help? Were those who gave practical help to tackle drug obstacles more successful than those who gave practical help to tackle social problems? Similarly, were those probationers who sought employment as a solution to obstacles relating to alcohol more successful than those who moved home?

Very few of the intervention types employed by officers, however, were found to be related to officers' accounts of whether the obstacle had made it hard for the probationer to stop offending.[8] This suggests that few particular types of intervention were any more likely to be effective than any *other type*, and that virtually all types were ineffective in combating obstacles. Similarly, none of the officers' reports of the probationer's actions were significantly associated with the 'successful' resolution of obstacles either. However, reporting that the probationer had *not* been motivated to address the obstacle was significantly related to it having *not* been resolved ($p < = .000$). In other words, from the officers' accounts of their own work and the actions of the probationer, it would appear that no particular types of intervention were more effective than any other in helping probationers to over-come the obstacles they were felt to face.

Of course, it may be hypothesised that those officers and probationers who actively *worked together* would be more likely to combat
successfully and overcome an obstacle than those who did not work
together. With this in mind, additional analyses were undertaken
which explored the *extent and nature* of co-operation between officers
and probationers. For each obstacle, a further variable, recording the
extent to which the officer and probationer worked together, was
created. A summary of these analyses is shown in Table 6.5.[9]

Whilst the numbers were small, some patterns did emerge. About a
third of the officers reported that they and their probationer worked
jointly on the obstacle. This degree of 'co-working' was in line with the
analyses presented in Chapter 5, which suggested that few officers and
probationers had identified the same obstacles. Co-working was most
common amongst those whom the officer had felt faced an obstacle
relating to their drug usage (19 out of 35), and least common amongst
those with friends/family obstacles (18 out of 74). Personal characteristics was the obstacle least often addressed – in over a quarter of the
instances in which the officer had identified the probationer as having
such an obstacle, no work had been undertaken (see the emboldened
text in Table 6.5). Obstacles relating to social problems were often left
to the probationer to take the lead in solving – one third of those
officers who had identified their probationer as facing an obstacle of
this nature reported that they had relied on the probationer taking the
lead or sole responsibility for tackling the obstacle.

In order to assess the extent to which working styles were related to
successful outcomes, officers' assessments of whether the obstacle had
or had not been resolved were cross-tabulated against the above
working styles[16] for each obstacle type. These analyses suggested that
there were *no* differences in terms of outcomes between officer-led/co-
working styles and any other style of work.[17] In other words, if the
probationers in the current study had been left to their own devices, or
if no interventions had been undertaken, they were just as likely to
have overcome the obstacle they faced successfully as they would have
been if their officers had led/co-worked with them.

These findings do not suggest that these efforts *never* produced
beneficial results but that they were just as likely to succeed as they
were to fail. In other words, the outcomes appear to exist independently of the interventions undertaken. Of course, one obvious limitation of
the analyses presented so far is that the probationer's perspective is
missing. Whilst officers can report their own understanding of the
probationer's response to the obstacle identified and the outcomes of
these efforts, it is important to understand probation supervision from

Table 6.5: Intervention styles sweep-one obstacles: officers' reports (numbers, with percentages in parentheses)

Intervention styles	Drugs	Alcohol	Friends/family	Personal characteristics	Social problems	Total
Officer took the lead[10]	0 (0)	3 (7)	0 (0)	3 (5)	1 (2)	7 (3)
Officer/probationer 'co-working'[11]	19 (54)	16 (39)	18 (24)	20 (33)	15 (30)	88 (33)
Officer/probationer working separately[12]	1 (3)	4 (11)	6 (8)	4 (7)	1 (2)	16 (6)
Probationer took the lead[13]	4 (11)	8 (20)	13 (18)	2 (3)	18 (33)	45 (17)
Was not addressed[14]	8 (23)	6 (15)	17 (23)	16 (27)	11 (20)	58 (22)
Change of officer, 'don't know', etc.[15]	3 (9)	4 (10)	19 (26)	15 (25)	8 (15)	49 (19)
Missing	0 (0)	0 (0)	1 (1)	0 (0)	0 (0)	1 (—)
Total	35 (100)	41 (100)	74 (100)	60 (100)	54 (100)	264 (100)

the probationer's perspective. Accordingly, the probationers' accounts of the work undertaken were the next subject of the inquiry.

Probationers' responses

Like officers, probationers were asked about the help which they had received from their officer in attempting to address the obstacle(s) concerned. Thirty-two per cent of the probationers said that the officer had been of 'little' or 'no help' to them in solving the obstacle which they had identified. However, over 50 per cent reported that their officer had helped them confront the obstacle which they had identified. In virtually every case this help consisted of advice: 31 out of the 48 probationers who said that their officer had helped said that their officer had given them advice.

The data derived from interviews with probationers were subjected to analyses which paralleled those reported above for officers. Table 6.6 outlines the probationers' reports of the extent to which they felt the obstacles which they said they faced had been resolved. Whilst *direct* comparisons between officers and probationers should not be made (as a minority had agreed about the nature of the obstacles faced), some general trends can be observed.

Probationers' ratings of the extent to which the obstacles had made stopping offending hard (i.e. were still unresolved) reveal some interesting findings (Table 6.6). Half the officers said that the 74 drug and/or alcohol obstacles they had identified had made it hard for the probationer to stop, and the same figure for probationers was very close (57 per cent). In fact, with the exception of 'other' obstacles,

Table 6.6: Resolving obstacles: probationers' reports [18]

Obstacle type	Identified at start and followed up (n)	Of which resolved (%)
Drugs/alcohol	28 (74)	57 (51)
Friends/family	24 (74)	38 (38)
Personal characteristics	17 (60)	53 (52)
Social problems	11 (54)	64 (52)
Finances	13 (13)	50 (50)
Other	8 (32)	77 (38)
Total obstacles	101 (307)	53 (48)

Note: Officers' reports in parentheses.

probationer's assessments for all obstacle types were very close to those of the officers (compare Tables 6.4 and 6.6).

Like the officers, probationers were asked to describe the work undertaken by their officer and their own attempts to tackle each of the obstacles which they had identified. Probationers' descriptions of their officer's work were re-coded into one of three variables: the officer did nothing/very little; officer gave me advice; and officer helped in another way.[19] The probationer's descriptions of their own efforts to resolve the obstacle they said they had faced were re-coded into variables similar to those used when exploring the officer's accounts of the probationer's activities (see footnote 8).[20]

Analyses of the types of interventions for *all* obstacles and for each obstacle type failed to uncover any statistically significant results – broadly in line with the same analyses performed using the officer's data. As with the officers, analyses were undertaken to explore the *extent and nature* of the co-operation between officers and probationers. For each probationer, a further variable recording the extent to which the probationer and officer co-operated together in solving the obstacle mentioned was created, again in line with those created from officers' reports. A summary of these responses is given in Table 6.7.

Again, the number of cases was very small, and drawing definitive conclusions from them should be avoided. However, it is interesting to note that almost half the probationers who reported that they faced a drug or alcohol-related obstacle said that they had addressed this *without* the assistance of their officers (i.e. that they did not co-work with their officer). In parallel with the officers, analyses were under-taken to assess the extent to which these differing intervention styles were related to outcomes. In none of the analyses undertaken on the officers' reports was statistical significance reached. This again suggests not that 'working together' *never* produced beneficial results, but that it was just as likely to fail to resolve the obstacle as it was to succeed.

From the foregoing analyses it would appear that whilst there were often attempts made to tackle the obstacles identified, these were not always successful – in so far that the obstacle still made it hard for the probationer to stop offending. This finding, initially observed when officers' accounts were explored, was confirmed when probationers' reports were examined. As stressed above, the interpretation of these findings is not to claim that 'nothing works', but rather to conclude that these reported efforts appeared to be just as likely to fail as they were to succeed.

Four possible explanations for this finding exist. First, although there were very few obstacles which officers said had not materialised, on

Table 6.7: Intervention styles sweep-one obstacles: probationers' reports (numbers, with percentages in parentheses)

Intervention styles	Drugs and/or alcohol	Friends/family	Personal characteristics	Social problems	Total
Officer took the lead[21]	1 (4)	1 (4)	2 (12)	0 (—)	4 (5)
Officer/probationer 'co-working'[22]	8 (29)	5 (1)	3 (18)	5 (46)	21 (26)
Officer/probationer working separately[23]	3 (11)	4 (17)	0 (—)	1 (10)	8 (10)
Probationer took the lead[24]	12 (43)	5 (21)	6 (35)	4 (36)	27 (34)
Was not addressed[25]	2 (7)	5 (21)	3 (18)	0 (—)	10 (13)
Cannot remember, 'don't know', etc.[26]	2 (7)	4 (17)	3 (18)	1 (10)	10 (13)
Total	28 (100)	24 (100)	17 (100)	11 (100)	80 (100)

which they had not worked, or which they felt unable to comment upon for various reasons, given the small cell sizes involved, the inclusion of data pertaining to these obstacles *may* have distorted the findings. Analyses, without these data, were rerun. The findings remained the same. Similar analyses were undertaken with the probationers' responses, this time 'dropping' from the analyses those obstacles which probationers had said did not emerge or about which they had forgotten what had been done. Again, the initial findings were supported.

Secondly, it could be argued that the officers and probationers identified a range of 'needs' rather than 'obstacles to avoiding further offending'. For example, unemployment *per se* does not prevent an individual from desisting. One can be unemployed and desist, or employed and offend. To what extent, then, were the obstacles identified by officers obstacles which could reasonably be thought to be related to offending? It is not possible to comment definitively upon this issue. However, on the basis of what is known about the correlates of offending, the obstacles identified appeared to represent the commonly observed 'risk factors' for continued offending. For example, the obstacles identified by officers were dominated by problem drug and alcohol usage, peer groups, poor employment prospects, financial difficulties and depression/low morale. None of these seem unreasonable features of an individual's life to identify as possible causes of further offending. Like the officers who supervised them, the probationers also did not appear to identify obstacles which bore no relation to offending. The hypothesis that officers and probationers identified 'social needs' rather than 'obstacles to avoiding further offending' is therefore unsupported.

Two remaining explanations remain to be explored. These form the focus of the following chapter, which deals with the role of motivation in tackling the obstacles to desistance identified by officers and probationers, and the subsequent chapter, which explores the impact of social and personal context on the efforts to tackle these obstacles.

Notes

1 These findings were replicated with officers' reports, again at the $p = < .000$ level.

2 Virtually identical results were obtained when officers' reports of whether obstacles had been resolved or not were cross-tabulated against desistance and persistence. Desisters here refers to those who did not offend, who

showed signs of desisting or who committed only trivial offences. Persisters are those whose offending was either non-trivial or appeared to be escalating.

3 All analyses (unless otherwise stated) employ responses from officers and probationers from their second research interview. For many cases this is, of course, the interview conducted during the second sweep of fieldwork. However, there were a small number of both officers and probationers who were not seen during sweep two, but who were seen during sweep three. For these 8 officers and 20 probationers, the responses which they gave in the third sweep are employed. For the officers this means that the total number of respondents is 198 and, for probationers, 157.

This chapter relies most heavily (but not exclusively) on the data collected when officers and probationers were interviewed for the second time (rather than *all* follow-up data). When the data collected at the third interview were analysed, it was observed that many officers and probationers reported little work having been undertaken between the second and third interviews. This is entirely understandable as, by that time, many probationers had to all intents and purposes completed their supervision and had been placed on nominal contact. In order therefore to make a meaningful comparison of working styles, the analyses rely most heavily on data from the second interviews.

4 Multiple responses possible.

5 Multiple responses possible.

6 More specifically: *practical help*; *talking*; *activities*; *family work*; *referrals* (including group programmes); and *'other' interventions* (including the use of a reporting scheme). In addition to these, variables for the obstacles which were either *not addressed* or which the *probationer overcame without help* were also created.

7 More specifically: *the probationer motivated him/herself* (such as the probationer 'realising crime was wrong', 'reassessing his or her life', 'started thinking more before acting' and the such like, all of which contained an element of the awareness that 'something needed to change' and that this change was, at least, initiated); *the probationer got a job* (which included getting work, getting better work, seeking work and joining the armed services); *the probationer addressed or changed his or her family situation in some way* (such as finding a new partner, leaving the old one, trying to get on better with *his or her* family or taking some similar action); *the probationer addressed or changed his or her drug intake* (mainly gave up altogether or reduced drug intake); *the probationer addressed or changed his or her alcohol intake* (mainly gave up altogether or reduced alcohol intake); *the probationer moved home; the probationer changed his or her friends; the probationer attended group work or other counselling; the probationer did not address the obstacle* and *I don't know what the probationer did.*

8 Including: talking to the probationer (associated with making obstacle resolution *harder*, chi. sq. $p = .005$) and referring the probationer (also

associated with making obstacle resolution *harder*, chi. sq. $p = .005$). Similarly, referring the probationer to a partnership for a drug-related obstacle was associated with making obstacle resolution *harder* than if the probationer had not been referred (Fisher's Exact Test = .009), as was the probationer attending a group programme (again associated with the obstacle making obstacle resolution *harder* than if the probationer had not been referred, Fisher's Exact Test = .013).

9 As financial obstacles and 'other' obstacles have been omitted from Table 6.5, the total number of obstacles is reduced slightly to 264.

10 That is, that the lion's share of the responsibility fell to the officer.

11 That is, that the officer and the probationer set about tackling the obstacle along similar lines, often in conjunction with one another.

12 Officer and probationer both tackled the obstacle, but employed different techniques.

13 That is, that the lion's share of the responsibility fell to the probationer.

14 This (often, but not exclusively) refers to the probationer failing to take up the officer's advice, referrals, offers of help and the such like. In a few cases, the probationer's 'presenting problems' were so pressing that they required they be focused on to the exclusion of all other obstacles, or one obstacle could not be tackled until another had been resolved first. In a very few cases the officers admitted that they simply had not addressed the obstacle at all, but gave no clear explanation of why this was.

15 In some instances, the supervising officer had changed and did not agree with the previous officer's assessment of the obstacle, or felt unable to comment on the work undertaken. In other cases the officer had changed his or her mind about the salience of obstacle and accordingly no work had been undertaken. Additionally, the obstacle may have been 'hypothetical' (i.e. 'if he lost his job') and the situation never arisen, hence no work having been undertaken.

16 These were re-coded with 'officer led' and 'officer/probationer co-working' against all other working styles. The hypothesis being that success was more likely in those cases where the officer took responsibility for solving the problem or where both parties worked together.

17 Chi square values for these tests lay between .505 and .866, far greater than even the least acceptable level at which statistical significance is commonly accepted (.050).

18 Multiple responses possible.

19 Such as gave counselling, taught coping techniques, changed my attitude, gave practical assistance or made a referral.

20 In some cases these codes were slightly different. For example, whilst there were three officers who said that their probationer had 'found god', none of the probationers interviewed reported this as a technique for tackling the obstacle in hand. Again, obstacles relating to finances and 'other' obstacles have been dropped from Table 6.7, bringing the number of obstacles to 80.

21 That is, that the lion's share of the responsibility fell to the officer.

22 That is, that the officer and the probationer set about tackling the obstacle along similar lines, often in conjunction with one another.

23 Officers and probationer both tackled the obstacle, but often employing different techniques.

24 That is, that the lion's share of the responsibility fell to the probationer.

25 This (often, but not exclusively) refers to the probationer failing to take up the officer's advice, referrals, offers of help and the such like. In a few cases, the probationer's 'presenting problems' were so pressing that they required they be focused on to the exclusion of all other obstacles, or one obstacle could not be tackled until another had been resolved first. In a very few cases the officers admitted that they simply had not addressed the obstacle at all, but gave no clear explanation of why this was.

26 In some instances probationers were unable to provide details about the work which had been undertaken. Where this was the case it was often due to their 'not remembering' what had happened or missing data. Like the officers, some probationers reported obstacles which were 'hypothetical' (i.e. 'if my wife left me') and the situation having never arisen, so no work was undertaken.

Chapter 7

Motivation and probation

Motivation to desist

Having the motivation to avoid further offending is perhaps one of the key factors in explaining desistance. As mentioned in Chapter 1, West (1978), Shover (1983), Shover and Thompson (1992), Moffitt (1993), Sommers *et al.* (1994) and Pezzin (1995) have all pointed to a range of factors which motivated the offenders in their samples to desist. These included the desire to avoid negative consequences (such as death or serious injury), realising that legitimate financial gains outweigh criminal gains, wanting to 'lead a quieter life', embarking upon a committed personal relationship and so on.[1] Burnett (1992: 66, 1994: 55–56) suggested that those ex-prisoners who reported that they *wanted* to stop offending and, importantly, felt they were *able* to stop offending, were more likely to desist than those who said they were unsure if they wanted to stop offending:

'more of those who desisted stated unequivocally at both the pre-release [from prison] and the post-release [interview] that they wanted to desist' (1992: 66).

Thus, in the current study, both probationers and officers were asked if the probationer wanted to stop offending and if he or she would be able to do so. As many as 95 per cent of the probationers said that they *wanted* to stop offending and their officers reported similar rates (see Table 7.1a). A slightly different picture emerged, however, when officers and the probationers were asked about *ability* to stop offending (Table 7.1b). Whilst most thought that the probationer would be able to stop offending, there was a significant minority of both officers and probationers who said that they did not know if the probationer would

99

Table 7.1: Motivation and expectation to desist

	Probationers	Officers
a Want to stop offending?		
Yes	94	96
Don't know	2	2
No	4	2
b Able to stop offending?		
Yes	80	68
Don't know	14	16
No	6	16
Total ($n = 199$)	100	100

Note: All figures are percentages.

be able stop offending (around 15 per cent for each). Officers were three times more likely to report that their probationer would *not* be able to stop offending than the probationers themselves (16 per cent as opposed to 6 per cent).

It would appear, therefore, that the probationers in the current sample were very keen to avoid further offending. Burnett (1992: 47) reported that 82 per cent of the prisoners in her study were motivated to desist – in the current study 94 per cent of probationers said that they wanted to stop. Similarly, Burnett's prisoners were less confident about their ability to stop offending (41 per cent of her study said they felt able to desist compared to 80 per cent of the current study). The explanation for the lower rates of 'confidence' amongst inmates in the Burnett (1992: 82) study is probably related to the fact that the prison inmates in her sample more frequently reported obstacles to desisting and had experienced long periods of incarceration (ibid.: 42, Table 3.1b).[2] The number of probationers in the study who said they wanted to stop offending and felt able to do so suggested that they were 'good working material' for probation officers.

When the officers' responses were considered, most of them also said that they thought that their probationer wanted and would be able to stop offending (68 per cent), but 16 per cent said they were unsure of their ability to so do, and another 16 per cent felt that, despite their probationer's motivation to stop, they would be unable to do so. They were therefore more cautious in their prognoses than the probationers.

More detailed analyses of officers' and probationers' responses concerning ability and desire to cease offending indicated that there were three groups of probationers:

1. Some 110 probationers who said that they wanted to, and felt that they would be able to stop offending *and* whose officers agreed with these assessments. These cases are referred to as 'the confident' (as both parties are confident of the probationer's desire and ability to desist).

2. A second group ($n=46$) of probationers said that they wanted to and felt able to stop offending, but their officers did *not* support this assessment – they either felt that the probationer did not want to desist, was unable to desist or both. These cases are referred to as 'the optimists'.

3. And 'the pessimists' (the remaining group of probationers; $n=43$) who said that they did not want to stop, would be unable to stop or both. In some cases, officers supported their assessments but, in others, they did not.

The stability of motivation

As well as being asked to describe the probationer's desire and ability to desist at the first interview, officers and probationers were asked identical questions during the second and third interviews. This enabled the progression of the probationers' motivation–expectation[3] during the order to be charted. Table 7.2 summarises the progression of the three groups throughout their orders.

For ease of presentation, Table 7.2 presents data relating solely to those cases for which *both* officers *and* probationers were interviewed

Table 7.2: Changes in motivation throughout the order

| | Motivation–expectation at sweep one | | | | | | | |
| | Confident | | Optimistic | | Pessimistic | | Total | |
	(n)	(%)	(n)	(%)	(n)	(%)	(n)	(%)
Sweep two								
Confident	34	(63)	10	(63)	6	(30)	50	(56)
Optimistic	11	(20)	4	(25)	5	(25)	20	(22)
Pessimistic	9	(17)	2	(13)	9	(45)	20	(22)
Sweep three								
Confident	45	(83)	6	(38)	8	(40)	59	(65)
Optimistic	5	(9)	9	(56)	3	(15)	17	(19)
Pessimistic	4	(7)	1	(6)	9	(45)	14	(16)
Total	54	(100)	16	(100)	20	(100)	90	(100)

at all three sweeps of interviewing ($n=90$).[4] Of the 90 cases selected for inclusion in the analyses reported in Table 7.2, 54 (60 per cent) were rated as being confident at the first sweep, 16 (18 per cent) were rated as being optimistic at the first sweep and 20 (22 per cent) as being pessimistic. (To this end, the 90 selected cases are skewed slightly towards the confident, mainly at the expense of the optimistic.)

The upper half of Table 7.2 indicates that at the second sweep, 63 per cent of the confident remained rated as confident, whilst 11 cases (20 per cent) had moved into the optimistic group (in other words, their officers felt *less* certain that they desired or would be able to desist). A slightly smaller group of confidents ($n=$ nine; 17 per cent) were now rated as pessimists (that is to say that the probationers themselves now felt that they could *not* desist). Most of those rated as optimistic at the first sweep (10 out of 16) had done sufficiently well for their officers to have become convinced that they could now stop offending and were accordingly rated as confidents. Of those rated as pessimists at the first sweep, almost half (9 out of 20) had remained pessimists, whilst the remainder had either started to believe they could desist ($n=5$), or both they and their officers now felt that they could desist ($n=6$).

When the responses from the third sweep were examined (the lower half of Table 7.2), some of the trends noted in the upper half of the table appear to have reversed. Most of the confidents that had been rated as either optimists or pessimists at the second sweep had 'returned to the fold', so to speak. Similarly, some of the optimists who had been rated as confidents were once again rated as optimists. Finally, some of the pessimists continued their progression towards becoming confident – with previously rated pessimists becoming rated as confidents or optimists.[5] Further analyses suggested that shifts in rates of offending, drug and alcohol usage, and changes in personal and social circumstances were the main reasons given by officers and probationers in accounting for the changes in their assessment of changes in the latter's motivation. In short, the assessments of motivation were fairly stable, although some cases initially classified as pessimists were later reassessed as optimists or confidents.

Variations in criminal history and social circumstances by motivation

These three groups, on closer inspection, were found to differ from one another in several ways, especially in terms of their socio-demographic characteristics and criminal histories. Table 7.3 outlines some of their characteristics.

Table 7.3: Motivation groups' criminal histories at start of order

Average for each group	Confidents	Optimists	Pessimists	All
Age at start of order	25 yrs	25 yrs	26 yrs	25 yrs
Age at first conviction	20 yrs	19 yrs	17 yrs	19 yrs
Previous convictions (*n*)	6	11	19	10
Previous probation orders (*n*)	0.5	0.6	2.4	0.9
Previous custody (*n*)	0.6	2.4	2.3	1.3
OGRS	53%	61%	68%	58%
Total	110	46	43	199

Whilst there was little difference in their age at the *start* of the orders, the pessimists were younger when *first convicted* (being on average 17 years old) compared to the confident (on average 20 years old) or the optimists (aged on average 19 years when first convicted). Consequently the average length of their criminal careers varied: confidents had the shortest careers at five years, optimists' average career length was six years and the pessimist had by far the longest, with an average nine-year criminal career. There were substantial differences in the average number of convictions recorded against each group: the confident were the least frequently convicted (averaging 6 convictions each), with the optimistic the next most convicted (averaging 11 convictions each) and the pessimistic the most convicted (averaging 19 convictions each). Their average number of previous probation orders and prison sentences also differed: the confident and optimistic had had little experience of either, whilst the pessimistic had had more experience. When previous custodial sentences were considered, the confident can be seen to have had very little experience, unlike either the optimistic or the pessimistic.

The confident, when compared to the optimists/pessimists, were more likely to be in the lower half of OGRS scores ($p < = .05$), to have had the fewest convictions ($p < = .000$) and to have never previously been in prison ($p < = .000$). When compared against the confident/optimistic, pessimists were more likely to have been in prison before ($p < = .000$). In terms of offending since the start of the order, the confident were less likely than either the optimists or the pessimists to have reported offending during the time (about seven weeks) since the start of the order (probationer report: $p < .05$; officer report: $p < = .000$). The pessimists, however, were more likely than either the confident or the optimists to have reported offending since the start of the order ($p < = .01$).

Table 7.4: 'Problematic' circumstances at the time of the offence: probationers' reports (%)

Social circumstance	Confidents	Optimists	Pessimists	All
Accommodation	29	39	54	37
Employment	56	57	51	55
Finances	48	65	51	53
Partner	38	28	21	32
Family	42	46	26	39
Alcohol	21	17	33	23
Drugs	27	46	37	34
Gambling	6	2	7	6
Feeling down/depressed	63	63	65	63
Other	27	30	40	31
Three or more problems	**43**	**50**	**56**	**47**
Total (n of sample)	110	46	43	199

Confidents reported that on average they had fewer problematic social and personal circumstances at the time of the offence than either the optimistic or the pessimistic (Table 7.4, emboldened row), although this difference was not statistically significant.

The confident were the least likely of the three groups to describe their accommodation and finances as being problems at the time of the offence. Their reporting of 'problem' drug usage was also lower than either the optimistic or the pessimistic. The optimists had the highest rates of reporting both employment and finances as problems, especially the latter. The pessimists were more likely than either the confident or the optimistic to report that their use of alcohol had been a problem. The confident were the group most likely to report that their relationship with their partner had been a problem. Feeling down, depressed or anxious appears to have been a feature of life common to all three groups.

The pessimists reported fewer employment, family or partner-related problems than either of confidents or the optimists. This could, in part, be explained by the pessimists actually having fewer relationships with partners and family members and, as such, these features of their lives not presenting immediate problems by virtue of their total absence rather than the inherent quality of these relationships for the pessimists.[6] Another explanation might also be that what is a problem for one person is less of a problem for another – the perennial dilemma for self-report studies.[7]

The three groups differed also with regards to the obstacles which they had been identified as facing at the outset of their orders. The confident were the most likely to have faced no obstacles (officer report: $p < =.05$; probationer report: $p < =.01$); their officers were also less likely to have described the confident as facing obstacles relating to their personal characteristics ($p < =.01$) or to be facing obstacles relating to their drug and alcohol usage ($p < =.05$) than either of the other groups. The pessimistic had been reported by their officers as being more likely to face at least one obstacle to desisting ($p < =.000$), whilst the optimistic had been more likely than either the confident or the pessimists to have been assessed by their officers as facing obstacles related to their personal characteristics ($p < =.05$).

These findings suggest an important conclusion: that the group of probationers felt most like to desist (the confident) is similar, in characteristics, to those identified in the general literature as being the least likely to be re-convicted. These, then, were a group of relatively non-problematic probationers; both they and their officers believed that they wanted to and would be able to stop offending and their socio-demographic and criminal history variables would appear to lend some weight to these assessments. More importantly, their self-reported offending, their officers' estimates of their offending and the frequency with which they identified obstacles supported the belief that they could and would desist.

The role of motivation in overcoming obstacles

What part did motivation play in the resolution of obstacles? Table 7.5 summarises the obstacles which officers and probationers identified at *all three* sweeps of interviewing and analyses this by motivation.[8] The table confirms that both officers and probationers reported that fewer of the confident faced obstacles which were related to their personal characteristics than the pessimists. For example, only 17 per cent of the confident probationers were reported by their officers to have faced such obstacles, whilst for pessimists the figure was 31 per cent (the emboldened text). However, there were few other outstanding differences in the reports of the obstacles faced by each of the three groups of probationers.

The resolution of obstacles

Table 7.6 reports the extent to which the obstacles identified had been felt by officers and probationers to have been resolved.[9] Again, it is

Table 7.5: Obstacles identified by officers and probationers

Category	Officer identified obstacles (n) (%)				Probationer identified obstacles (n) (%)			
	All	Confidents	Optimists	Pessimists	All	Confidents	Optimists	Pessimists
Friends and family	152 (22)	81 (26)	36 (18)	35 (20)	35 (18)	18 (21)	9 (23)	8 (12)
Financial reasons	36 (5)	13 (4)	13 (8)	10 (6)	31 (16)	17 (20)	7 (18)	7 (10)
Drugs and alcohol	150 (22)	68 (22)	47 (24)	35 (20)	54 (18)	23 (27)	16 (41)	15 (22)
Social problems	140 (20)	74 (24)	42 (21)	29 (16)	30 (16)	11 (13)	4 (10)	14 (20)
Characteristics of the probationer	155 (22)	**53 (17)**	43 (22)	**55 (31)**	28 (15)	11 (13)	1 (3)	16 (24)
Other responses	57 (8)	25 (8)	19 (10)	12 (7)	14 (7)	4 (5)	2 (5)	8 (12)
Total no. of obstacles identified	690 (100)	314 (100)	200 (100)	176 (100)	191 (100)	84 (100)	39 (100)	68 (100)

Table 7.6: *Was the obstacle resolved?*[11]

| | Officer assessment (n) (%) | | | Probationer assessment (n) (%) | | |
	Confidents	Optimists	Pessimists	Confidents	Optimists	Pessimists
Yes	176 (79)	74 (58)	84 (68)	45 (71)	16 (59)	29 (63)
No	48 (21)	54 (42)	40 (32)	18 (29)	11 (41)	17 (37)
Total obstacles identified	224 (100)	128 (100)	124 (100)	63 (100)	27 (100)	46 (100)

important not to overstate the findings, especially in the case of the self-reported data pertaining to the optimists (for whom cell sizes are small), but trends are nevertheless discernible. A higher proportion of the obstacles faced by the confident were felt to have been resolved (by both probationers and officers). The least likely to have resolved their obstacles were the optimists, although they were very similar to the pessimists. There *does*, therefore, appear to be something of a variation by motivation in the rates with which obstacles were felt to have been resolved. The obstacles identified as facing the confident were the most likely to have been resolved, whilst those facing the optimists and the pessimists were the least likely.[10]

However, the relationship between motivation and obstacle resolution, such that it is, appears to have existed independently of probation work: when working style and amount of help received were examined they varied only slightly between confidents, optimists and pessimists. As mentioned earlier, officers and probationers were asked to describe how they had attempted to tackle the obstacles which they had identified. Table 7.7 reports their accounts of the *extent and nature* of co-operation between officers and probationers and relates these assessments to their motivation. Although cell sizes were small, some trends emerged. As noted in Tables 6.5 and 6.7 in Chapter 6, there were relatively few officers and probationers who worked together to tackle obstacles (typically around a quarter to a third). When the same data were analysed by motivation, there appeared to be little variation when officers' reports were considered: officers reported that they had co-worked with the confidents, the optimists and the pessimists to an equal extent (between 34 and 40 per cent of officers reported co-working with their probationers – see the emboldened text in the left-hand side of Table 7.7).

The probationers, on the other hand, presented a slightly different picture. Similar proportions of the confident and the pessimistic reported having co-worked with their officers, but far fewer of the

Table 7.7:   *Working styles used to tackle the obstacles identified at sweep one*[12]

Worked together?	Officer reports (n) (%)			Probationer reports (n) (%)		
	Confidents	Optimists	Pessimists	Confidents	Optimists	Pessimists
Yes	**43 (34)**	**30 (40)**	**22 (35)**	14 (39)	**2 (12)**	9 (32)
No	82 (66)	45 (60)	41 (65)	22 (61)	**14 (88)**	19 (68)
Total obstacles	125 (100)	75 (100)	63 (100)	36 (100)	16 (100)	28 (100)

optimistic reported co-working. Only two of the sixteen optimists who identified obstacles and were followed up reported working with their officer – see the emboldened text in the right-hand side of Table 7.7. However, there were few other differences between the officers' and probationers' reports of their work together and there appears to have been little influence of motivation on the extent to which officers and probationers 'worked together'. With the exception of the optimist's reports of their own work with their officers, it would appear that co-working was uniformly distributed and therefore cannot account for the variations in resolution rates reported in Table 7.6.[13]

A model of desistance is starting to emerge from the analyses reported so far here and in Chapter 6: solving obstacles was related to desistance (Chapter 6), but it would appear that the type of probation intervention was *not* associated with resolving obstacles (Chapter 6). Motivation, however, *did* appear to influence the extent to which obstacles were both faced and overcome. These relationships are presented diagrammatically in Figures 7.1 and 7.2 – which chart the progress of each of the three groups of probationers towards desistance.[14]

Fewer of the confident (40 per cent) faced obstacles than either of the other groups, whilst half the optimists and eight out of ten of the pessimists faced one or more obstacles. Of the few pessimists who faced no obstacles, 67 per cent desisted. However, 64 per cent of those pessimists who faced an obstacle but *overcame* it desisted, whilst even fewer – only 31 per cent – of those pessimists who faced an obstacle but did *not* overcome it desisted. For the optimists and pessimists, solving obstacles was particularly strongly related to desistance: of the six optimists who overcame the obstacle they faced, all but one desisted. On the other hand, of the 11 who did not overcome the obstacle they faced, five desisted and five did not (one was lost during the follow-up). Desistance rates were highest amongst those groups that faced no obstacles and lowest (with one exception – the confident) amongst those who faced obstacles but did not overcome them. This suggests that overcoming obstacles is successively more important for each group. Most of the confident desisted regardless of their resolving their obstacles. However, 64 per cent of the pessimists who resolved their obstacles desisted, compared to 31 per cent of those who did *not* (Figure 7.1). Data from the officers (Figure 7.2) support this model.

How and why did motivation effect the resolution of obstacles? In order to explore further the relationship between motivation, solving obstacles and desistance, case studies of individual probationers need to be examined.

Steve [020] was a confident who desisted. He was in his 30s when he started his order – imposed for theft. He had been wandering around looking for something to steal in order to raise money to buy heroin for himself and his girlfriend, Suzie. Spying some scrap metal in a disused railway siding, he attempted to steal it, but was caught leaving the yard by a security guard.

By the time of the first interview both Steve and Suzie were on methadone and had stopped using 'street drugs'. Steve and his officer said that he wanted to stop offending – both also identified the same motivation: he and Suzie getting their children back from the social services. Although Steve did not identify any obstacles to him desisting, his officer said that if they did not get better access to their children or if he slipped back into drug use Steve might offend again. The first of these, she said, she could do little more than advise upon, and the second she was unsure exactly how she would approach, but thought that a de-tox might offer a possible solution.

By the time of the second interview, Steve and Suzie had been given increased access to their children and had stayed on the methadone course. Steve said he was wary of coming off methadone too quickly, as it could see a return to his using street drugs. His officer said that in general Steve was 'responding well and making reasonable prog-ress'. In terms of their access to their children, Steve's officer confirmed that access had been increased, and added that she had advised Steve about how to approach the social services department and suggested that he enrole on a college course to improve his 'image' with social services (which Steve said he was going to do the following autumn). Drugs de-tox was still on the agenda, but Steve's officer understood his reluctance to come off methadone too quickly. Neither Steve nor his officer identified any further obstacles to his desisting.

At the third interview, both Steve and his officer reported that things with social services had continued to improve, and that Steve and Suzie were planning to go to court to seek more contact with their children. Both Steve and his officer said that he now wanted to work

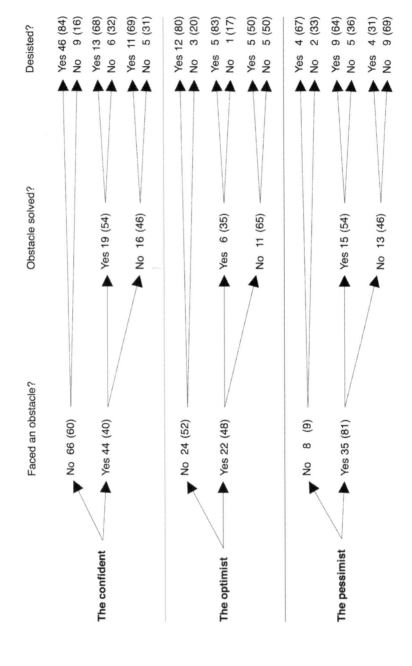

Figure 7.1 Motivation, obstacles and desistance: probationers' reports. All figures are N (%).

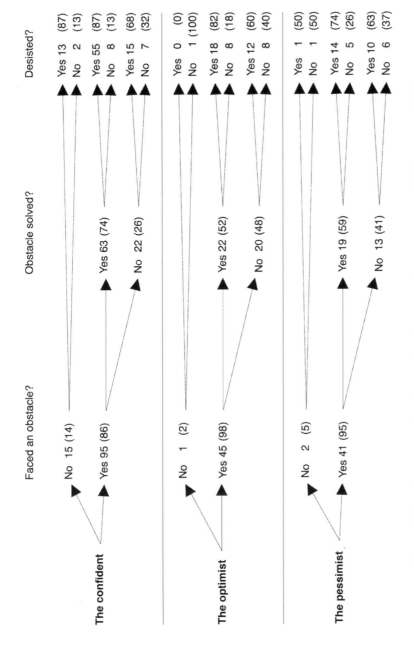

Figure 7.2 Motivation, obstacles and desistance: officers' reports. All figures are N (%).

and seemed in a better position to do so. Neither identified further obstacles to his desisting and both reported him to have desisted by the time of the end of the order.

Dave [061], on the other hand, was an optimist whose offending was little affected by his time on probation. He did not desist and was rated as a continuing non-trivial offender in the schema outlined in Chapter 4. Dave was 17 when he breached his Community Service Order and 18 when he started the probation order imposed to replace it. (The CSO had been made originally for an affray.) Although Dave said that he was both able and wanted to stop offending, his officer disagreed with him on both counts, saying 'he will do the same thing again if the same circumstances arose' adding 'he will not accept that he may be wrong'. Dave said that the only obstacle he faced in stopping offending was that he 'lived in a bad area'. His solution was to live in 'a nice area', but he saw 'no reason why I should have to move house'. He did not think his officer would be able to help him with this matter. His officer said that the obstacles which Dave faced were his 'attitude' (not understanding that he had done wrong) and his poor level of literacy. The first of these would be hard to address as Dave was 'very reluctant to work with probation'. She planned, however, to tackle his illiteracy by finding him a course in reading and writing.

At the second interview, Dave said he had in fact moved house and foresaw no other obstacles. Again, he said that he was able and wanted to stop offending. He had arranged a college course for himself – 'having got fed up waiting for probation to do it for me'. He also complained about not having seen anyone from probation for 'ages' and said that he had had 'very little contact'. His officer had left, and he had been seen by a number of Probation Service officers – who only saw him for a few minutes at any given appointment. On the third occasion he was seen, Dave said that his officer had 'talked down to me all the time' and recounted how he had once walked out of her office. Dave smoked cannabis throughout the course of his order and, at the third interview, reported that he was being taken to court for possessing an offensive weapon (a knife) which he had been carrying after being threatened on several occasions. It was on the basis of this last offence which he was classified as a non-trivial offender.

Les's [177] offending escalated during the time he was on probation for assaulting a police officer. He and his wife had separated, and he had been ordered by the court to stay away from her home. However, she phoned him and asked him to come round to help her look after their daughter, who was mentally handicapped. According to Les, his daughter started 'smashing things up and screaming', and a neighbour called the police. When they arrived they assumed that Les had started the trouble and a fracas broke out, during which Les punched one of the constables.

In terms of Les's desire and ability to stop offending, neither he nor his officer felt he was able to desist. Les said: 'The problem is that I don't sit down with idiots. I can't help it, I kick off. I'd love to be able to change, but I can't help it'. Les did not identify any obstacles that would prevent him from desisting. However, his officer said that his attitude towards others presented a problem:

> he has this strong sense of being a 'man', protecting his family and wife which increases his violence. I am trying to show him how this can be both negative – i.e. getting him into further trouble – and positive – i.e. taking care of his daughter without being aggressive to others. He is still very defensive when challenged about his use of violence. He sees himself as a strong, protective father. The thing is to make him see that he can be himself and have values without 'kicking off'.

However, by the time of the second interview, Les had reoffended. Driving to the home of someone he was intending to 'get even with', Les was stopped by the police, who suspected him of being drunk. When asked to provide a specimen, Les refused and was arrested. Found guilty, he was given a custodial sentence. Prior to this, Les had threatened his original probation officer after she had contacted the local social services about his behaviour. She described him as being very resistant to any challenges from her and that he still saw violence as the fault of others. Although Les was contacted during the fieldwork for the second sweep of interviewing, he told the interviewer to 'fuck off' and hung up the phone on her.

As a pessimist, it is hard to find a better example than Les. He didn't think he could stop offending; neither did his officer and there seems to have been little constructive work between them. The obstacle which his officer had identified appears to have been only too accurate in the light of subsequent events.

These case studies suggest that motivation at the outset of supervision was associated with desistance because it influenced the way in which probationers approached the obstacles they faced. For example, Steve took a cautious approach to his drug problem and understood the importance of making a 'good impression' with the social services. Dave appeared to be reluctant to engage with probation supervision and got on badly with his officer. Les appeared to have made no efforts to 'change his ways' and to have even ruled out the possibility of such a change. However, these case studies also suggest that other factors may have been present. Steve's motivation appears to have been supported by both his partner and their desire to rebuild their family. Similarly, Dave's attitude to probation and Les's attitudes towards other people did little to help them desist. As well as probationers' approaches to the obstacles they faced varying by motivation, it would appear that other social and personal factors influenced the extents to which impediments were overcome, and it is to a consideration of these that we now turn.

Notes

1 On the motivational factors associated with not committing an offence, see Tunnell (1992: Chap. 7).

2 Of the respondents in Burnett's sample, only 8 of 107 (7 per cent) said that they felt that they would not face any obstacles in stopping offending – in the present sample the figure is far greater (49 per cent). There is, of course, an additional wealth of literature which posits a direct relationship between experiencing a custodial sentence and problems in resettling in the community after a custodial sentence.

3 The term 'motivation–expectation' is something of a mouthful, and so 'motivation' is used in its place at points through out the text.

4 Identical analyses were undertaken employing data from all cases followed up during the second sweep ($n = 137$) and all cases seen during the second and third sweeps ($n = 106$) and all cases seen in the first and third sweeps (also $n = 106$). These analyses confirmed the results shown in Table 7.2 and described in the main text.

5 All the results reported were checked against frequencies for *each* of the three groups across second and third sweeps to ensure that by selecting just those cases for whom both officers and probationers had been seen at *all* three sweeps had not distorted the findings. The results were confirmed.

6 This certainly appears to have been the case with partners – whilst around 15 per cent of both confidents and optimists reported being single, the same figure for the pessimists was 21 per cent.

7 Indeed, when officers' reports of the problems faced by these three groups were examined, they appeared to have faced similar levels of employment, family and partner-related problems.

8 In the following analyses, *all* reported obstacles are used (including those identified during the second and third interviews) so as not to reduce cells sizes too much when controlling for motivation.

9 By focusing on those obstacles which were resolved, the data analyses are limited to just those obstacles reported during sweeps one and two, as

those obstacles identified during the third and final sweep could not have been followed up.

10 The optimists do less well than one would have expected. Had the relationship between motivation and obstacle resolution been perfect, one would have expected to see the optimists overcoming fewer of the obstacles than the confidents, but more of them than the pessimists did. The general rule that the optimists 'fall between these two groups' is confirmed by a number of other tables. See, for example, Tables 7.3 on their criminal histories; 7.4 on the total problems faced by each of the groups; 10.2 on the rates with which they desisted; 11.1 on the rates with which they offended; 11.5 on the amount of offending they were reported to have committed; and Table 11.4 on the rates with which they offended controlling for type of offence. To this extent, Table 7.6 represents something of an oddity.

11 Multiple responses possible.

12 These responses are identical to those used above, and described in Chapter 6. The data analyses use only those obstacles identified during sweep one because, as noted in chapter 6, footnote 3, when those obstacles identified during sweep two and which were followed up during sweep three were analysed, it emerged that little work had been undertaken in the period between sweeps two and three.

13 In any case, as reported in Chapter 6, co-working was not associated with resolving obstacles.

14 For those who faced more than one obstacle, the overall extent to which all the obstacles they faced was used to determine whether they were counted as having their 'obstacle solved'. For cases which had equal numbers of obstacles solved or unsolved, the outcome of the main obstacle was used.

Chapter 8

Probation work: content and context

This chapter takes the investigation started in Chapter 6 a step further and explores the role played by social and personal contexts in mediating the outcome of the attempts to tackle obstacles successfully. Instead of concentrating on the *type* of intervention, the extent to which officers and probationers *worked together* or the extent to which these were associated with the probationers' motivation, the focus is on the social and personal contexts in which the efforts to tackle obstacles were embedded. In so doing, more light is thrown upon the content of probation work. This process of illumination offers an explanation for one of the clearest findings to emerge from the study: that probation interventions appear in many cases to have had little impact on either the obstacles faced by probationers or their lives more generally. The explanations for this would appear to be that much probation work is negated by aspects of the probationers' lives, is aimed at tackling obstacles which are enduring and therefore very difficult to address or that the proposed solutions and the manner of their delivery appeared to be irrelevant to the needs of the probationers.

The manner in which 'contexts' were approached and operationalised in the current study drew heavily upon the work of Pawson and Tilley (1997: 69–70), who have argued that contexts can be crucial in understanding the outcomes of social interventions:

> programmes are always introduced *into* pre-existing social contexts and ... these prevailing social conditions are of crucial importance when it comes to explaining the successes and failures of social programmes. By social context, we do not refer simply to the spatial or geographical or institutional location into which programmes are embedded. So whilst indeed programmes are initiated in prison, hospitals, schools ..., it is the prior set of social

rules, norms, values and interrelationships gathered in these places which sets limits on the efficacy of programme mechanisms.

Thus the 'context' and, in particular, the social context, as developed by Pawson and Tilley, is not just the 'where' and 'when' of an intervention, but also the attitudes, socially 'appropriate' activities, approach to life and social relationships which existed prior to and during the period of supervision. To this can be added person-specific contexts: the personal histories, lifestyles and life chances of the specific individuals who were the focus of the programme in question.

In order to assess the role of such contexts in mediating the outcomes of the obstacles probationers faced, detailed analyses of officers' and probationers' accounts of how they tackled these obstacles were examined. In the case of officers, attention is focused upon two types of obstacles – drugs and the personal characteristics of the probationer – although these findings were replicated with regard to other obstacles.

One officer [233] described how his efforts to combat one confident probationer's heroin problem ultimately came to nothing:

I referred him to [a local drug team] and discussed with him the bad effects of drugs and methods for overcoming his addiction. He attended the drug team, got methadone scripts from them, but failed to turn up again [and] was never seen again. He was on the [methadone reduction] programme from the start of the year until March.

The investigations undertaken by both his supervising officer and the author aimed at ascertaining why the probationer 'disappeared' so dramatically, and suggested that poor housing, drug use and unpaid fines were all possible contributory factors. Another officer [006] recounted how she had referred her probationer – an optimist – to a local drug rehabilitation scheme only for him to be convicted for an earlier offence two months into his order, and for which he received a custodial sentence. In the time he had been on probation, the probationer had been to the drug scheme just once and had continued to offend, albeit of a trivial nature. Even following referrals, officers often had to contend with the probationer's own inactivity. As some officers said of their respective probationers:

He did nothing. Went nowhere [049].

[She did] very little – carried on associating with other drug users [141].

[He did] a de-tox, but started using again. Initially avoided users, but drifted back into the scene [172].

As recounted by their officers, the lives of each of these three probationers present a similar set of underlying reasons for failing to complete, or even start, the schemes to which they had been referred. In the case of 049 – an optimist whose offending escalated – the officer said that he had been consistently missing appointments for the last five months of his nine-month order and had been using heroin throughout that period. When asked to describe the biggest change in his life since the first interview, she said 'no change – that was the problem'. The circumstances surrounding the work undertaken with case 141 – a confident whose offending also escalated – portray the violent and exploitative side of heroin-user networks. The officer at the first interview identified two obstacles to her desisting: using heroin and her friendship with a local dealer. Despite referrals for drug counselling, the officer reported that it was: 'hard to engage the probationer in work whilst on probation, very difficult to persuade her that she had a problem' and that advice 'went in one ear and out the other' [141]. Within two months of the start of her order, she was abducted by three or four men – possibly her dealer and some accomplices – and 'gang-raped'. Following this she received death threats from these same men, required an abortion and suffered a nervous breakdown, resulting in her eventual sectioning under the Mental Health Act. Her officer was unable to see her for some six months because she had been sectioned. At the time of the second interview, the officer had placed the probationer on monthly reporting and had, in effect, ceased to work with her.

In the opinion of his officer, case 172 had only stopped using heroin for a brief period following a residential de-tox. Case 172 was another confident whose offending escalated. It would appear that he started probation heroin-dependent, burgled his parents' home, started and successfully completed the de-tox and was then heroin-free, was then convicted for the burglary and, as a result, expelled from his parents' home. This in turn led to the probationer living 'rough' on the streets and his eventual return to heroin use.

This scenario highlights the part that families can play in fostering or hindering change. Another probationer (086 – an optimist whose offending escalated) commenced his order after moving home to his parents' in an attempt to avoid heroin users. His officer duly set about arranging appointments with a drug counsellor for him. He did not, however, keep these appointments. As a result of an argument with his parents, he left their home, returning to the area in which he had lived previously. The argument with his father, be it either as the *result* of his continued drug use or the *cause* of continued use, had left the probationer living close to the old drug associates he had been trying to avoid. His officer said:

> I think that he is more at risk of getting back into heavy drug use and re-offending – in terms of stealing – because he has gone back to where he knows a lot of drug-using people. That was why he left in the first place, to get away from that scene.

Not all families reacted in these ways, however. In the case of one of the probationers (105 – a confident whose offending initially escalated but had ceased by the time of the end of her order), her family (*not* her officer) worked together in order to arrange and pay for her admission to a rehabilitation clinic. Her officer said:

> They're all involved. Her Uncle, her Aunt's research [about the clinic] – it's a team ... a family commitment. She seems to be rising to meet their support – even her grandfather is helping. [She is] committing herself to the rehabilitation programme in a genuine way [105].

Her officer, who had only recently started to supervise the case, said that she was supporting the probationer's decision to enter the clinic. Another officer believed that her probationer's concern to repair his relationship with his family had been the reason why he had addressed his drug use:

> He made a big effort at getting off heroin. He tried to cut down and arranged to de-tox. The motivation was there to repair family relationships. This was the main focus of the work that I did with him, so we discussed all aspects. I guarded him against complacency too, I warned him that it would be a long process [227, an optimist who desisted].

The officer supervising case 060 – an optimist – recounted the following sequence of events as the probationer failed to come off heroin:

> I ensured that she had access to treatment – her GP and [a local drug partnership]. She got methadone from her GP and the local drug partnership gave her acupuncture and counselling. She was

119

aware of these facilities anyway, but we discussed them regularly. I've offered her 'time out' in a crisis, which she's not taken. I've seen her jointly with her mum. [The probationer] went to her GP, to [the local drug partnership] and another clinic, but the counter-influences, particularly this man have been very powerful. This man – an ex-boyfriend – re-emerged. He was a bit of a wolf in sheep's clothing. In the end they both ended up using heroin quite heavily. He was very controlling. She lost her self esteem and got back into heroin in a big way. She couldn't turn her back on him.

At the time of the follow-up interviews, the probationer was thought to be using heroin again and in breach of her order – there was a warrant out for her arrest as a result of her failing to maintain contact with her officer:

> She's gone to relatives in . . ., but it was not done in a positive way. I would have given my blessing and transferred her. But it is the same way of her thinking as with heroin treatment – when she gets an idea into her head it has to be done instantly. Last time I heard from her was when she rang our duty officer while I was away and wouldn't give her address. In a way, she did the right thing, but in the wrong way.

For some people, however, the decision to come off heroin was made for them. One officer recounted how the probationer he was supervising – a confident who desisted – had almost died as a result of injecting into an artery in his groin:

> He was so desperate for heroin that he injected in unsafe conditions. He knew he'd hit an artery, but rammed it in anyway. I had to physically go round and take him to hospital. He wasn't going to move. His doctor said that if he'd stayed in the flat one more day he'd have lost his leg – two more days, his life [153].

This event had, at least in the officer's opinion, removed the probationer from the street and placed him in a safer environment – the hospital.

Not all officers reported events as unpleasant as some of those discussed above. One officer said that his probationer – a pessimist who was classified as a continuing trivial offender – 'may relapse into drug use'. When asked what had been done to prevent this from happening, he replied: 'Not much. It hasn't been necessary as he is clear now. I do rely on his reporting if there was any change. We've talked about it a few times, but it hasn't been a problem at all' [168]. When asked how much he'd been able to help the probationer with this obstacle, he said 'not much', adding that this was 'more a reflection of what [the probationer] has achieved *rather than the work of probation*' (emphasis added). The probationer had a new partner and had moved in with her. His officer reported that his new partner was in full-time employment and was a good influence upon him.

Other officers reported their experiences of 'gently nudging' their probationers towards total drug abstention:

> We're having discussions for a longer de-tox programme.[1] I am trying to encourage him to take the next step, but he doesn't seem to be ready now. He has cut down a lot on his methadone. I think he is afraid to give it up completely in case he gets weak and falls back to serious drugs again [020, a confident who desisted].

> I can only encourage [her], I can't march her to the drugs agency. She has reduced her intake, but she is finding it difficult to go the last fence and give up altogether her methadone. Her GP has reduced it forcefully, even when she didn't want it reducing any more [058, a confident who desisted].

Another officer reported a gradual improvement in her probationer's use of drugs:

> It's much better now. [I referred him] to [a local resettlement centre] and through there he got on a methadone programme. There was a case conference to resolve things with the doctor, and he now gets his prescriptions from another GP. He now uses methadone and not heroin [013, a pessimist who desisted].

A similar set of processes were detected when officers' accounts of their work aimed at tackling those obstacles related to the probationer's personal characteristics were examined. Many of these obstacles concerned the probationers' mental health or their 'attitudes'. Officers' work in such cases often revolved around making referrals: 'I spoke to the mental health specialist in the [probation] office and she took her case to the Mentally Disordered Offenders Panel. They agreed that a psychologist would see her with a view to counselling' [110, a confident who desisted].

Other responses suggested that officers had placed an emphasis on helping the probationer balance his or her medical needs. One officer, who reported that her probationer was suffering from depression and that this represented an obstacle to him desisting, described how she had: 'Tried to encourage him to keep in contact with the hospital and to stop self-medicating. To discuss things with his doctor. We looked at trying to keep busy and focused on things outside of his relationship.[2] I referred him to our Mental Health Team, but he did not attend' [127]. The probationer, a pessimist whose offending escalated, had: '. . . gone full circle. He is realising that he needs more help – maybe he will take it. In relation to his depression, he has come off pills willy-nilly – tried to do it alone – but it is too much for him by himself. He needs medical help.'

In this case the officer's efforts were nullified by the probationer's actions (failing to attend the Mental Health Team and coming off his medication haphazardly – both symptomatic of his depression perhaps). In other cases mental health problems either failed to materialise or were in someway suppressed by factors outside the officer's sphere of influence:

> [his mental health] is still a problem, but now dormant. It is there, but he got employment. If he loses the job, the depression will come back. Psychiatric service help is still in the pipeline, but it is up to the service to contact him. He got the job himself [and] he's bloomed. It raised his self-esteem and financial 'muscle'. He threw himself into work [077, an optimist who desisted].

> Cutting down on alcohol made her less depressed. Circumstances also slightly improved, which had a positive effect[3] [152, an optimist who desisted].

> Apart from offering advice and support, I couldn't do much about [his mental health]. He was taking his medicine before he got put on probation [119, an optimist who desisted].

Obstacles relating to immaturity, low self-esteem and attitudes appeared to be especially hard for officers to tackle successfully. In the following report of the work undertaken, the officer discusses how, between them, he and the probationer had addressed two obstacles – stress in the probationer's life and his low self-esteem:

> He creates stress. There are problems in his relationship – not showing any affection to her. I discussed parenting skills with both

of them. He listened, but it was short-lived. [In terms of his self-esteem], we've focused on the times when he handled things well. He had been a main-carer for their children at one point, and his self-esteem was high at this time. He went on a sex chat line – thought it would give him confidence, but it contributed to his dissatisfaction with his partner, and the result was a pile of sexual problems with her – from his point of view [118, an optimist whose offending escalated].

Other officers reported similar problems:

We've discussed his attitude. He has no respect for girlfriends, so finds the work hard to take in. I just tell him not to hit women [102, an optimist who desisted].

Not done much [about the probationer's immaturity] really, except talk. But it is difficult to get into the pattern of work with him. He brings in other crises[4] [107, an optimist who desisted].

I've tried case-work, aiming at behaviour modification. Getting him to identify his own mood patterns and to understand how he got himself out of these patterns. He continued to believe that moods were 'inevitable' and 'uncontrollable' [016, a confident whose offending escalated].

Obstacles associated with poor temper control or anger management were only identified by officers in six cases and appeared to be no easier to tackle than inappropriate attitudes:

I hoped to get him on a course, but wasn't able to do that. I'll just continue to expose issues related to this in supervision, but there hasn't been continuity, and with him being at work I didn't want to increase contact. He is willing to look at these issues when he comes here. There's a lot of back-log to work through. There's a lack of time now. I was hoping that if he was convicted of this assault[5] I could get him on an order with a condition, but the charge has been withdrawn [220, an optimist whose offending escalated].

We looked at some of his past instances of losing his temper. But this got side-tracked by him losing his accommodation and job. These then became the focus of the work. He walked out of his job after a conflict at work. He doesn't see it as a problem –

the 'problem' is other people's behaviours [193, an optimist whose offending escalated].

In some cases, the officer's attempts to tackle the obstacles they had identified were rendered impotent by the probationer failing to maintain contact (see Farrall 2002, on unauthorised absences). The officer supervising one probationer [146] had identified three obstacles at the first interview: his addiction to gambling; his accommodation; and his low self-esteem. However, the probationer – a pessimist whose offending escalated – moved away and there was little the officer could do to intervene with any of these obstacles. In some instances, characteristics of the probationer themselves presented impediments to effective work. Gary [202], in his early 20s at the start of his order, had been found guilty of a number of counts of arson, which appeared to be the result of his father's recent death and excessive drinking on the probationer's part. As a result of some of the concerns expressed by his officer, the probationer was assessed by a clinical psychologist, who reported that he was 'borderline education-ally disabled' – a fact which appeared to have hindered all efforts at working with him:

SF   Last time we met, I asked you if you thought there was anything that might make it hard for Gary to stop offending. You said that there was only one obstacle – another possible trauma like the death of his father previously. Have there been any [traumas]?

PO   Not that I am aware of – and I wouldn't necessarily agree with my own view six months later. There clearly must have been some kind of catalyst to set of this chain of offending that occurred . . .

SF   [*Interrupting*] Sorry, I thought he was only convicted of two arsons?

PO   I think he was convicted of one with 'recklessness to whether life endangered' and one 'without . . .', but there were probably more fires than the two that he is convicted of. In fact there were probably quite a few more . . . What was thought at the time was that it was a combination of the trauma and the unresolved grief of the bereavement and the excessive use of alcohol that had actually brought about the offending behav-iour. Nothing has been done to address either of those issues – or nothing significant. What he said – that he was not able to articulate his feelings in any way . . . so certainly if he did experience a trauma of any nature, the risk of re-offending would increase. But he hasn't. I do feel less inclined to accept that this was just about that trauma than I did six months ago. *Why?* I think there is probably a more long-standing problem – but I am not sure what it is. Certainly a bereavement, if you *are* stressed and anxious, you are going to get *more* stressed and anxious – I'm not saying it was insignificant. But I'm more inclined to think that we ought to be looking much further back at something that . . . maybe not a one-off event but something about the way . . . I don't know. Something that has been happening to him through out his life probably.

SF   You said that you haven't been able to make any progress with issues around bereavement or alcohol, is there anywhere where you have been able to make progress?

PO   No, not really. The fact that he attends appointments and goes to education [classes], which, I think, is positive. And I don't think that we'll always be in this position of not being able to make progress, well we may be, but if we are we will know why that is. I am much more inclined today than I would have been six months ago to believe that actually one of the major reasons for lack of progress is Gary's reluctance to engage in anything too demanding.

Gary did not face any further traumas and attended well for the rest of his probation order (some 18 months). He appeared genuinely remorseful when discussing his past offending – which, it appeared, had been limited to just the arsons referred to above. He did not offend again during the time of the order (two years). However, given the difficulties his officer faced when working with him, it is hard to find evidence that his supervision played a part in accounting for his desistance.

Probationers' responses

Thus far, the analyses undertaken have relied upon officers' accounts of the work undertaken. In this section, the probationers' perspective is developed. Because probationers generally reported fewer obstacles than their supervising officers, the following analyses draw upon *all* obstacle types identified by probationers rather than just drugs and personal characteristics, as was the case with officers.

Some of the probationers reported instances when their officer had been able to help them directly with the obstacle which they had identified. In one case, the probationer reported how his officer helped him 'change his lifestyle' (the obstacle he had identified):

> She has helped me getting the place where I am now. It is a resettlement unit run by the Salvation Army. [I've also] kept away from certain people. Resisted being tempted to use heroin and occupied my time by doing voluntary work and going to college three days a week [013, a pessimist whose offending continued at a high rate before he desisted].

Another probationer had identified the 'trouble in the area since my friend was killed' as something that could make it hard for him to stop offending. With regard to this obstacle, he said, his officer had helped him to understand: '. . . my feelings at the time when I almost attacked this guy.[6] She made me aware of the "warning signs"[7] and made me aware of the consequences' [068, a pessimist who was classified as a continuing non-trivial offender].[8]

In other cases it is clear to see how the direct influence of the officer helped to avert situations which would almost certainly have led to further offending by the probationer. Samantha (028 – a confident who desisted) recounts how her officer intervened to support her efforts to avoid a drug-using and violent ex-partner:

> He came back from Holland and moved here. He had a nice job, his own house and money and said he had gone straight and drug-free. He made a lot of promises but then he went back to drugs and offending. When I tried to get rid of him, he started beating me up. I didn't want him in my life because I knew he would get me back on drugs. It killed a few months of my life. I got depressed and ended up taking pills. I lost a lot of weight and my life was in a mess. [My officer] made a home-visit to see why I was missing all my appointments. When I explained, she phoned the domestic violence people and got back to me with their advice. She also called the police and told me to let him [boyfriend] know. I phoned the police like she told me to do and I made a complaint because of his violence. This stopped him because I told him. He still lives around the area, but he's not bothering me anymore. I was scared at some point that I would get back into drugs because of him.

For the following probationer – another confident who desisted – the influence of his officer was apparent to him, even if he could not articulate exactly how she'd helped him with his depression: 'It is not

something that I can say in words – not just something she said . . .'
[027]. Other obstacles were confronted and overcome in slightly more
roundabout ways, as this quotation from a young male probationer
(who had identified his 'temper' as an obstacle) illustrates: 'She tried
to make me see "the light" – anger management helped, but it was
really related to cocaine use, and [I] calmed down when I stopped
using. I stopped using coke, but before I stopped I didn't realise it was
related to my temper' [071, a pessimist who desisted]. The probationer
had earlier in the same interview identified 'stopping taking coke' as
the biggest change since the previous interview, which he put down
to: 'My girlfriend was getting pissed off. At work I was knackered if I
couldn't score. I started reducing then stopped'[9] [071].

Another probationer (who had identified alcohol as his obstacle to
stopping offending) said:

> My officer referred me to [a local alcohol partnership], my GP and
> the Alcohol Dependency Unit at the hospital. My GP told me to
> cut down as I had alcohol related diabetes, so I had no choice. I
> was also in and out of court all the time for 'drunk and disorderly',
> which I got fed up with [030, a confident who desisted].

Again, locating the driving force for this abstinence is hard. The GP,
his officer and his own growing irritation at being in and out of court
could all claim some role in it.

Despite these cases, which all show the influence of probation
supervision in helping probationers confront the obstacle which they said
they faced, there are equally compelling accounts of how, despite the work
of officers, wider social and personal contexts hampered the complete
resolution of the obstacle mentioned. One probationer (193 – an optimist
whose offending escalated) reported at the first interview that he felt that
'having no money, no job and no home' would make it hard for him to stop
offending. When interviewed for the second time he said that although his
officer had helped him get somewhere to live and given him ideas about
work and despite his own efforts to find work, his several previous
convictions had made getting work hard. In other cases, the probationer
appeared either not to have sought advice or to have ignored it:

> We didn't discuss [drugs]. I de-toxed myself and got a job [072.
> Obstacle: 'drug use'. A pessimist whose offending escalated].

> She gave me advice, but I didn't really take it. I find it difficult to
> let go. She couldn't have done more. The decision has to come

from myself [206. Obstacle: 'if boyfriend gets back on drugs'. A confident who desisted].

She didn't have much chance to help me because I told her it wasn't much of a problem. We discussed gambling, but I thought I was cutting down – I now realise I wasn't. If I'd asked her she could have set up appointments with Gamblers Anon. I didn't ask because I thought I could stop myself [146. Obstacle: 'gambling'. A pessimist whose offending escalated].

Others denied that probation could ever be of help. The following probationers, when asked: 'has being on probation helped you stay out of trouble?', said:

No. Probation does not help, it's up to the individual. I've been on probation for years and it doesn't stop me from offending. It may help some people, but not me. It's okay, but it doesn't keep me out of trouble [226, a pessimist whose offending escalated].

I don't know how she can help me with it.[10] Just talking to her is a positive experience, but in practical terms she has no effect. Though I like her as a person and I'd hate to disappoint her, she's of no consequence to me, nor me to her, so ... I've changed my lifestyle a little, sacked a few friends, been more considerate, curbed a bit of my routine. I've looked at my future, long and short term and made plans, been more responsible [019, a pessimist whose offending initially continued before showing signs of desisting].

Life events (such as marriage, child-rearing, employment and so on) have long been associated with desistance by those researching criminal careers (see Chapter 1). Similar processes can be seen in the lives of probationers as they overcame some of the obstacles which they had identified:

I'm still on methadone prescriptions, but nothing else. Not much [has been done by my officer]. We've talked a lot about it, but that's as far as it goes. I didn't get much help. I was already pregnant last time I saw you. I knew I had to stay out of trouble for the baby's sake [PR 134. Obstacle: drug use. An optimist who desisted].

She suggested things – like anger management, but nothing happened. Because life's generally better, I can cope easier. I split up from my boyfriend. It was my decision to end it – it was destructive for both of us. I've been a lot better, before I was stressed out, I'm no longer stressed [PR 110. Obstacle: temper. A confident who desisted].

I don't normally see my friends so much during the week. I'm with my girlfriend. It is still a problem because when I see them at the weekend I need . . . like . . . they all start smoking and I just can't resist it really [039. Obstacle: drug use. An optimist who was classified as a continuing trivial offender].

Looking at obstacles from different sides

So far, the analyses have focused on officers and probationers in isolation from one another. This style of analysis was driven by the fact that very few officer and probationer pairs had identified the same obstacles as one another. We turn now to consider the instances where officers and probationers agreed about the obstacles faced. Probationers' battles against drug addiction (usually heroin) have formed a recurring aspect of the analyses. One officer [008] described the work he had undertaken with his probationer: 'I have negotiated with the [drugs dependency team] and tried to get him to be honest about the extent of his drug use.' However, when asked to describe what the probationer had done, the same officer said: 'He got himself back on the programme [with the drugs dependency team], and then played silly buggers with the methadone doses!' Things were not all doom and gloom, however. The probationer's partner had had their second child, which the officer described as having 'spurred him into getting a job', which the officer said the probationer seemed quite happy about. In addition, the couple's first child, aged 3, was 'getting some awareness of "Daddy's" frequent use of the toilet'.[11] Whether it was due to the arrival of the new baby, the older child's growing awareness of his father's drug use, the somewhat stymied drug programme or the probationer's growing sense of needing to provide for his family (hence the job) is hard to ascertain with any certainty. What can be said, however, is that he went from being a pessimist when first seen, to an optimist and finally a confident and was classified as a desister. The probationer himself described his officer's efforts at helping him give up drugs as: 'He just talks to me really. When I stopped going to the [drugs dependency team], he was keeping in touch with them, checking how many times I was going there.' Of his key-worker at the team and the team generally he said: 'I came off drugs with the help of the team. I didn't get on with my key-worker, he was a pain in the bum. I stopped going, but things are alright now.' When asked to describe the biggest change in his life, he said 'giving up drugs'. When prompted to discuss why he had given up drugs he referred to his new baby and added that his wife had said she would leave him if he did not stop using heroin. Indeed the role of his wife appeared to be a key factor in understanding why he had ceased using heroin. His officer said: 'In recent months he's felt under pressure. Fluctuating motivation of attending the [drugs dependency team]. She had quite a big influence on him actually turning up.' This account was supported by the probationer himself, who said of a recent threat of breach from his officer:

> When I didn't go a couple of times, he sent me a letter warning me that if I didn't go he'd have to report me. Still I didn't go, but [my wife] panics too much and made an appointment for me to go and see him – which I did.

In another case, whilst both officer and probationer agreed about the obstacle faced by the probationer, and even agreed on the course of action required to combat it, other factors negated action:

> I encouraged her to go to the Employment Training Officer, but she wants to wait for her daughter to start school before doing so [PO 058. Obstacle: unemployment].

> We've talked about it, but with a little girl I can't do anything work-wise at the moment [PR 058. Obstacle: unemployment].

In other instances, whilst there was an agreement about the obstacle faced, the solutions proposed by the officer and probationer were different. In the following case, the probationer was a pessimist who was classified as a continuing non-trivial offender:

> Well, to tell you the truth, I could get a job anytime I want. I have got to a stage where I didn't really want to work. I'm quite happy. Then it came to the stage where I wanted to start working again. If I really put my mind to it, as soon as I get out of here,[12] I could have a job within a few days [PR 204. Obstacle: unemployment].

> I remember him saying that he was most likely to offend late at night and in the morning and that if he could find a nightshift job it would stop him re-offending, but he never did find a nightshift job. I don't think, however, for me, that was the solution. It might

have helped him break a pattern, but he needed to learn ways of not offending other than finding a nightshift [PO 204. Obstacle: unemployment].

In yet other cases the treatment offered was not felt by the probationer to fit his or her requirements:

I made appointments for him with a drug counsellor, he failed to attend these [PO 086. Obstacle: drug use. An optimist whose offending escalated].

She tried to get me on a day course. I'd been on one before but it didn't do any good before, so I didn't go on it, which she accepted. I said I needed residential care all along. They are asking me to do an unrealistic thing – to get off drugs while I'm out here.[13] Everyone you know is doing it, so the temptation is too much. But they won't put me on a residential rehab [PR 086. Obstacle: drug use].

In any event, as reported earlier, the probationer left home after a row with his parents and moved home – taking him to another probation area altogether.

A case study: a pessimist who desisted

In this section, the work of one officer–probationer pair is examined in detail. The purpose of investigating this case is to illustrate both the nature of the work undertaken as part of probation supervision and the role of other individual and social contexts in mediating such work.

Anthony [094] was in his late 20s when he started his 12-month probation order – imposed after he had been found guilty of actual bodily harm. He had been working on a confectionery production line when another employee approached him and started to pass remarks about Anthony's hair style. Anthony head-butted this man, breaking his two front teeth. Anthony said that at the time of the incident he had been getting on badly with his wife, who had just given birth to their first child; he hated his work and was generally stressed, mainly about the new baby, which was keeping him awake. He said that he spent about £50 a week on cannabis and amphetamines. His officer confirmed this portrait, adding that Anthony 'drank heavily with his friends'.

Between the offence and the first interview, Anthony's lifestyle changed. He had left the home he had shared with his wife and child to live with his sister, and divorce proceedings had commenced. Anthony said that he 'occasionally snogged birds', but was not in a steady relationship. He had a new job (having been sacked from the previous one as a result of the assault), but was drinking and smoking cannabis much more, both of which he attributed to his divorce. He said he was also feeling 'down', again due to the divorce. His officer painted a similar picture.

Anthony identified two obstacles to his desisting: if he saw his wife with her new boyfriend, and his drug use – which he said was not something he would address as 'no one will stop me smoking drugs'. With regards to the first obstacle he said he had 'told her not to bring her new fella near me'. When asked directly whether probation could help him with this obstacle, he said: 'No. There's nothing they can say or do that would stop me attacking him – it's a pride thing. She shouldn't see someone in front of me.'

Anthony's officer also identified two obstacles: his 'way of thinking' and his friends, whom he described as a 'bunch of ruffians'. In terms of tackling the first of these, he stated that Anthony got angry quickly and that they would use some of the exercises from 'Targets for Change' to deal with this. However, the second obstacle – Anthony's friends – would be addressed less directly: 'I won't do too much. The more you tell someone not to do something the more they'll do it. I'll try to empower Anthony to do something himself – give Anthony an insight into the consequences of knowing these people.'

By the time of the second interviews, Anthony's circumstances had changed again: he had moved home again and was now living on his own which he liked, as it gave him more independence; he had also been off sick from work, after he hurt his leg in a fight; and he was drinking more. The obstacles he had identified during the previous interviews were revisited:

SF   Last time we met, I asked you if you thought there were any problems that might make it hard for you to stop offending, and I remember you said 'if you saw your ex with her new bloke you'd flip'.

PR   Yeah, I would, I probably would still now. Lucky I haven't seen him – I don't want to see him. I keep telling her 'don't bring him anywhere near me. If I see you in town with him – I will'. 'Cause inside [of me] I know I will. I can sit here now and say 'nah I won't do nothing', if they walked past that window now, I'd have my trainers on going down there getting him. It's inside you, you know what I mean? You can't stop that. I'm not going to go stalking him or anything, or anything like that, it's just that if I see him in a pub or in the street, I'll hit him or whatever – I will. It just . . . it's a matter of principle. When I split up with my wife, within six weeks, she was seeing him. As far as I know, she could have been seeing him before hand. But she swears blind she weren't. But I still got that doubt. It will always be there – until I get it out, get it out of my system, actually give him a kicking, it will always be there.

SF   You said earlier that you'd talked to [officer] about how you felt about that, is there anything else that he could have done?

PR   No, no. At times when I talked to him about it, I was for going round there, kicking the door in giving him abuse. Waiting for him to walk out of work and jump him. But [officer] was saying that was a stupid thing to be doing – 'you'll get inside, you'll miss your kid'. That's right, yeah, but if I saw him in the street, I wouldn't stop it anyway. It's just inside – I'd just flare up. I can stop myself from going to get him, I can stop myself from stalking and getting him, but if I see him . . .

Although Anthony's officer had identified him as being 'quick-tempered' at the first interview, he said during the follow-up that he had actually done very little work with Anthony on this topic as he was due to start an anger management course. With regards to Anthony's domestic arrangements he observed:

He felt that the situation at home [when he had been living with his wife] was . . . well, that he didn't want to stay in it, and he moved out – which was his right. And I wouldn't try to put him back there. I wouldn't try to encourage him to go back there cause it is not what he wants. He thinks he has got a temper, and I think he has got a temper, although when he comes to see me he has a placid way of co-operating. And we can discuss lots of issues. I think if he was pushed emotionally he would react. And he did say to me before that he was looking forward to going on the anger management programme as he hopes that by the end of the programme he would be able to develop strategies to deal with his anger and his temper. Which he recognises is a problem for him . . .

The second obstacle to his desisting which Anthony had identified was his continued use of drugs and, in particular, cannabis:

SF   The other thing that you said that might make it hard for you to stop offending was the fact that you were smoking dope.

PR   Yeah. I reckon that . . . well . . . I'm not going to give up dope whether they make it legal, illegal, whether they ban it. I'm still not going to give it up. It's my prerogative. They're allowed to get pissed up on whiskeys,[14] I'm allowed a spliff. That's the only way I mean, if they made it legal tomorrow, I wouldn't be breaking the law smoking a spliff. They're making me a criminal by doing that. That's one reason why I ain't giving up dope – I enjoy it too much. I'm not giving up no drugs – I like this, I like pills and I like coke. That's like, when I go out at the weekends, I'll have a few drinks, and I'll have perhaps some whizz.[15] Between that I'm smoking spliffs – spliff after spliff after spliff. Cause everyone I know smokes. Skins up, well one every ten minutes. Well, I smoke all the time . . .

SF   Remind me again, did you talk to [officer] about dope?

PR   He says, I've spoke to him about it like – there's not a lot wrong – he don't say it's right. He just says there's not a lot wrong, a few spliffs here and there. He said if it don't agree with you, just have beer . . . he don't actually condone it, but he don't actually say 'don't do it'.

This report was supported by Anthony's officer who said 'well, he smokes cannabis, he tells me that. Only now and then, but it is not a major problem'. Anthony's officer had outlined two obstacles to his desisting. One of these, his temper, has already been discussed. With regards to the second obstacle – Anthony's friends – the officer said:

Well, I know some of the people he associates with, and I know of the [pubs and clubs] that he goes to to relax, have a game of pool and a few pints. It is a well known establishment in town. I have seen him around the town centre with others who I know, through my work as an officer. He is associating with these people and since the offence [for which he received the order] he hasn't come to the notice of the courts. So I think he . . . it appears he is managing alright. Whilst I want to be able to wish him well for the future – I am skirting around it here – I don't want to be judgmental, he has known these individuals for a long, long time and they are friendships that were nurtured at school, very hard to shake off. You can still have relationships with people who are offending and not offend yourself. I would like to believe that that is the case.

The topic of Anthony's friends was returned to repeatedly during the interview:

SF   Has Anthony been involved in any offending since the last time we met?

PO   Not to my knowledge. But I do know . . . I am concerned about some of his peers . . . that are known to me, known to the [probation] service. I see him around the town . . . and I do see him in the company of others that I would rather he didn't associate with. But that's . . . he is happy in their company, and so far he hasn't come back he hasn't re-offended so I suppose it is not like that . . . but I would rather he didn't associate with some of his peers.

When the focus of the interview fell upon the officer's own efforts to intervene he said that he had done very little. This is entirely understandable, and exactly as he had predicted:

SF   Just thinking about the friends, which strikes me again and again as being your primary concern about Anthony's future, is there that anything that you or the probation service can do?

PO   I don't think that you can legally prevent anybody from associating with anybody in this country really. It is a democracy after all. We can befriend whomever we please. In this particular case, as far as probation goes, all we can do is to raise . . . my concerns and then it will be entirely up to him if he wants to or not.

SF   Have you raised your concerns about his friends with Anthony himself?

PO   Not recently. He did tell me of some individuals that he knows, and he knows that I know these individuals as well. And we talked about the merits of actually being with them. I did actually say to him that he should be a little more self-aware than that, and he actually said he wouldn't associate with them, but we never talked in depth about it. *How did he react to your suggestion that he be more . . .?* Basically I didn't want to put too much of a point on it. I didn't want to sort of make it the main focus of anything. I just mentioned it and allowed it to stay with him and let him deal with it. I don't want to do the big brother thing and sort of 'don't do this'. I felt I would just mention it and allow it to stay on the agenda and perhaps to come back to it another time. Give him time to think about it.

135

At the end of the second interview, both Anthony and his officer were asked to identify further obstacles facing Anthony and to reflect on how they might tackle these. Anthony's officer said that Anthony's friends would still pose a problem, but because Anthony was going into group-work for the rest of the order, they would be seeing very little of each other. Anthony himself identified his involvement with drugs and friendships:

SF   Tell me a bit more about some of the things you think might get you back into trouble.

PR   Oh, there's definitely drugs and that. Like even being in work, like my mates – like they're drug dealers. Like I'm in a car with him a lot of times, and he's got drugs in his car, I'm in that car, I'm nicked with him. He's not gonna say it's his, he's gonna say 'humpf – I don't get that' – you know what I mean? And I'll be sat next to him, so there's another way of getting nicked. I also, the pubs I go in as well, the other pubs I go in, most of the pubs near town, you get a lot of trouble, like people coming in Saturdays and things like that. Too much uncertainty – it's all 'ifs and buts'. But it is possible, it is easily possible. There's many different ways of getting arrested for silly things. Some of them are not so silly and some of them are. *Is there anything you can do to sort of . . . stop that? Yeah.* No. You can't. There's no way you can do it. The drugs for instance, that's my social life. That's the people I deal with and hang around with. That kind of thing – that's just life. Its part of life. If it wasn't for drugs, if they weren't illegal, then . . . then, I wouldn't be breaking the law. Fighting for instance, that you can't stop, that's gonna happen whatever, the poshest bloke in the world or the lowest bloke in the world – if someone hits you you're gonna hit back. So that kind of thing you can't stop.

The third sweep interviews took place shortly after Anthony was due to have completed his order. However, at that time it became apparent that he had attended very few of the anger management sessions. The officer interviewed (who had taken over the case after the previous officer had left the office) had never met Anthony and could provide little information about him. He noted that Anthony had been reported by the officers running the anger management group to have appeared 'withdrawn' at the two sessions he had attended, but that he had not approached either of these officers about this. Anthony was breached and a warrant was issued for his arrest. His account of his 'disappearance' was the first thing discussed when he was seen for the third and final time:

SF   So, you're technically no longer on probation, that all finished.
PR   Yeah that all finished. *When did that finish?* Well, I assume, when I never went to anger management (laughs). Cause I moved from that address, they never contacted me. All my mail must have gone to that address and I never heard nothing, so I assume that I have been breached. *I saw you in July, and you were still seeing [original officer] then.* Yeah, I was. Once a fortnight I was seeing him then. *And, what happened?* Well, I just sort of moved house, didn't go to my appointments when I was supposed to. And stuff like that really. He sent a few letters saying 'turn up at such and such a time'. *This is [original officer]?* Yeah. Once I knew I'd lost me job, and was in debt to my rent, I just thought 'fuck it, fuck everything'. Move away from the area, move away from the city centre sort of thing, and just forget everything, forget the anger management, forget probation, and just move on. I don't think I need it anymore, personally speaking.
SF   You went to some of the anger management sessions.
PR   Yeah I went for 11 weeks. *And what were they like?* Stupid. They were based on an American thing. It is a trial thing over here really. It is basically, they ask you stupid questions of situations which never happen and how you are going to respond to them. Like, I'll give you an example: one of them was 'you're with a bunch of Jewish people, you're being chased through a village, and there are German soldiers chasing you, they run into this house and one of the women's got a kid. The kid is crying, it's going to give away your position, and the Germans are going to come in and shoot you all, what do you do? Do you kill the kid or . . .?' Do you know what I mean? Do you give yourself up for the sake of the kid? What a stupid question. I refused to answer it . . .[16]

Anthony was asked to discuss the obstacles which he had identified:

SF   When I spoke to you last time I asked you if you thought there was anything that might make it hard for you to stop offending and you said 'knowing people who use drugs'.
PR   Yeah – cause I am constantly around people who smoke dope all the time. It is like a different social world to everyone else's.

Like everyone else who don't smoke dope, they got their friends and such and such, they go out for a drink with the friends, or play cards, or whatever they do with their friends. When you got smoking friends, you go round their houses, you sit down, you smoke a few spliffs, you get stoned with them, you have a laugh, most of the people I know, nearly everyone I know, smokes dope. It is a different social background. So, I go in drug dealers' houses all the time. I have a smoke in there – if I'm in there and they get busted, and there's loads of drugs around, I'm dragged in with it. That is a risk you take. It is only cannabis – it is not heavy drugs. But if they legalise it, then no one would be criminals.

So, in effect, he had done nothing about the obstacle which he had identified. In sum, neither he nor any of the officers he'd had contact with had directly addressed his 'temper'. His officer had not wished to tackle it directly, for fear of ruining the work to be undertaken in the group-work sessions, and the officers running the group did not appear to have impressed Anthony in any way. At every one of the three interviews, Anthony reported having been in numerous fights (usually associated with drinking). His drug use continued and he was 'hanging around' with other users and dealers.

Yet despite this, Anthony would appear to have received (and by all accounts listened to) advice from his officer. For example, he discussed with his officer his ex-partner and her 'new fella' and how he should react to this situation and, accordingly, he had not gone to her new home and 'jumped' her 'fella'. Anthony remembered sufficiently well what his officer had said to be able to recount it when interviewed, had realised that his officer's advice was worth heeding and had started to get on better with his ex-wife.

Whilst he had continued to become involved in fights, at the third interview he estimated that his last fight had been six months prior to the interview. At around that time, Anthony's life changed dramatically: not only did he leave the area (near the city centre) in which he had been living to move to a suburban part of the same city, but he started to live with a new girlfriend, Cleo. During his final interview, Anthony discussed the influence of Cleo, probation supervision and other normative life events:

SF Any other trouble that you've got into since I saw you?
PR No, not really. I've stayed off the drink as much. Now I'm with Cleo like, I don't drink as much as I used to. I drink a bit

indoors, but I don't go out pubbing it no more. I don't need to. The only reason why I used to go out pubbing it was to socialise. Meet girls. Get drunk, y'know. I don't need to since I met her. I just stay in with her – become a quiet life again.

And again:

SF   Can you describe for me your life when you first started probation, back that year or so ago.

PR   Well, when I got [probation], just before Christmas in December I got sentenced. It must have been just after I split up from my missus. Back that time I probably needed someone like [officer], like I said, it felt like counselling, you could go in there and say to them and it felt better when you left there, like 'fucking bitch won't let me see my kid'. And he'd say 'well, you ain't gonna see your kid if you speak to her like that'. He'd make you look at it that kind of way. So it was all right for that sort of reason. The counselling. It helped with my personal problems. As for re-offending and stuff like that, as I said before, everyone breaks the law everyday, it's just that people do it in different moderations.

SF   That was your life then. Tell me a bit more about your life now.

PR   Now I'm unemployed. I'm not really looking for work at the moment. After working for five years on two shitty jobs, I want about a year off. Have a break. I'm a lot happier now that I've got Cleo. I don't go out with attitude no more. When I was single and that, I used to go out with attitude and that. It was all about getting a name for yourself and all stuff like that. Which I already have, but its all image when you're on your own. But when you are with someone you don't give a fuck about anything, you just think 'ahhh fuck it. I'm with her and that's it', it's as simple as that. So you can relax more. You can take little digs at you a lot easier. Like before you'd bite on them – you'd say 'what was that you fucking said?', but now you just think 'yeah, yeah, go away you prick', you know what I mean. You just brush it off easier now.

SF   Those changes, that you just described to me from between when you started probation and now, was that anything to do with probation or was it things away from probation?

PR   Nah. Its away from probation. I done it myself. Probation didn't really help me. The only thing they really did for me was like I said – counselling type of thing, helped me see my kid and things like that. It helped me . . . use it . . . the right way about going about things. Like going round there blowing up, putting windows in and trying to get the kid and stuff that way, he made yer sit down and think about it. And that's about it really. But, then I never really talked to him about crimes or anything, 'cause he is an officer, you know what I mean. You can't say 'yeah, I go out smoking dope', 'I'm doing "this" all the time . . .', cause he'll just go 'oh, yeah? oh yeah? – you're breached, you're not supposed to commit offences whilst on probation. So you can't really say nothing like that to him. You can talk to him to a certain extent, but not to the full extent – not like you – you're in confidence,[17] they're supposed to be confidential too, but if they know that you're breaking the law, a serious offence, they'll scratch that straight away.

These extended extracts reveal the influence of Cleo. Anthony claimed that the changes in his life and his frequency of offending were due to Cleo – and certainly no other major changes could be detected. Probation was, he admits, helpful at the start of the order, when he had somewhere to go and 'sound off' about his wife, and the advice of his officer may have been of use. Certainly it would appear that having someone to talk to did help Anthony at that time.

Anthony's experiences were chosen as an example of the situated context of probation work because whilst he and his officer had identified different sets of obstacles, similar themes – peers, the 'ex-' and anger – permeated their discussions. They had also discussed together possible ways of resolving some of these (the 'ex-' and peers being the obvious examples), *and* it would appear that Anthony had taken on board some of the advice given to him – in particular concerning his 'ex-'. Nevertheless, it is hard to come to the conclusion that probation was the *driving force* behind Anthony's offending reducing in the way it did. He claims his offending (i.e. fighting) was greatly curtailed around the time that he ceased to attend probation, moved away from a particular area and started to live with Cleo. In other words, changes in Anthony's personal and social contexts appear to have been the features of his life which encouraged desistance, rather than probation supervision alone.

Summary

This chapter has developed the analyses started in Chapter 5, which explored the outcomes of the attempts to tackle the obstacles to desistance faced by probationers. After finding that variations in the formal interventions made by officers played little part in accounting for whether obstacles were resolved or not, this chapter has considered the role of personal and social contexts.

This discussion has demonstrated a number of important issues concerning 'successful' and 'unsuccessful' attempts to tackle these obstacles whilst on probation. There were very few instances where failure was due to inexcusable *inaction* on the part of the officer. However, even when officers did intervene to help their probationers overcome the obstacles which they faced, their efforts did not often appear to have been of help. There appeared to be a tendency for officers to 'talk about' the obstacles which their probationers faced, rather than actually take action (see Table 6.3). Officer 107 reported that he had talked with his probationer about his immaturity yet, as he noted, it proved to be very hard to make much headway with this approach. The officer supervising Anthony reported that he had '. . . just mentioned [Anthony's friends] to him . . .' as he '. . . didn't want to make it the main focus of anything'. One is left with an impression of circuitous discussions between officers and probationers during which officers 'drop hints' about 'issues', the lessons of which are not brought home to the probationers. Contrast this approach with case 113 (in Chapter 10), where the officer 'continually' spelt out to the probationer the need for him to change. This interpretation is borne out by quotations from the probationers themselves – see case 134 earlier in this chapter on how she and her officer 'talked about it', but that was 'as far as it went', or case 110 who reported a discussion about anger management but that 'nothing happened', or case 008 who reported that his officer 'just talks'. There appears to be a consensus amongst officers that 'talking about' obstacles to desistance with probationers will resolve them. It may well be that this is the first step towards resolving them, but it would *not* often appear that this approach actually *solves* these obstacles in and of itself.

What, then, would appear to help probationers to overcome these obstacles, and thereby increase their chances of desisting? The answer could lie in not talking, but *acting*. From the qualitative data presented in this chapter, examples of 'good work' (i.e. intervention which led to some positive outcome for the probationer) by officers would appear to consist of *action*. Consider, for example, the officers who helped probationers to find accommodation (see earlier this chapter); went round to the probationer home and assisted them, either by telephoning other agencies on their behalf, or who physically took the probationer to another agency. Other examples of similarly 'good work' being equated with action rather than talk will also be found in subsequent chapters: by, for example, telephoning family members to ask them to help probationers, case 153 (in Chapter 9) or case 054 (in Chapter 10). This not to say that talking is *never* good, but that too often it is all that is relied upon and that more, by way of action, is required to maximise probation supervision. Consider the events reported by officer 060 (this chapter). She reported that she and her probationer 'regularly discussed' heroin and that the probationer was offered 'time-out' – but nothing was done to address the 'counter-influences', namely, an abusive boyfriend. Contrast this with the reports of the action taken by another officer in a very similar situation (case 028, this chapter), who intervened in a very direct manner and achieved a positive outcome.

This is not, of course, to ignore wider social and personal contexts or their influences on the probationers. There were several instances of the probationers' social and personal contexts intervening in such a way as to influence the 'success' or 'failure' of the attempts made to deal with the obstacle. Arguments and reconciliation with family members usually occur independently of probation supervision; decisions to leave home, return home, 'runaway' and so on are made for reasons other than their 'rehabilitative' tendencies. Gaining employment – often associated with reductions in offending – losing work and getting better work are also open to influence from factors outside probation supervision. Hitherto, evaluations of probation work have largely ignored the role of these factors in encouraging or inhibiting desistance from offending. Whilst the discussion above has not investigated the *magnitude* to which social variables impacted upon the general outcome of probation supervision (this issue is discussed in more depth in Chapter 10), it has demonstrated that the outcome of the work aimed at tackling the obstacles identified by officers was influenced by the social and personal circumstances of the probationer.

Another theme which emerged from the responses given by the officers was that 'successful' and 'failed' attempts to tackle obstacles were often the result of the probationer's inability or reluctance to confront or resolve the obstacle *as well as* the influence of the probationer's social and personal life. Probationers, by their own admission, failed to seek advice – or sought advice but then did not follow it – or attempted to tackle obstacles in ways other than as their officers had suggested.

Of course, motivation, social and personal contexts and probation work do not exist independently of one another. Similarly, social and personal contexts are fluid – as some of the data presented in this chapter have demonstrated. A probationer's employment status may alter, his or her family relationships may change and so on. The next chapter explores the most frequent changes in probationers' social and personal circumstances and the ways in which motivation, changing contexts and probation supervision interacted with one another.

Notes

1 The probationer was already on a methadone reduction programme.
2 The probationer in question was in the process of separating from the mother of his children.
3 The probationer had been given better terms of access to her children, who were living in care.
4 Although the officer did not mention specific crises, it is clear from the interview that the probationer had problems with the following aspects of his life, any of which could readily have thrown up crises: unstable accommodation; unstable employment; financial problems; problems with access to his children; a tendency to drink large quantities of alcohol; and depression.
5 The probationer had faced charges, which were eventually withdrawn. The officer's recall of the events surrounding the offence were hazy (due to the case being withdrawn), but it appears that the probationer and his partner were in a pub where he assaulted her after a dispute. The charges were withdrawn by the probationer's partner shortly after the event took place.
6 The probationer had recounted how he had met one of the people involved in his friend's death and come close to assaulting him.
7 Which he described as 'how I feel when I get angry'.
8 Although the probationer had gained insights into his offending, being 'known' in the area frequently resulted in him having to resort to violence to protect himself and/or his friends.
9 On the role of his officer in this process he said: 'she didn't know [about him giving up cocaine] until I stopped.'
10 The obstacle identified by the probationer was his 'pride'. He is expanding on this point by saying: 'If I say I'm going to do something, then I get it done. If someone kicks my fucking door through, and I say "I'm gonna get you", then I will.'
11 In order for him to inject heroin without the child seeing him do so.
12 The probationer was in prison at the time of the second interview.
13 In the community.
14 It is unclear who the 'they' refers to – but at the time of the interview, it appeared to refer to judges or magistrates.
15 Amphetamines.

16 The probationer recounted this same tale during the second interview. He'd started the course previously (as part of this order) and not completed it then either.

17 Anthony was referring to the interviewer at this point.

Chapter 9

Motivation, changing contexts and probation supervision

This chapter builds on the previous two chapters in two ways. The recent literature on the effectiveness of penal interventions has emphasised the need to take account of dynamic variables[1] (Andrews 1989; Jones 1996: 58). This chapter therefore investigates the most common changes experienced by probationers and the impact these had on their lives. It then moves on to consider the role of the officer in helping to foster these sorts of changes and, in so doing, 'brings together' the analyses of motivation, probation supervision and changes in personal and social circumstances.

Change and development in social and personal contexts

All officers and probationers seen during the follow-up phases were asked to describe the 'biggest single change in the probationer's life' since the previous interview. The most common responses – those which accounted for more than 10 per cent of all changes – are reported in Table 9.1. Two of the most common changes reported related to employment and family formation. When individual case studies were examined, it was found that the reported changes of home were usually incidental to other changes. For example, many of the moves of home were in fact to addresses close to the probationer's original address and were the result of changes in employment status or family formation. This is a fairly obvious finding – as people start work, set up or end relationships, they often move home. Changes in substance use were also often usually found to be the result of changes in employment and family formation. For these reasons, this chapter focuses primarily upon changes in employment and families. There are, however, other good reasons for focusing on employment and

Table 9.1: Probationers' 'biggest single' life change since the previous interview

Category	Officers		Probationers	
	(n)	(%)	(n)	(%)
Change in employment[2]	41	(12)	45	(18)
Change in family formation[3]	44	(13)	35	(14)
Change in substance use[4]	34	(10)	33	(13)
Change in home address	43	(13)	34	(13)
No change/don't know	76	(22)	31	(12)
All other changes	103	(30)	77	(30)
Total	341	(100)	255	(100)

family. As well as being amongst the most common indicators of 'adulthood' (Hogan and Astone 1986; Graham and Bowling 1995), and hence of 'maturity' and 'responsibility', the acquisition of stable employment and family formation have been linked with desistance from offending in several previous studies (see Chapter 1).

In terms of its impact on an individual's life, paid employment has the potential to achieve all the following: a reduction in 'unstructured' time and an increase in 'structured' time; an income, which enables 'home-leaving' and the establishment of 'significant' relationships; a 'legitimate' identity; an increase in self-esteem; use of an individual's energies; financial security; daily interaction with non-offenders; for men in particular, a reduction in the time spent in single-sex, peer-aged groups; the means by which an individual may meet his or her future partner; and ambition and goals, such as promotion at work.[6]

The descriptions obtained from officers and probationers of the latter's gaining work, getting more stable work or being promoted at work illustrate some of these processes. Employment brought a number of changes to probationers' lives – one of the first of these was to reduce the amount of 'unstructured' time:

[the probationer's drinking] is moderated by the fact that he is working. I think that if he wasn't working, he'd be drinking more [PO 194, a confident who desisted].

I've got a job. I've always got money. When you've got money you've got things you can do, so I can go out and that instead of going out, like, on the streets drinking, causing trouble [PR 067, a pessimist who desisted].

I mean, obviously if I'm at work, I can't smoke [heroin]. You know, I can't go out for a drink every ten minutes or I can't have a line of coke every hour you know. So really, it's quite good because it's controlling me ... [PR 164, a pessimist who was classified as a continuing trivial offender].

In addition, some jobs physically removed people from the situations which had previously led them into trouble. One person, on probation for assaulting his partner, gained employment which took him away from their home during the week:

Well, for one thing, he is not living [at home], and so the opportunities for discord between him and Nina is limited – 'cause he has been working away. It just takes him out of the environment doesn't it? Working all across the country, his mind is preoccupied with other things and so relationship problems are not magnified. Maybe he is more able to be more objective about the relationship than if he was not at work and hanging about ... [PO 098, a confident who desisted].

Indeed, one of the probationers who said that he had lost his job reported that he had become: '... bored. I take it out on my girlfriend – we're in each other's faces twenty-four hours a day. Makes me lazy. I'm in bed 'til four o'clock most days' [PR 022, a pessimist whose offending escalated].

Several respondents reported that employment encouraged the probationer to take a 'more responsible' attitude towards consuming drugs and alcohol:

I've cut down a lot [on drinking]. I only get really drunk one night a week. Before I would have had a few cans whilst getting ready to go out, now I don't [PR 014].

I've been promoted in my job. I have got more responsibility now, so obviously I can't smoke [cannabis] during the week – which I was before. I have to concentrate because I work on the railways [PR 039, an optimist who was classified as a continuing trivial offender].

As well as reducing the 'time available' for 'aimless hanging around' which may lead to offending (especially amongst young men: Wallace 1986, 1987) and encouraging reductions in drug and alcohol usage, employment 'keeps one occupied':

Because I have work, I have got things to do. Because, before, when I committed crimes, I didn't have a job and I was just going around just to make money and that and I had time on my hands so I was drinking all the time. Now I have got a job and that I am working all the time and I haven't got time to drink [PR 067, a pessimist who desisted].

Long hours, which served to tire the probationers, appeared to be something of a recurring feature: 'I'm working a lot – I enjoy it' said case 014, whose officer added: 'he works long hours – 'til seven or eight at night.' Long hours spent at work, in many cases, served to reduce the probationer's desire to do much but relax after work: 'If I am not too tired I jump in the shower, get dressed and go and see [my daughter]. If I come home knackered, I have a shower and relax, I don't go anywhere!' [PR 036, a pessimist who desisted].

Fieldnotes made after interviewing another probationer supported the idea that work not only occupied the probationer's time, but also left some with little energy to do much else:

He was very tired. He said that he had to get up at six in the morning to get to work and it was twenty to eight in the evening before he got home, where the interview took place. It must be said that he did look pretty tired [PR 067].

For Jamie, a pessimist who desisted, it appeared his employment had imposed a gruelling routine upon his life:

by the time I get home, it is six or seven o'clock in the evening, I go out, back in by eleven o'clock, then [get up for] work again. And weekends – means you can't do nothing [PR 115].

I visited him twice at his home. Always five p.m.-ish. I would wait for him to come in and yeah, he wouldn't have the energy. He'd just sort of [officer mimics a slouch]. Three hundred and fifty pounds was good money, but he worked for it [PO 115].

Both the officers interviewed about this probationer reported that his self-esteem had been increased as a result of his gaining employment:

the conversations we had at supervision were very positive, much more vibrant . . . much more definite tones in his voice about what his life was about and how he was going to do this and that . . .

When he had the job he was much more positive. Plans for holidays, plans for this ... things I'd never heard him talking about [PO 115, second interview].

He seemed to be really motivated about these jobs ... He had an identity with the job, he apparently enjoyed the job, he was working very late, getting rid of his energy that way. It appeared to me that the employment was where he got his identity and got a role for himself [PO 115, third interview].

Employment not only changes an individual's image of him or herself but it also changes others' opinions of that individual. One officer reported how, by starting work, his probationer's family no longer saw him as 'a druggie':

because he is now working and providing for the household, all his pressures [with his family] have gone down. He was on the verge of actually being thrown out, and [made] homeless, by them. And that has receded 'cause he is becoming – from their point of view – a productive and constructive member of the family, and therefore working *with* them instead of *against* them. Which is often the perception of families with drug addicts – 'no matter what they do, they still end up on drugs' [PO 150, an optimist who desisted].

As some probationers remained in work, and started to perceive their employment as something from which they derived benefits, they came to realise that staying in work could be jeopardised by further convictions:

what was coming through [in supervision] was that he was thinking about drinking, thinking about not putting himself into vulnerable situations because his job is heavily dependent upon him driving. He is delivering books all over the South West [of England], so he can't lose his licence. So he has been thinking 'I will not make myself vulnerable, I will get a cab home or I will think how I will get home now' [PO 034, a confident who desisted].

the only time I got behind the wheel of a car was to start my dad's car up in the driveway 'cause he was under the bonnet, and that was it, and I got straight out of it when I started it up ... I wouldn't do it. 'Cause I know that if I got caught I'm going to lose my job [PR 194, a confident who desisted].

Work also introduced probationers to people they would never otherwise have met – as one [014] said, 'you get to meet people, see different perspectives on things'. Similarly, one of the officers [066] explained why he felt employment was associated with reductions in offending: 'when people work they tend not to go out so much, they tend to be a bit more focused. A bit more able to relate to . . . a bit more of the world and society'.

The following case study illustrates further the role of employment. Sandra [063], a confident who was classified as a continuing trivial offender, was 23 years old when she started her probation order, imposed after she had been found guilty of theft from her employer. 'I was working as a waitress in a cocktail bar,' she said, when she started drinking heavily. She stole around £2,500 from the till in order to buy drinks, and was consuming several cans of lager and a bottle of spirits a day around the time of the offence. Sandra said that she liked neither her work nor her home life. Until shortly before the offence, Sandra had been living with her parents, but had left home and was staying with friends whilst looking for more settled accommodation. She said that at this time she had been feeling down and confused over 'where she was going in life'.

At the second interview, Sandra had found employment. Following a self-initiated referral to a local alcohol counselling service which also ran an employment and re-skilling course, she had applied for work in the accounts department of a large firm. This was a daunting prospect for someone who had little prior work experience, and none at all in the previous six months: '[Work is] okay. It's getting better – the longer I spend there, it's getting better. The first week I was there I was thinking "urrrrgggggghhh – what am I doing here?" I was ready to [quit], but I stuck at it and it is going good.'

Sandra's officer recounted how nervous Sandra had been about applying for the position, and described her own efforts to reassure Sandra:

I think she thought that nobody would want to employ her again because the offence was actually for dishonesty – which was against her employer. So in fact it was a breach of trust, in employment . . . so that did present some difficulties when she went for this job. But in the end they decided to give her the job because they got a fairly favourable report from the employment and re-skilling project that she was attending.

I tried to explain that that was one department [internal security] that was putting up the stumbling block [regarding her previous conviction]. And yes, she was a bit down sometimes about it, but she tried to remain positive, 'cause she went for the interview, and I said 'well, at least you passed the interview stage, and if it comes that you don't get the job . . .' I tried to be positive – I said 'well, you know that it is not because you are not *capable* of going through the interview process. You've done the application, you've done the interview . . .' I said 'you *know* you are capable of doing it'. So I said, 'if you don't get it, don't let that stop you'. So I think she started to feel a little bit better about it. I said 'there will be another firm that maybe won't have somebody that is so pedantic. Yes, they will need to know [about the conviction], they'll be aware of it and can work with that, but . . .' I think it was the first job she applied for.

Sandra described her reaction to finishing her first week in her new job:

The very first Friday I worked it was 'yeeerrrse! Down the pub, down the pub!' I got absolutely rat-arsed, and felt so really ashamed of myself on the Saturday. I thought, 'okay – that is allowed, that is your first Friday, first full week at work. Okay, it is not going to happen next week'. And it didn't and it's been cool. I'm going away on holiday on Thursday. *Oh, where to?* Tunisia. When I first started work, one of the things that worried me was having money again would just be a ticket to going down the pub every night. But it hasn't been. I want to learn to drive, I want to get out of home, I want these things. So I am just going to have to save up and do it like everybody else.

Sandra's officer described the changes in Sandra which she had identified since she had started working again:

I think it has done her the world of good. The first time she came in she had really made an effort – she had done her hair up, dressed a lot smarter, her whole attitude and . . . what's the word I am looking for? When she comes in she doesn't look so *down* about things . . . she's really happy. She is really pleased about it.

Sandra's employers also appeared to be pleased with her efforts at work, and shortly before she was interviewed for the second time had given her a positive appraisal:

Last week, they told me that they are happy with my work – which has given me a boost. Up 'til then I was just getting along with it and I didn't know if they were happy with what I was doing. So that was good – they reassured me. 'We're really happy with you – keep it up'.

Sandra admitted that she had continued to smoke cannabis throughout the course of her order, but said that her usage was 'nothing serious'. At the third interview she said that she 'felt like a normal person' and was still enjoying work. When asked to describe her plans for the next six months she said she had enjoyed Tunisia and was 'going to South America in the summer'. When asked about longer-term plans she said 'to stay employed, progress in employment as far as I can and start driving lessons'.

Clearly, gaining employment will not guarantee that an individual will cease to offend (and, indeed, several studies have demonstrated that work can increase the opportunities for offending, e.g. Ditton 1977; Henry 1978). But evidence suggests that gaining work serves to reduce offending (e.g. Farrington *et al.* 1986; Horney *et al.* 1995). The reason for this is not simply because people commit crime because they are out of work, and employment takes away the need to offend. For many, employment structures their daily lives in such away as to reduce some of the opportunities for offending. Additionally, it gives people a sense of 'identity' and 'a role in society'. Commitment to work, that is to say, believing that one's job is beneficial in some way, serves in time to reinforce reductions in offending. Because most jobs demand physical presence at set times, and repeated transgressions of this may lead to disciplinary action being taken, commitment 'shapes' people's routines, often leaving them little opportunity to offend.

Changes in family formations also produced dramatic changes in probationers' lives. Several probationers had, either as a result of their engagement in offending, or for other reasons, 'fallen out' with their parents and had left home or were living independently and had little or no contact with their parents. Becoming reconciled with parents and a return to the parental home, often described as a 'temporary arrangement', provided one context in which families acted to support probationers during either moments of crisis or prolonged attempts to desist from crime.

One officer recounted how the probationer he was supervising (153, a confident who desisted) had eventually started living with his mother again after over ten years of living independently. Some of the circumstances surrounding the probationer concerned have already been referred to in Chapter 8. He had almost died as a result of injecting into an artery in his groin and had had to spend several weeks in hospital. Whilst he was in hospital, his officer spoke to his mother. Initially she had been reluctant to allow her son to come home to live with her, but consented when she realised that he would be homeless otherwise. Realising how close he had come to dying, the probationer resolved to stop using heroin and accepted his mother's offer of 'a bed'. When he was interviewed for the third time he was still living with his mother and reported that he had stopped offending as he had given up heroin.

Sandra [063], whose case was discussed above in relation to her employment, also moved home. Although she had not got on well with her parents for some years, and had not told them of her conviction, for fear of incurring their disapproval, her relationship with her parents had improved after an uncle had been diagnosed with cancer. When her own accommodation plans fell through, Sandra turned to her parents:

> I wasn't going to move back home – I had a flat lined up, I was going to move in with somebody. It was somebody from the alcohol sessions. He'd been dry for a long time. And we got on really well. He lived 15 minutes away from where I worked, so it was all dandy – it was going to be cheap, it was all perfect. I was meant to move in there on the Saturday, and I rang him up and he was drunk. So, that was it. I couldn't afford to put myself in that situation. He was older than me – he'd gone through an awful lot more. He was further along in the alcohol line than I was – much further along. I couldn't put myself in that situation. So my only option was to go home. At first it was ... like going backwards, but then, after speaking to a few people, I realised it is not going backwards, it is going sideways. It is just putting things on hold for a little while and doing things more sensibly.

As well as providing a 'refuge' in times of emergency, some families also appeared to offer practical assistance that could help probationers avoid further offending. For example, case 103 (a confident who desisted) reported how his wife drove their family around after his conviction for drink-driving. However, the most striking examples of intervention by families again concerned their attempts to assist probationers, usually their sons and daughters, in their attempts to give up drugs and/or alcohol. In one case this consisted of driving the probationer around in an attempt to find a drug rehabilitation clinic of her liking (092, a confident who was classified as a continuing trivial offender). In other cases far more urgent action was required. Two cases in particular (052, and 105,[7] both females in their mid-20s and both with family living abroad) provide examples of this sort of help. On learning that their daughters had developed heroin habits, both sets of families returned to the UK and rallied to support the women in question. In both cases this entailed finding the money to fund lengthy stays in drug rehabilitation clinics. However, not all families were as supportive – exclusion from parental homes resulting in increased risks of returns to drug usage were not unheard of (e.g. cases 086 and 172, Chapter 8).

Until this point, most of the discussion has focused upon the probationers' families of origin – that is, the families of which the probationers were the off-spring. Some of these families had been able to offer practical help, funding for rehabilitation programmes and temporary accommodation to 'wayward' sons and daughters. Similarly, families of formation – that is, those families which the probationer had formed via marriage, partnership and child-rearing – also offered the motivation to avoid further trouble.

Karla (134, an optimist who desisted) already had two children in social services care by the time her third child was born. Although she said she had given up heroin at the very start of her order, the child was born methadone dependent. Karla's officer reported that:

> there was an overall improvement in her self-esteem. Also the baby has increased her motivation, she's got a serious reason to avoid the risk of custody. Previously, she lost the care of her other two children and she does not want this to happen again. She has been very co-operative with the social services, who have told her she'll be able to get the baby back once she has her own accommodation and has remained drugs free.

Karla responded to this advice and established a close relationship with the baby – visiting him every day whilst he was in the hospital. Her officer described the baby as 'her main motivation to stop using drugs'. By the time of the third interview, Karla had found settled accommodation and had care of her baby and was seeing more of her children in care. Her officer said that she 'didn't want to lose what she's got now'. Although Karla could not be traced at the time of the third interview,[8] her accounts during the previous interviews support this general picture. Her motivation to stop offending (in effect, get off heroin) appeared to be high, and she reported that she did most of the work in achieving this by herself, saying 'I didn't get anything from probation, not even from the women's group'. Her officer supported her assessment: 'no matter what we do, it's mainly down to her. She's been highly motivated and she's made a lot of effort [to get off drugs]'.

Clive (076, a pessimist who desisted) had had a drink problem for a very long time. He was in his 30s when he started probation, and his officer said that he had had a drink problem for over 20 years. When first interviewed he was still drinking 'heavily', but by the time of the second interview, Clive's partner was pregnant: 'This is my fourth child, but it is like I get a second chance with the relationship. I can't "destroy" it this time. It gives me determination to make it work.'

His officer said that expecting another child had made Clive determined to tackle his alcohol problem and had helped him to stay out of trouble. Clive had contacted a local alcohol support group and was spending more time at home with his partner. By the time of the third interview the baby had been born, and Clive was spending even more time at home:

> I spend more time at home now. I have more things to do with myself. It also keeps me out of trouble. It's my own choice – I don't want this life for my baby, I still haven't given up drinking, I don't think I ever will, but things are not so bad now.

> I've tried to stay out of trouble, in order to prove to the social services that we can look after the baby. I only drink a couple of times a week now, and it's only outside the house.

As well as providing something which could be jeopardised if plans to desist are not kept to, families also provided a means of 'enforcing' such plans:

> [My partner] wouldn't let me re-offend anyway. Like, if I say 'look, I'm going to go with my mates today . . .', like if I told her about a certain person like, and she knows I am going round there, like, basically she won't let me go round there . . . She doesn't like to see me getting into trouble in any way [PR 036, a pessimist who desisted].

Another young male probationer (039, an optimist who was classified as a continuing trivial offender) said that seeing his girlfriend during the week (instead of his friends) limited his consumption of cannabis to the weekends. In addition, his girlfriend did not approve of his drug use and this also stopped him from using during the time he spent with her.

Having a girlfriend and, consequently, spending less time with friends also 'interrupted' legitimate pursuits which *could* place the individual at risk of offending. For example, one probationer (194, a confident who desisted) reported how he now spent less time with his mates drinking in pubs as a result of seeing his girlfriend (see also Warr 1998). Even when probationers did go to pubs, they were now often accompanied by their partners, which could also alter their behaviour. Anthony (see Chapter 8) reported during his third interview:

> I'm a lot happier now that I've got Cleo. I don't go out with attitude no more. When I was single and that, I used to go out with attitude and that. It was all about getting a name for yourself and all stuff like that. Which I already have, but it's all image when you're on your own. But when you are with someone you don't give a fuck about anything. You just think 'ahhh. Fuck it. I'm with her and that's it', it's as simple as that. So you can relax more. You can take little digs at you a lot easier. Like before you'd bite on them – you'd say 'what was that you fucking said?', but now you just think 'yeah, yeah, go away you prick', you know what I mean. You just brush it off easier now [094, a pessimist who desisted].

Families as 'something which could be lost' and as 'supportive' were two topics which recurred during the discussion of the ways in which families served to assist people in desisting. The following case study of Dominic (227, an optimist who desisted), who was in his mid-20s when he was given a six-month probation order for possession of heroin, illustrates both these themes. Dominic had been an addict for about two years and was spending about £80 a day on heroin. He had managed to keep his addiction secret from his wife and their children (all of whom he lived with) and his wider family. Following his arrest, however, he was no longer able to conceal his heroin use, and his wife refused to let him stay in their house. His parents had initially 'disowned' him too and Dominic was living with friends: 'They sort of disowned me when they found out about my drug habit. But now they are supporting me, hoping to get me off heroin.' Dominic's officer appears to have played some part in encouraging him to foster links with his family: 'I encouraged him to be open with his family and through this to ensure their support.'

By the time of the first sweep of interviewing, Dominic's expenditure on heroin was down to £20 a day. At the time of the second interview his officer said that Dominic had 'made a big effort at getting off heroin'. From his own descriptions of his life at that time, Dominic had indeed successfully tried to cut down on his heroin use and was now 'clean'. The motivation for this appeared to have been his desire to return to his family. Dominic himself said that he was 'off drugs' and had moved back with his wife and children. His parents, however, were still suspicious of him: 'If I look pale one day, they think I'm back on drugs again. I don't talk to them. After they found out about my habit, they started to accuse me of stealing things, like they thought it was me who stole their neighbour's bike'.

At the third interview Dominic was still living with his wife and children and they were considering a move away from the area in which they had been living, in order to make it easier for Dominic to avoid other drug users and dealers in that area. Dominic, however, had largely managed to avoid these people anyway. By this time also his parents had started more readily to accept that Dominic had stopped using heroin. They had even gone as far as to pay off the money (around £1,000) which he owed to various dealers and were 'coming round for hours and being really nice' to him. Dominic said that he felt 'quite shocked' at this turnaround in their attitude, which he likened to being 'given another chance'.

Employment and familial arrangements are two of the key determinants of an individual's lifestyle. For those lucky enough to have it, employment, as well as providing a wage, provides a structure to one's days and weeks. Similarly, familial arrangements organise a daily routine. As well as representing something which could be jeopardised by further conviction, families help to structure time and activities. Lifestyles and, in particular, the ways in which these are organised by family and employment, are the focus of this section. 'Lifestyle' (following Blaxter 1990) is interpreted as being not just the *voluntary* aspects of an individual's life, but also those aspects of their life which are, in some way, prescribed for them, or at the very least aspects over which they have limited choice.

The extent to which their lifestyles were not simply a matter of choice for probationers was made several times during interviews with officers:

I'd say [being unemployed] is a problem for anyone who has been unemployed for a long time and has no recent job reference or job experience, and somebody who is in and out of prison doesn't have any qualifications or any saleable skills ... [017, an optimist whose offending escalated].

It's very understandable why people in her situation drift into these problems [claiming benefit whilst working] because they've

157

no skills, they actually can only get very, very low-skilled employment, unskilled employment ... I think the employers make use of this by employing them erratically as and when it suits and then laying them off for days unexpectedly. I've noticed several probationers have had this very erratic employment pattern [and] because the employers will only take them on for a time, [they] end up claiming benefits, letting the benefit continue because they really don't know whether or not they are going to be given a day's work here there and whenever [079, a confident who desisted].

When he came out [of prison], he had nowhere to live, a girlfriend who was pregnant, he was on drugs, so bottom of the list was learning to read and write [070, a confident whose offending escalated].

Lack of employment, family support and, in general, a lack of 'structure' which organised the lives of probationers were frequently referred to as often leading to 'trouble', whilst the acquisition of such a 'structure' was associated with a reduction in the likelihood of being involved in trouble:

I think ... not having a constructive use of her time – it is not a job *per se*, if she was in college, if she had something where she had to get up and spend time with non-offenders, I think that that would be really positive. I think the fact that she has an awful lot of time on her hands and no money certainly increases the risk of offending [PO 054, a confident whose offending escalated].

A lot of his depression was an unstructured lifestyle. And not having any real work. In actual fact, he did work in the past, but he lost that work for bad time keeping. Either he had got himself so chaotic, that getting into a routine was difficult for him so he lost it, but somehow this new [job], he has been more capable of getting it together [PO 150, an optimist who desisted].

I know what I am doing. I got everything in perspective ... I got everything productive. I can sit down and say 'yeah – this is happening, this is happening ...' Before, it was one of those days where you take it as it comes. The first person who comes to your house, that is the person you are going to be for the rest of the day [PR 212, a confident who was classified as a continuing trivial offender].

Changes in lifestyles, particularly when associated with gaining employment, promotion at work or family were often observed to lead to increases in 'responsibilities'. Looking after younger siblings, ensuring that one's work is satisfactory, providing for one's family and an increased understanding of the consequences of further convictions were all amongst the factors which were cited as examples of increasing 'responsibility':

> I'm twenty-seven. I can't be doing with that going to court all the time. I got a little boy, I need to be around for my little boy. The misses and that . . . just . . . settled. Like if I was single and that, it wouldn't bother me in the slightest, not in the slightest, I could hack going to prison, it wouldn't bother me at all. But it is not me who it affects now, well it is, but it goes deeper than that. It would affect the little 'un and that. It has got more implications now. The most of the trouble that I have ever got in, has been when I have been on me own and that and I have had no one to like . . . It didn't matter whether I was locked up or not – it's not going to really affect anyone. But now it would [PR 098, a confident who desisted].

> I am more grown up for a start. More responsible, with regards to the children and my wife. *You're married now?* Yeah. I've been married – I've forgotten already – it was only [seven months previously]. But I've got kids from another relationship. I've got one living with me now – the boy – I've got custody of him. But . . . Yeah, the responsibilities. It is just basically everything in life. What goes on in my life – job, family, my home, it is all more important. And I can understand why it is more important [PR 032, a confident who desisted].

> I am working now and I got this course, so work can help me save money, plus I help pay for the bills . . . It helps my brothers get to school and all that. I help my mum with the money . . . I give my mum – I get £110 or £120 a week, depending on what hours I do – so I give my mum £40 a week. So it is less for her to pay. *Did you say you chipped in for the electricity too?* Yeah. And the phone. It's just so that it is less for her to pay [PR 212, a confident who was classified as a continuing trivial offender].

These quotations (taken along with some of those reported above – see, for example, case 039 on the 'responsibilities' of working on the railways) illustrate how responsibilities were not merely *situated* within a wider social context, but were *invoked* by that context. No one can take responsibility for children or employment he or she does not have. Responsibilities were also understood in terms of 'appropriate' behaviour given the role in society which that individual occupied: for example, being a 'father' meant not going to prison; similarly, being a 'worker' meant paying for household bills. The social context surrounding individual's lifestyles and changes in that social context (either 'real' or 'perceptual') were often the starting points for the adoption of responsibilities.

The adoption of a 'stable lifestyle' (which appeared to entail regular employment with the same employer, living at the same address, often with a partner and/or children) was often cited by officers as being a key factor in the ability of probationers to 'avoid trouble' (i.e. avoid offending) or moving towards a position where an individual was more able to avoid trouble:

> Well I think that all of [the probationer's social circumstances] can have an impact. Take the housing. I have always felt that that was a fundamental ... having him in some stable housing that he could cope with, where he wasn't feeling that he was still under the threat of being a victim, which at one [address] he was ... Employment will have a knock-on effect, actually being in work and with a decent income. I believe that being integrated within the community and therefore the quality of contact with his family, and giving him more stability in that respect may well also be a fundamentally positive factor for him as well [PO 232, a confident who desisted].

The roles of motivation and supervision

The analyses reported thus far have focused upon changes in the lives of the probationers and very little has been said directly about the roles of motivation and probation supervision in these processes of change. This section of the chapter brings together motivation, probation supervision and changes in social and personal contexts.

As noted in Chapter 5, the role of probation supervision in tackling obstacles to desistance appears to have been slight. However, as the case studies in this chapter have demonstrated, improvements in employment and family relationships were associated with positive life changes. In order to assess the extent to which officers were able to assist probationers in fostering changes in their employment and family circumstances, data relating to those officers who had identified such obstacles were re-examined.[9] Data were coded to record whether the problematic aspects of the probationer's family and employment circumstances had been overcome by the end of the order. For an obstacle to have been overcome, families had to have been reunited, for example, or a previously unemployed probationer found work. Reports of having overcome employment and family obstacles were associated with desistance ($p = .021$), confirming the earlier qualitative analyses which suggested that improvements in employment and family circumstances were associated with positive life changes, in this case desistance.

Table 9.2a reports whether employment and family-related obstacles had been *overcome* during the course of the order, who the *main instigator* in overcoming the obstacle was, and the *amount of help* that officers said they had given the probationer in tackling the obstacle concerned. It can be seen that whilst most of these obstacles (57 per cent) were overcome during the course of the orders, this was, according to the officers themselves, due mainly to the efforts of the probationers, rather than their own efforts (see the emboldened row in Table 9.2a).

Table 9.2: Resolving employment and family obstacles: main instigator of solution and amount of help given by officer

	Not overcome		Overcome		Unclear		All	
	(n)	(%)	(n)	(%)	(n)	(%)	(n)	(%)
a Main instigator of solution								
Officer	7	(78)	2	(22)	0	(—)	9	(12)
Probationer	**3**	**(7)**	**41**	**(91)**	**1**	**(2)**	**45**	**(60)**
Both	3	(23)	9	(69)	1	(8)	13	(13)
Neither	10	(91)	1	(9)	0	(—)	11	(15)
Unclear	4	(20)	3	(15)	13	(65)	20	(15)
Total no. of obstacles	27	(28)	56	(57)	15	(15)	98	(100)
b Amount of help								
Little/none	16	(36)	**26**	**(58)**	3	(7)	45	(46)
Some/a lot	4	(15)	**21**	**(72)**	1	(4)	26	(27)
Unclear	7	(26)	9	(33)	11	(41)	27	(28)
Total no. of obstacles	27	(28)	56	(57)	15	(15)	98	(100)

Note: All percentages are *row* percentages, except for those in the rightmost column, which are *column* percentages.

In the nine cases where the officer *alone* was the main instigator of the attempts to resolve employment and family-related obstacles, only two attempts were successful. However, 41 of the 45 instances where the probationer was the main instigator resulted in the obstacle being solved. This is not to suggest that the impact of probation supervision is 'nought' but, rather, that it is *extremely limited*, a point reinforced by Table 9.2b. When officers said that they had done nothing or little, 58 per cent of these obstacles were overcome *anyway* (see the emboldened text in Table 9.2b). However, when they *were able* to assist the probationer, there was evidence that their help was associated with higher levels of overcoming obstacles (72 per cent). In other words, the work of the probation officer *supplemented* the probationer's work.

This begs a further question: what was the attitude – i.e. the motivation – of the probationers who instigated the attempts to resolve these obstacles? Table 9.3 suggests that it was those who had been confident or pessimistic at the beginning of their order. Half of both the confident and the pessimistic took the lead in solving the obstacle themselves, compared to a quarter of the optimistic. However the cell sizes for the pessimists and optimists are probably too small for meaningful conclusions to be drawn from them; hence they are collapsed together (on the grounds that in both categories their officers had had doubts about their chances of desisting).

When one compares the confident and the pessimists/optimists (the emboldened text in Table 9.3), a small difference in the extent to which probationers took the lead in solving the obstacle at hand emerges. Thirty-eight per cent of the pessimists/optimists took the lead, compared with 54 per cent of the confident, although this difference was not statistically significant. It must be remembered, however, that the probationer's motivation was not the *only* factor in resolving obstacles (see Chapter 8) and that around 40 per cent of those classified as pessimists at the outset of their orders were classified as confidents by the end of it (Chapter 7) – in other words, a sizeable proportion of those classified as pessimists in Table 9.3 may have been closer to being confidents. In addition, in a third of the cases it was unclear who had taken the lead in solving the obstacle and the data do not include the probationers' perspective (see footnote 9). Therefore, whilst in no way conclusive, the data were *indicative* of a variation by motivation and as such warrant further investigation.

The qualitative data presented in the earlier sections of this chapter suggested that positive life changes were associated with changes in employment and family relationships. As probationers gained work, were reunited with family members or developed attachments to new

Table 9.3:   Main actor in overcoming obstacles by motivation

	Officer		Probationer		Main actor Both		Neither/unclear		Total	
	(n)	(%)	(n)	(%)	(n)	(%)	(n)	(%)	(n)	(%)
Confident	3	(6)	**27**	**(54)**	6	(12)	14	(28)	50	(51)
Optimists	5	(19)	**7**	**(26)**	5	(19)	10	(38)	27	(28)
Pessimists	1	(5)	11	(52)	2	(10)	7	(33)	21	(21)
Pessimists and optimists	6	(13)	**18**	**(38)**	7	(18)	17	(35)	48	(49)
Total no. of obstacles	9	(9)	45	(46)	13	(13)	31	(32)	98	(100)

partners or children, so they refrained from behaviours likely to result in offending – drug use, excessive drinking, 'aimless hanging around' or general aggressiveness. The quantitative data have suggested that those probationers who took the lead in addressing the employment and family-related obstacles they faced (itself indicative of possessing the motivation to confront and resolve problems) were also those most likely to have solved such obstacles by the time the order had been completed (Table 9.2a).

These analyses, taken together, suggest that the outcome of probation supervision is the result of a series of interactions between motivation, probation supervision and social and personal contexts. Gaining employment would, from the descriptions of officers and probationers, appear to have brought about dramatic changes in the lives of the probationers. Similarly, families of formation appear to have acted as a motivating influence on probationers' desires to desist, whilst families of origin appear to have offered an avenue of support in achieving this change.

When the role of probation supervision in helping probationers to achieve these changes was considered, the themes established in Chapters 7 and 8 re-emerged. That is, that whilst officers would appear to have identified appropriate obstacles and taken appropriate steps to tackle these obstacles, and whilst most of the obstacles identified *were* indeed resolved by the end of the order, this appears more often to have been the result of the probationers' own actions and their own circumstances rather than as a result of the actions of the officer (see also Crow 1996: 60).

As such it is possible to develop further the model of desistance outlined in Figures 7.1 and 7.2 (Chapter 7). Figures 9.1 and 9.2 introduce to the model summarised in Figures 7.1 and 7.2 the issue of social and personal contexts.[10] The introduction of social and personal contexts, especially the extent to which these circumstances remained stable or either improved or worsened, has the unfortunate effect of reducing cell sizes. However, by including change in social circumstances, one is able more readily to grasp the extent to which some probationers started in a more advantageous position and the extent to which improvements in social circumstances were related to both the presence of obstacles and the resolution of obstacles.

Consider, for example (in Figure 9.1) the confident who faced no obstacles: of those who were living in good contexts at the start, 79 per cent were still living in good social circumstances at the follow-up. Of the confidents who did face obstacles, more were living in poor rather than good social circumstances (61/39 per cent). Living in social

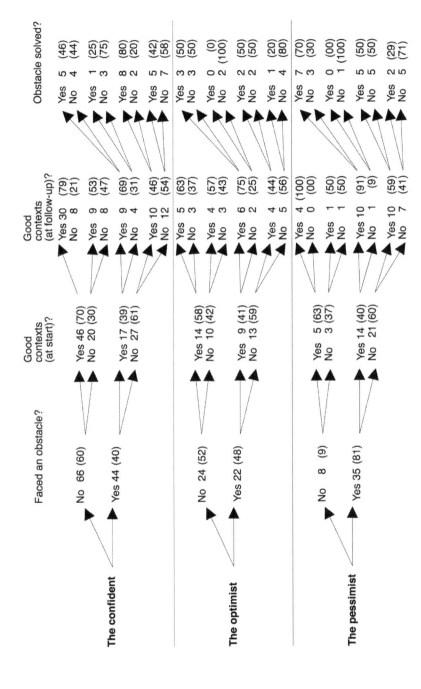

Figure 9.1 Motivation, obstacles and social contexts: probationers' reports. All figures are N (%).

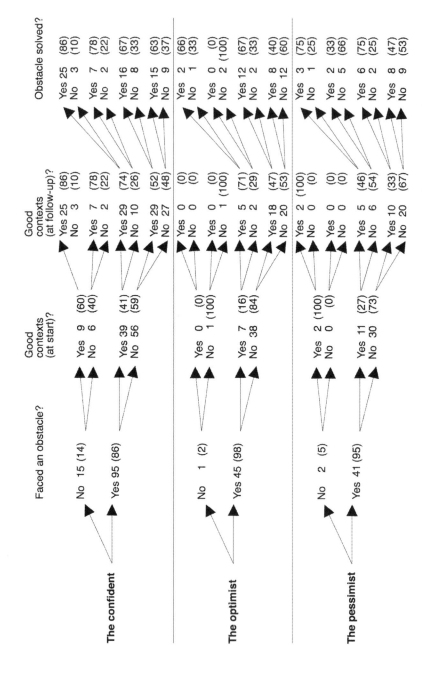

Figure 9.2 Motivation, obstacles and social contexts: officers' reports. All figures are N (%).

circumstances which were initially good, but which deteriorated was, irrespective of motivation, more frequently associated with *failing* to resolve obstacles than with resolving obstacles. For example, of the four confident probationers who faced an obstacle and who were initially living in good social circumstances which worsened, only one resolved the obstacles which he faced. Similarly, of those confidents who faced an obstacle and *never* lived in good circumstances, 58 per cent did not overcome the obstacles they faced. However, of the ten confidents who faced an obstacle and were initially in poorer circumstances but which *improved*, eight overcame the obstacles they faced.

These figures confirm the analyses reported earlier, namely, that motivation and contexts were important in understanding obstacle resolution rates, and that these co-varied. For example, 57 per cent ($n = 63$) of confidents reported that they were living in good contexts at the start of their orders; rates for optimists and pessimists were lower, respectively: 50 and 44 per cent ($n = 23$ and $n = 19$).

But which is more important to resolving obstacles – contexts (and changes in contexts) or individual motivation? The answer is that it is virtually impossible to disentangle the two from each other. The probationers who appeared most motivated to desist – the confident – started in a more favourable position, with, for example, shorter criminal careers and generally fewer problem social circumstances (see Tables 7.3 and 7.4 in Chapter 7). Those who were motivated to address the obstacles and seemed capable of doing so appeared to receive help from their partners and families, which in turn appeared to sustain the probationer's motivation to desist and belief that he or she were able to do so. For example, Dominic after initially being rejected by his family, proved he was able to cut down on his heroin use and was eventually 'given another chance' by them. Similarly, another case [065], who was recognised as having more potential than many of his fellow employees, reported increases in his self-esteem and feelings of 'self-worth' after his promotion to a management position. In turn this appeared to have helped him in his relationship with his partner. Other examples of what is essentially a feedback loop between good social and personal contexts and motivation to avoid further trouble were not hard to find: reports of probationer's families supporting them after they found work or probationers becoming more motivated as a result of working or of praise at work litter the accounts referred to above. In short 'nothing breeds success like success'. An example of the reverse of this – a confident probationer who failed to find employment, did not receive the encouragement of her family and who did not desist – will be presented in chapter 10 (Tracy, 054).

This chapter brings to a close the investigation of the roles of motivation, probation supervision and contexts in helping probationers tackle some of the features of their lives which were felt to be possible sources of further offending.

Chapter 5 outlined the obstacles faced by the probationers as they commenced their supervision. Chapter 6 explored the outcomes of the efforts of probationers and officers to tackle these obstacles – finding little evidence of probation interventions 'working'. Chapter 7 considered the motivation of the probationers concerned, and found that whilst motivation did not appear to influence the extent to which officers and probationers 'worked together' to solve obstacles, the rates with which probationers were reported to face obstacles and were felt to have resolved these were related to motivation. Chapter 8 explored the contexts in which these efforts were located and found evidence to suggest that social and personal contexts played crucial roles in mediating the outcomes of probation supervision. This chapter has explored *changes* in these contexts, in particular employment, familial relationships and lifestyles. The data have suggested that changes in employment and family relationships can radically alter individual lifestyles and offending trajectories. Additionally, the quantitative data (Table 9.2b) have suggested an important finding for probation supervision:

> When officers reported that they had given the probationer 'some' or 'a lot' of help in tackling employment and family-related obstacles, the obstacles were more frequently solved (Table 9.2b, emboldened cells), suggesting that help with these obstacles reaped benefits.

This is encouraging news for probation services. Whilst motivation and social and personal contexts appear to be the dominant forces in determining whether the obstacles facing probationers are successfully resolved, there was evidence that the work of probation officers could *improve* the chances of success.

Notes

1 For example, whether a probationer has had a previous custodial sentence is *not* a dynamic variable as there are no circumstances under which this can be altered. However, employment or marital status is a dynamic variable, as these aspects of the probationer's life *can* change.

3 Includes starting work; starting a 'better' job; getting more stable work; losing work; joining the armed services; and starting full-time education or training. The majority of responses were, however, 'started work' (25 of the 41 officer responses and 25 of the 45 probationer responses).

3 Includes started seeing a (new) partner; stopped seeing the old partner; got back with an ex-partner; getting on better/worse with family; probationer/ probationer's partner had/expecting a child; and got better access to child(ren). The single most common was 'probationer/probationer's partner had/expecting a child' (17 of the 44 officer responses and 16 of the 35 probationer responses).

4 Includes gave up alcohol; gave up drugs; cut down on alcohol; cut down on drugs; used drugs more; started to use hard drugs; and started to drink. The single most common change was giving up drugs (13 of the 34 officer responses and 17 of the 33 probationer responses).

5 This included a 'hotchpotch' of changes, including deaths of close relatives, learning to drive, having more money to spend and so on.

6 Full-time education or voluntary work may also provide many of these features.

7 052 was classified as a confident who had continued offending, and 105 a confident whose offending escalated but had ceased by the time of her order.

8 Karla would appear to have deliberately 'covered her tracks' in order to 'start again'.

9 There were 82 officers who reported that the probationer they were supervising faced either an employment or a family-related obstacle (or both), making in all 98 such obstacles. When probationers were considered, it was found that there were only 14 who identified family and/or employment obstacles. Between them they identified 16 such obstacles. Although data collected from the probationers were examined, it was hard to draw any definitive conclusions from them.

10 These measures were summations of the social and personal circumstances which probationers reported were 'problems'. Those with three or more problematic circumstances were classified as not having good contexts.

Part 3
Persistence and Desistance

Chapter 10

Desistance, change and probation supervision

This chapter focuses explicitly on desistance from offending and, in particular, deals with a discussion of the role that probation supervision may have played in helping some probationers to desist. The largest group of probationers were those who, on the basis of their self-reports throughout their orders, were classified as 'showing signs of desisting' or who were reported not to have offended at all whilst on probation. Of all 199 probationers interviewed, 46 per cent fell into these categories. From the officers' reports, the corresponding figure is even greater: 70 per cent of the sample were classified as either 'showing signs of desisting' or having avoided offending altogether.

For the purpose of all further analyses, the groups outlined in Table 10.1 were divided into two groups: 'emerging' desisters (comprising non-offenders, those showing signs of desisting and trivial offending groups) and 'persisters' (consisting of those whose offending was non-trivial or escalating). Those cases seen only once were deemed impossible to code and were dropped from all further analyses.

Table 10.1: Desistance (all)

	Probationers		Officers	
	(n)	(%)	(n)	(%)
No offending	64	32	105	53
Showing signs of desisting	28	14	33	17
Continued offending (trivial)	20	10	15	8
Continued offending (non-trivial)	18	9	15	8
Continued offending (escalating)	27	14	30	15
Impossible to code	42	21	1	—
Total	199	100	199	100

Table 10.2:   Desistance by motivation

	Confidents (n)	Confidents (%)	Optimists (n)	Optimists (%)	Pessimists (n)	Pessimists (%)	All (n)
Probationer report							
Desister	70	(78)	22	(71)	17	(52)	109
Persister	20	(22)	9	(29)	16	(48)	45
Total	90	(100)	31	(100)	33	(100)	154
Officer report							
Desister	92	(84)	33	(72)	28	(67)	153
Persister	18	(16)	13	(28)	14	(33)	45
Total	110	(100)	46	(100)	42	(100)	198

Exploratory regression runs (not reported here) suggested the 'sorts' of probationers who were desisting. Those with fewer previous convictions and in lower OGRS bands were more likely to be amongst the desisters (probationers' reports), as were those with fewer social problems and, in particular, those fortunate enough to have experienced stability in terms of both their employment and accommodation[1] (both officer and probationer reported). Motivation was also related to desistance: those who were pessimistic at the start of their orders were more likely to be amongst the persisting group, as Table 10.2 confirms.

Of the confidents, 78 per cent desisted according to their self-reports (84 per cent when officer-reports were considered). The optimists were very similar to the confident in terms of the proportion which desisted. As probationers were classified as optimists when *they* expressed the desire to and belief that they would stop offending and their *officer* expressed doubts about their desire and ability to desist, this finding suggests that their officers underestimated optimists' abilities to desist.

Another of the findings to emerge from Table 10.2 was that around half the pessimists had desisted. Given that the pessimists had rather longer criminal careers than either the confident or the optimists and had an average OGRS of 68 per cent (see Chapter 7), the finding that about half the pessimists were desisting, despite their original gloomy prognosis, should be regarded as 'good news'.

Gender did not appear to be a salient factor in desisting: not only did it not enter during the regression runs, the proportions of males and females classified as desisters was not significantly different (68 per cent of males and 86 per cent of females were classified as desisters;

$p = .083$). Similarly, desistance did not vary by race (69 per cent of whites desisted compared with 79 per cent of ethnic minorities;[2] $p = .316$). Age was also amongst the variables which appeared to be of little utility in accounting for desistance.[3]

The role of probation in desistance

From the analyses reported in the previous chapters which have dealt with the impact of probation supervision on obstacles to desisting (especially Chapters 5 and 7), it would appear that there was little evidence to suggest that interventions by officers often played very much of a *direct* role in desistance. In any case, as Chapter 6 suggested, much of the work of officers was limited by the actions (or inaction) of probationers themselves, or as a result of the circumstances in which the probationers lived.

There is, however, a further reason for the limited impact of probation supervision: probation officers actually spend *very little* time with their probationers. Imagine a probationer on probation for 12 months who sees his or her officer *exactly* as directed by National Standards. The probationer would see his or her officer once a week for the first three months of the order, fortnightly for the next three months and monthly for the remaining six months. Suppose too that his or her meetings lasted an average of 45 minutes. This amounts to 20 hours of contact. During one calendar year there are 8,760 hours, of which one third of these (lets say) would be spent asleep – leaving 5,840 hours of 'wakefulness'. Of the 5,840 hours the probationer is awake, he or she would spend about one third of 1 per cent of this time with his or her officer. These figures suggest two important things. First, that the actual amount of time spent with officers relative to the time engaged in other activities is very small and therefore perhaps not too much should be expected of probation supervision. Secondly, that the continued concentration upon 'what the officer/probation service does' inevitably misses a huge number of other factors which are at play when people desist or persist.

It should be noted that the calculations above probably have a tendency to *overstate* the amount of contact: few probationers will attend *every* session and not all sessions will last as long as 45 minutes. It is probably for this reason that others who have made similar calculations have reported much lower levels of contact. Philip Bean, writing a quarter of a century ago, reported that most probationers would get about 11 hours of supervision a year (1976: 76). In fact, the limited amount of contact was referred to by officers and probationers themselves:

> We are seeing someone for an hour a week. There are another six days and twenty-three hours of that week to go. We are on 'the surface', and sometimes an awful lot more is expected of us than is . . . I think we do very well in very difficult circumstances [PO 066].

> . . . all I had to do was go and show my face every three weeks. I just went in there, showed my face, they asked me if I had any problems, I said 'no' and that was it [PR 121].

However, whilst it is true that the impact of probation on desistance would appear to have been rather minimal, and whilst there are good reasons to believe that probation 'is but a drop in the ocean', it must be noted that case studies of individuals' experiences suggest that there *were* instances in which probation supervision was a significant factor in helping some probationers desist (see also the concluding discussions in Chapters 8 and 9).

In the section below, attention is turned to the role played by probation supervision amongst three groups of probationers:

1. those pessimists and optimists who nevertheless *desisted*;

2. those pessimists who *persisted*; and

3. those confident and optimistic probationers who, against their own predictions, *persisted*.

These groups of probationers were chosen for analysis for a number of reasons. Persisting confidents and optimists were grouped together because the optimists and confidents shared the motivation to and expectation that they would desist – yet they did not do as well as expected: what went wrong for them? The persisting pessimists similarly did not 'do well' – they were however not expecting to do well. Which processes prevented them from desisting? The desisting pessimists and optimists, on the other hand, were the real success stories: their officers were not expecting them to desist, yet they did: what changed about their lives to enable this? It is with these success stories that the analyses commence.

Table 10.2 suggested that of the 43 pessimists, between a half and two thirds showed signs of desisting. There were 12 probationers who were classified according to both their own and their officers' reports as desisters. These 'unanimous' desisters are compared against the 16 pessimistic probationers who reported continued offending.[4] In addition to the 12 desisting pessimists, 20 desisting optimists are considered, albeit briefly.

The desisting pessimists: what changed?

The individual case histories of the 12 pessimists who showed signs of desisting revealed a number of processes which appeared to be associated with changes in offending trajectories. These included gaining employment; changes in the probationer's family life; and, to a lesser extent, the influence of their probation officer.

Gaining employment, a topic already dealt with in some depth, appeared to play a large part in desistance for some people. Jacob [057] was 21 years old when he started his probation order. He had received his first conviction when 15 years old and had in all ten convictions for a range of offences. When he was seen at the second interview he was asked to describe the 'biggest single change in his life' since the previous interview. He said 'getting a job', which he said had: 'given me security, money, something to aim for. It's made me "come out of my shell". Made me behave myself because now I have more to lose.' Jacob was working in a bakery as an assistant manager, a job which he got through a friend who offered him work. At the third interview Jacob reported how the bakery was opening a new shop and in which he would be given a 50 per cent stake of the profits. When asked again to describe the biggest change since the previous interview, Jacob said that he was 'developing, maturing in myself' and described himself as being 'more confident' (a fact which he attributed to having started work). On the influence of his officer, Jacob was less enthusiastic, saying that he had been 'stringing her along for a long while' and that she 'could have helped me, but I didn't want to be helped'.

Malcolm [180] was 25 years old and already had eight previous convictions when he started his 18-month probation order. Like Jacob, he too pointed to gaining employment as the explanation for his desistance. When asked (at the third interview) to explain how he had managed to avoid offending since he had started probation, he said: 'A job, that's it. Most of the time you're at work, and when you ain't you've got money. Plus, when you get home from work you just want to get some food and go to sleep. I do ten hours a day, plus travelling time.'

His officer reported that Malcolm had 'always said that if he got a job he would stop offending' and that her approach had been to point out to him the link between drinking and offending. However Malcolm himself reported little assistance from his officer saying at the third interview that it 'hadn't really affected me'.

Another factor which encouraged desistance amongst the pessimists appeared to have been the influence of 'meeting someone'. Kevin [071] was 17 years old when he started his order. At the second interview he reported how ceasing to take drugs (in this case, cocaine) had been the biggest change in his life since the previous interview. He attributed this to his girlfriend, feeling tired at work and a short 'coke drought'. Kevin's reduced cocaine intake left him 'feeling better'. His cocaine use had made him less able to control his temper, affected his work and eaten into his money. However, it was not until he had stopped using cocaine that he realised this. When asked to describe how probation had helped him stay out of trouble he said it 'makes no difference' and that he 'didn't like coming here [to the probation office] and having to talk a load of rubbish'.

One of the findings from the quantitative analyses was that stable accommodation (especially when also experienced with stable employment) was associated with desisting. One of the officers [163] reported how his probationer, after getting stable accommodation, was able to use that as an address from which he could apply for work – which he got. The officer's role in this appeared to consist of discussing with the probationer the limitations of what could be expected from the local housing associations and renting agencies.

Other probationers reported more direct influences of probation supervision. One [113] said that his officer had 'consistently spelled out that if I don't change my act, I'd be back in prison'. The probationer (who had amassed 26 convictions in 15 years and was by that time in his early 30s) said he felt he needed to be told this regularly as it helped him to stay out of trouble. He went on to say, however, that 'most' of the reason he had avoided trouble was because of his fear of a return to prison. He added that, in his opinion, prison did not help people confront their behaviour, but served only to make it worse. Another probationer [067], when asked to explain how he had managed to avoid trouble, said: 'a mixture of probation, like talking to me about what could happen if, like, offences are committed again and things like that, and me stopping drinking really.'

Clive [076], who was referred to briefly during Chapter 9, was, in his own terms, 'an alcoholic' who was given probation for attempting to steal vodka from a supermarket. At the first interview Clive said that he wanted to stop offending ('I never wanted to offend in the first place – it's like having a double personality: sober and drunk'), but said he did not know if he could. At the second interview he said he still wanted to stop and was still unsure if he could. However, at the time of the third interview he said he had stopped and, when asked whether he could 'stay stopped', he said 'I can only answer that for when I'm sober'.[5]

What happened to Clive during the course of his order which helped him move from being a regularly offending[6] pessimist to a non-offending and slightly more 'upbeat' individual? As noted in Chapter 9, Clive had had an alcohol problem since he had been a child, and this formed a large part of the work which his officer undertook with him. When discussing how he saw being on probation in relation to his alcohol problem, Clive said:

> I see probation as a step forward for me. It helps me as an individual. There is someone there for me now and I need it. I would have been in prison now. That would destroy me completely. If I ended up in prison I would have been even worse. Of course, I am forced to come [to the probation office]. If it was my choice I wouldn't be here, but it helps to keep me away from the streets and of course the drinking.

The answers which both Clive and his officer gave suggested that Clive had benefited greatly from his period of supervision:

> I've learnt more about people and communication and how it affects me. I never used to be like that but people [at the probation office] were asking me if I'm well and how I'm getting on and now I [ask others] too. Before I wouldn't talk. I've learnt that if I get in trouble, that will be it – I'd lose everything I've tried for.

> [My officer] is the best one I've met. He wasn't pushing me or screaming at me, but still was telling me what I needed to do. Other officers want to control you, but [he] is not like that. He's told me what I have to do and reminded me things I would forget without trying to control me.

Towards the end of the second interview, Clive was asked about the obstacles he saw standing in his way to desistance. He said 'if anything went wrong with the social services, or the baby or anything'.[7] When asked if probation could help with this he said: 'Yes. Just talking to [my officer] makes me feel better. It helps me release all my stress. When there's nobody there you suppress your feelings and let it come out differently. He also helps with communicating with the social services.' Clive's feelings about his period of supervision did not change when he was seen for the third time. When asked if he had been able to avoid the situations which had previously got him into trouble, Clive said:

> Yeah, probation had a lot to do with it, because of the specific officer. All of my other experiences on probation were bad. I wouldn't listen to the other officers because I didn't like them. Drinking is still a problem, I get on the edge[8] from time to time, but now I can control it.

In addition to praising his officer, at the third interview – by which time Clive's partner had had their baby – he said, perhaps most telling of all: 'I've got a family now. I want to be responsible.' It would appear from these accounts that the arrival of the new baby and the influence of his officer *both* contributed to Clive's steady progress as a recovering alcoholic. However, the role of his officer was not referred to extensively in the passage in Chapter 9 as it appeared to play no part in strengthening Clive's family. Similarly, in the discussion above concerning the role of Clive's officer, the arrival of the baby is suppressed. Clive's case indicates the fact that social circumstances and probation supervision can both assist in positive change without actually 'connecting' in any way.

The desisting pessimists appeared to desist as the result of either changes in their family or employment circumstances *or* because of the advice of their officers. In a few cases, such as Clive, changes in family life and probation supervision would both appear to have been of importance in accounting for their desistance.

The desisting optimists appeared to desist for reasons which were – in the main – associated with family and employment changes. Of the 20, seven reported that they had desisted because they had started to get on better with their families, or had embarked upon new relationships. In all some five reported that employment had in some way encouraged or enabled them to desist. Giving up drugs and/or enrolling on methadone schemes were cited by another three probationers. The remaining cases referred to stressful situations passing, spending more time at home after illnesses and 'growing up' as the reasons why they had desisted.

The persisting pessimists: the failure to change

This section considers the reasons which lay behind some pessimists' failure to address their offending behaviours. Five explanations for continued offending amongst the pessimists emerged: the probationer failing to respond to the order (seven of the 16); a feeling that 'nothing had changed' in the probationer's life (six cases); the probationer being 'addicted' to shoplifting (four cases); the probationer continuing to rely upon substances (five cases); and the probationer being a 'professional criminal' (one case).[9]

Seven of the 16 persisting pessimists showed signs of having failed to respond to probation – often they reported that they felt that the order had been 'a waste of time' and, on occasions, their officers also noted their reluctance to engage with probation. One probationer [022] said that probation had 'done my head in, coming here speaking about bollocks to them'. His officer reported that he had 'kept us [the probation service] at arm's length'. Another probationer [005] recalled how he had found supervision 'patronising', a 'wind up' and described it as having 'no point'. The following extract is taken from the third interview with a probationer who was seen in prison at the second interview, was on licence at the third but was being supervised by his original officer:

> ... at the end of the day, what we are doing is ... what are we doing though? I come in here, she says 'are you alright?' I say 'I am alright', that's it. What is actually happening? There is nothing happening, is there? It seems to be like ... I dunno, a useless exercise really. I come down here for ten minutes, five minutes, and [my officer] says to me 'are you alright?' I say 'yeah I'm fine, and I'm this and that', and she writes it down in the little book and then she says to me 'what are your chances of re-offending?' and I'll just say 'nil', and she'll say 'well, what do you think ...' ... and it just seems to be ... I dunno, it just seems to be pointless. A whole pointless exercise 'cause I don't think that coming into probation for five minutes once a week and then every fortnight after a while is really going to do anything for you [PR 204].

Six of the 16 persisting pessimists appeared to have shown no signs of having changed their lives; they continued in much the same vein as before: 'Well, that's the problem with [probationer]. There hasn't been any change' [PO 168]. It is hard to account for the lack of change, but reading the interview transcripts one gains a sense of fatalism on the part of the probationers, and from the officers a sense of being unable to help. One officer [127] reported how the probationer she was supervising had 'gone in a full circle' but was starting to realise that he needed more help. She said she had tried to encourage him not to expect too much of himself. At the final interview the same officer reported how the probationer would come to the probation office, but not when scheduled to do so. When asked how much probation had impacted upon the probationer, the officer said 'nothing tangible' and the probationer said 'nothing really'.

Another group of four pessimists who persisted referred to their own 'addiction' to shoplifting. One probationer [007] reported how shoplifting was: '. . . addictive. It is not planned, it happens. If I go into town I get an adrenaline rush. There is no explanation, last week I pinched a £4.99 plate, I took it because I can.' Whilst others said:

> I think that it's a bit of an addiction. I used to get a buzz out of it, but not anymore. I find it hard to stop because I'm so used to doing it. It's easy money, like a job [PR 146].

> I feel that if I stop [stealing], some part of me would die. It gives me a buzz [PR 022].

Interestingly, none of the officers supervising these probationers reported them to be 'addicted'.

A reliance upon (or unwillingness to give up) a particular substance such as alcohol, heroin or cannabis was another of the factors which emerged when persistence amongst the pessimists was considered. Probationers either refused or were unable to give up drugs, or continued to drink heavily. There appeared, again, to be little that the supervising officer could do to encourage these probationers to change their ways. One of the probationers – in prison at the time of the interview – reported that he and his family were 'professional criminals' who were involved in the large-scale importation and distribution of drugs.

The persisting pessimists appeared to represent a group who were unlikely to respond well to probation supervision because they were not motivated to do so, either 'addicted' (real or otherwise) to a substance or to shoplifting, or were incapable or unwilling to engage with probation. The desisting pessimists, who on the whole also suggested that probation had not had *very* much of an impact on their lives, nevertheless had found a job or a relationship which they valued sufficiently for them to wish to change some aspects of their behaviour. Probation supervision (for the desisting pessimists) appeared to have been 'in the background' offering advice, ideas on how to find work or spurring the probationer on in some way. However, the persisting pessimists did not experience the sorts of life changes which might encourage desistance, or were in some way incapacitated. Nor did they respond positively, it would appear, to probation supervision.

The persisting optimists and confidents: what went wrong?

The most worrying group of probationers identified during the course of the investigation were the confidents and optimists who continued to offend. Eighteen officers reported that the confident probationer they were supervising had persisted, and 20 of the confidents themselves reported persistent continued offending. Nine optimists also reported continued offending, as their officers had feared. An examination of the reasons cited for their offending suggested a number of explanations: continuing drug or alcohol use (cited by eight officers and 11 probationers); anger management problems and immaturity (cited by seven officers and nine probationers); mental health problems (cited by three officers and three probationers); lack of alternative career opportunities (cited by two officers and four probationers); and a range of other unique explanations.

Drug use appeared to be particularly problematic. One probationer [035], who had been using heroin for seven years, reported how despite coming off heroin for several weeks, he drifted back into heroin use. 'I'll always find a reason to use again,' he said when seen shortly after his order had ended. Although his use of heroin had stabilised, he said that he was unsure if this had been due to probation as this 'could have happened anyway'. His officer said that they had had 'discussions about drugs and [I] constantly reminded him about the dangers of drugs'. However, the officer did not refer the probationer for treatment until towards the end of his order, which perhaps goes someway to explaining the probationer's assessment of his order: '[probation] was a footnote – it came and went, neither good nor bad.' The officer cannot, however, be blamed for not referring the probationer sooner. When interviewed the probationer said: 'I denied using heroin, but then again that is what he wanted to hear.'

Another of the probationers [105] reported how 'intoxicated with valium, heroin and booze' she stole a CD player whilst out shopping in order to help her pay her rent arrears. Similarly she acted as a fence for her friends who also used heroin: 'People I knew who were on gear would bring me stuff – all part of a circle . . .' Her officer confirmed these events – for which she was given a further probation order. Boredom and a 'lack of something to do' were often referred to by recovering heroin addicts as factors in their return to heroin use, but for some officers a more significant problem was the probationer's lack of sustained motivation:

I don't think he can [stop offending]. He can't accept that he can do without [heroin]. He would probably say it's because he can't get the help he wants, but it has been offered to him. Much was on offer: prescriptions, being detoxed in hospital, but he didn't take it and went back on drugs. It's a way of life for him now, he needs a dramatic change in his lifestyle and he's not motivated at this time [PO 172].

Whilst continuing drug use was often associated with property crimes, continuing engagement in violent behaviour was frequently the result of alcohol problems. For example, one probationer [095] recounted how his fighting was related to his alcohol use: 'when I drink, my "fuse" goes right down. Also I'm known in this area – I've got to fulfil people's expectations, I've got to hit them first or they hit me.' The probationer went on to say he still had a bit of a drink problem, that he liked to drink everyday and that, in his opinion, he should have had more alcohol counselling.[10]

Another probationer [083] who was on probation for robbery and carrying an offensive weapon, beat up drug dealers who were operating in his local area. He said that he had been angry at them selling heroin in a children's park which his children used. He admitted that he could have gone to the police instead, but said that he had not as 'I'm not a grass'. He also reported how he had been charged with using threatening words and behaviour towards his partner after a row at their home to which the police were called. His officer, although she did not report any offending on his part, did acknowledge the potential for him to become involved in confrontations: 'He lives in an area where certain groups are seen as volatile – he is [volatile] too – this leads to a process to expect trouble and to respond accordingly.'

Other examples of 'violent' offending suggest not so much an anger management problem, but a degree of immaturity. One probationer [167], who was on probation for a minor assault on a police officer, reported how he had 'tapped' someone:

Saying that, I did hit someone. *Right, in the street?* No. He walked back to my friend's house and he was going to beat up the guy that was already there so I sort of told him not to. And things were getting out of hand. I was just sitting on the couch watching it all and it was all getting out of hand. Then they started attacking each other. It was a really big guy against a little guy. So I just give him a little tap to end it. And it ended it quite nicely. *Right, I see.* And they all stopped misbehaving. *And you actually did that, you said 'a little tap'?* Stopped it all, yeah. *What do you mean by that?* Well, I just give him a little tap because I told him not to have a fight. I said: 'Look, you have got to leave the guy. He's smaller than you.' We'd been out drinking all night and had a laugh and we have come back to this house. 'He's here and you are picking on him,' I said, 'and I can't watch that happen.' So I gave him a couple of warnings. *And you hit him?* Yeah.

The same probationer reported similar events when seen towards the end of his order – again using violence to end or prevent confrontation. Another officer [026] reported how his probationer (a young man aged 20) was eventually breached for failing to report, failures which his officer put down to his immaturity:

he does behave like an adult when he's in a club or whatever and girls are talking to him, whatever, he's very, very adult. But when he's at home, his mum's giving him grief, then he's very much a child. And he's moving from one stage to another so he's not yet got the adult responsibilities of turning up to appointments when he's supposed to and organising his life and stuff. So we have been working on that transition and bits of his life that are adult and bits of his life where he's still a child ... Probation is a pretty boring place to come to. It's not somewhere he would choose to come to. But it's just with all this other stuff going on in his life he doesn't prioritise or see it as very important and that is quite a childish response on his part because the offence he committed, he could well [have gone] to prison for it. And he needs to know that. [Theft from employer] is extremely seriously regarded by the court and he was very lucky not to go to prison in the first place. It was only because it was his first offence and his immaturity that they didn't give him prison.

As it transpired, the probationer was given a short custodial sentence for his failure to attend. When interviewed after he had been released on licence the probationer hinted at a growing awareness that he had been immature in his earlier approach: '[officer]'s shown me ways, like ... because now I am over 18, I have to start being an adult, not being a child or anything'.

Other probationers' continued offending appeared to be related in various ways to their mental health. One probationer – originally on probation for sexual offences (rubbing himself against women in crowds) – reported how he had 'heard voices'. His officer reported a deterioration in his mental health prior to his offending again: 'His mental health deteriorated and he was sectioned and held in a hospital. After being discharged, he was found a place in a hostel, but two weeks later was found masturbating in a churchyard' [PO 016].

In other cases mental health problems appeared to be related to continued offending in a rather roundabout way. One probationer [037] reported how his depression prevented him from working. His officer confirmed this, reporting that for several months he was very depress-ed and reluctant to leave his home for prolonged periods. His inability to hold down regular employment meant that the probationer was reliant for much of his income on acting as a drugs courier for friends of his. His officer reported that his mental health posed a considerable problem to the work she had planned to do – mainly aimed at looking at his relationship with his wife – and confirmed that he was indeed too ill to work. She added that during their conversations about his drug-dealing friends he had said to her 'these are my friends, this is where I grew up, who else would want to know me?'

Other probationers reported how they had continued to offend as they saw few other means of surviving economically. One of them [082] recounted how he regularly drove without insurance or tax as he was unemployed (due to being partially disabled) and could not afford to insure his car. Other confident probationers who continued to offend did so for a variety of reasons. One probationer [091] reported how he continued to drive despite being disqualified because he enjoyed driving and liked to drive around his friends – none of whom could themselves drive. Another officer [143] felt that the probationer she had been supervising had not been able to stop offending because of his past reputation. The probationer, who was placed on probation for drink-driving and possession of offensive weapons, was later charged with a serious assault after returning to a area where he used to live. The assault charge related to a fight with a former associate which, in the probationer's words, was part of a long-running 'vendetta'. Although they had discussed his reputation, his officer acknowledged that it would always be a potential cause of further trouble. When asked to summarise why he had not been able to avoid trouble, another probationer [080] replied: 'I'm not working. I've never really had a job – I don't know nothing else.'

In some cases, despite the best efforts of the officer, and the probationer's motivation to avoid further trouble, offending persisted. Tracy [054], the subject of the following case study, was 23 when she started her probation order, imposed after she had been found guilty of common assault. Tracy and her officer both reported that she wanted and was able to stop offending when they were first interviewed and maintained these beliefs at every subsequent interview. As her officer explains, initially things went well for Tracy on probation:

> She was coming every single week. She was doing job skills, computing, and she was at a sort of partnership agency. She was seeing our employment officer. You know it was very active and things were happening and she really . . . like she was, you know, trying to achieve positive change. I think, I suppose it happens sometimes, it goes down to fortnightly appointments, doesn't it? A bit of momentum. By six months in the order, Tracy herself, I think, let things drift an awful lot and I suppose perhaps probation ended up chivvying her along or refocusing her. Do you know what I mean? And I think, she came in today and we were both sitting here going 'Oh God, everything has drifted. Shall we go back to fortnightly appointments?' And she was quite keen for that. I mean, she is aware of it herself. *How do you mean things have drifted?* Well, she stopped going to the education, for the computing. There was the New Deal,[11] it might be taken under the New Deal umbrella, and I think that is quite slow-going anyway because it is a new system going into place.

Tracy declined to be interviewed at the second sweep, and at the third sweep (when she did agree to an interview) it transpired from her officer's account that she had been involved in heroin use and theft:

> SF It sounds like from what you have said that Tracy hasn't been able to stay out of trouble. What would you say have been the things that have prevented her from staying out of trouble?
>
> PO I think her motivation wavers. Sometimes I see her and she is very motivated to work, to go to college, to do things. I think she is very isolated, she lives in a flat by herself that she can barely afford to run. She is very bad at managing her money. When stressed she is extremely vulnerable. In the summer, after this drugs thing, she started to see her GP, who was prescribing her quite high dosages of diazepam and valium and she kinda lost it again. She was going to him saying 'I can't cope' and she was on quite a lot of sedative medication which caused other problems. And then probably during that time we had two or three appointments that . . . 'cause I think I have always said to you that 'there's something going on and I don't

187

know what it is' – I think it was very obviously that she feels, I can't remember how old she was when she moved to this country, but she has felt very isolated. She feels that she was never consulted about her family moving here, she feels that the rest of her family have settled and she has felt quite alien here, she feels her mother and sister have a good relationship, from which she feels excluded, and she really feels this kind of 'differentness', not belonging and I think she is very isolated and it makes her vulnerable to people like this bloke.[12]

SF   Would you say that – since I saw you last – that Tracy has learnt anything as a result of being on probation?

PO   Erm ... there are times when she has felt *very* supported by probation, and I think it is probably the only people who do support her. There are times when she has felt quite angry with probation 'cause it feels like we are adding more ... y'know, quite strict about her attending appointments and so on. We're adding more pressure when she has got enough. I think that she is quite clear about what she needs to do. I think she is unrealistic about how difficult it is to do it. And I think originally – both the last times I have been interviewed, I have overestimated her abilities to manage an independent life. She presents as quite able and she can be quite eloquent and she'll express motivation to sort her life out, which I believe is genuine. But I think that she underestimated and I think that I underestimated how difficult she finds it ... say, she is always wanting jobs, but they never work out. Nothing ever seems to work out. I think that there is a real problem with wavering motivation. She is just very vulnerable, it doesn't take a lot and she is back to square one.

SF   Since I saw you last in July, do you think that there is anything that you have said or done that will help keep Tracy out of trouble in the future?

PO   I think that one thing that I did when she came – it wasn't an appointment – she came here very, very distressed. And she felt – it was a Friday, she had nothing, she felt completely isolated, no where to go, nothing to do all weekend, didn't know how she was going to cope. And I actually made 'phone calls to her mother and her sister and explained that I thought that she was trying, but did need some support, and the latest I've heard is – it's tentative, but I think communication ... y'know sometimes people take notice if a probation officer rings them up and says 'I'm concerned about your sister – she does need a helping hand here', and I think that that is probably one thing that I have done. It is still very fragile of course.

At the third interview, Tracy herself recounted this story about how she had come to probation 'in a right state' and her officer had 'phoned her family to ask them for their support on her behalf: 'she rang round my family and helped me out with bus fares.' It was clear that a lot of time and effort had been expended in helping her feel less isolated. There was also evidence of the much more practical assistance offered by her officer:

SF   [At the previous interview] you said that there were two obstacles to Tracy stopping offending. The main one was that she didn't have a job. Has that continued to be a problem?

PO   It is more of the same problem. Her problem ... I think the problem now is ... it is not just as straightforward as employment ... she is having difficulty achieving *any* sort of permanent occupation, whether it be college or ... she has done bits and pieces with college, it is that staying power and organisational abilities. It is not ... if someone put a job in front of her I would think 'yeah, that would be it', but it is ... there is a big gap even before ... she is not prepared enough at the moment to hold down a job ... there is foundation work that needs to be carried out. *Have you looked at work with Tracy?* She has quite regular appointments with our employment officer. Who has kinda put her into different ... y'know she was doing some computer training, and has pulled out other kind of resources and it is Tracy's lack of ... success in following any of those through which kind of causes warning bells all the time. *Is Tracy still doing the computer training course which she was last time?* No. That has finished. That resource has finished within the probation service, but she had bombed out before then anyway. *So she didn't complete it?* No. She didn't attend on a regular enough basis. She was always half looking at other options. I suppose you get lulled – 'oh well, at least she is looking at something'. It takes a long – it sounds like I am really slow on the uptake – but it takes a long time to realise that a pattern is emerging of everything is bombing. A few weeks ago she walked in and she said 'oh I have got agency work starting tomorrow, I'm coming off my benefits', and part of you wants to believe it and part of me was wise enough now to think 'we've been through this before'. So when she came in last week and said 'it never really worked out', there was no surprise, and I had – when she said 'I'm going to start work tomorrow' – started to be thinking 'well, let's look at what has failed before'. I think she wants a job now, and ... my experience of her would be that she needs to build up more slowly and at the moment she isn't showing the motivation or consistency to do that.

SF   How much would you say you have been able to help Tracy with the issues around her work?

PO   She has missed several appointments with [the employment officer], and I don't think that that has been helpful. And I think a good example, like last week, Tracy turned up and she had some note of a course that was starting today and wanted to get me sorted to get her on it. I encouraged her, I tried to make the 'phone call, I couldn't get through, I said 'this isn't the way to do it, this is where you are falling down all the time, let's book you in to see [employment officer] next week' and I am sort of encouraging her to ... I suppose it is every aspect of her life, not just employment. [She needs] to take planning, to think about what might go wrong, try and think of ways, rather than 'I need a job, I'll do it today' and then it all falls down. And then she didn't turn up to see [employment officer] last week. So, I think that it is going to take a lot more reinforcement ... 'you need to plan'. *Would you say that not having a job has made it hard for Tracy to stop offending?* Yes. I mean, I think ... not having a constructive use of her time – it is not a job *per se*, if she was in college, if she had something where she had to get up and spend time with non-offenders, I think that that would be really positive. I think the fact that she has an awful lot of time on her hands and no money certainly increases the risk of offending.

Despite all the efforts which her officer went to, Tracy neither managed to get stable employment nor to stop offending. This is not to suggest that had she got stable employment (or, as her officer notes, a college course) she would have stopped offending. What might have happened, however, was the disruption of her daily agenda by the routine of work or college such that she had less free time to spend with people like her boyfriend. The lack of a good informal social support network (like a family) to which she could regularly turn for help only served to exacerbate Tracy's isolation. A 'phone call to the officer after the fieldwork had been completed revealed that Tracy had been 'on and off' heroin around the time of the third interview and had offended again.

The range of factors associated with persistence amongst confidents and optimists appeared to be not too dissimilar from those associated with persistence amongst pessimists. Substance use in particular appeared to be a particularly salient factor. In some cases there was an apparent failure on the part of the probationer to be honest with his or her officer about the problems he or she faced (e.g. case 035 who denied using heroin) or to maintain the willpower to address the sources of his or her offending (e.g. case 095 who could have sought further counselling for his alcohol use, but chose not to).

This raises the question why these probationers were so confident of their ability to desist. The author was fortunate enough to have interviewed many of the confident probationers who persisted. The majority of these probationers appeared to be articulate and had insights into the problems they faced, and it is easy to see why they might have been felt by their officers to want and be able to stop offending. This, coupled with an element of wishful thinking on their own part, may go much of the way to explaining why both they and their officers believed that they would be able to desist. It was also noted that none of the confidents and optimists who persisted were *both* working *and* in a relationship, and that the majority of them were neither working nor in a relationship.

This chapter has dealt with the extent to which the probationers in the sample can be said to have desisted from offending and the factors associated with desistance. Around about half the sample self-reported rates of offending which were indicative of what has been termed 'emerging desistance'. When officers' reports were considered, over 80 per cent were reported to have shown signs of desisting. Stability of employment and accommodation, and initial motivation appeared from quantitative data analyses (not reported here) to be the variables which best accounted for desistance. Probation supervision appeared, for many probationers, to play a very slight part in whether or not they desisted, although a small number of probationers did appear to have benefited substantially from probation supervision.

Those pessimists who did manage to desist appeared to do so as a result of either finding employment or attachment to a partner *or* receiving help from their officer. Persistence amongst pessimists appeared to have been the result of various factors: an unwillingness or inability to engage constructively with their officers; or an 'addiction' to theft or substances such as heroin or alcohol. The confidents and optimists who persisted also seemed to have either failed to have addressed their drug or alcohol use or to have reacted violently in particular circumstances. Additionally none of them reported stable employment or partners when seen during the course of their orders.

Notes

1 If an officer or a probationer reported that the probationer's employment was a problem at two or more of the sweeps he or she was classed as having experienced 'employment instability'. The same procedure was repeated for accommodation.
2 Ethnic minorities (of which there were 35) were made up of Asians, Afro-Caribbeans, those of mixed parentage, others and unknowns. See Table 3.4 in Chapter 3 for the relative sizes of these groups.
3 Various age groupings were employed – none of which produced a relationship between age and desistance, suggesting that this finding was a 'true' finding rather than the result of coding decisions.
4 The fact that 11 of these 16 probationers had officers whose reports suggested that the probationer had or was desisting is not a major concern. As noted in Chapter 4, officers were bound not to know of all offences committed by probationers. The reverse (probationers claiming to have desisted whilst their officers reported persistence) was less often encountered.
5 Which has been interpreted as meaning 'yes, but I'm not in control of my actions after I've been drinking and I might offend whilst drunk'.
6 Clive's first conviction had been when he was 16 years old. He was 30 when he started his order. In the period between his first conviction and the start of his probation order, Clive had amassed 23 convictions, amounting to an annual average of 1.6, or about three convictions every two years.
7 Clive's partner was expecting their fourth child. The previous three were in the care of social services.
8 It is ambiguous what Clive is referring to when he says 'on the edge'. It could refer to getting close to offending, getting close to drinking too much or some other, less tangible, 'stressed out state'. However, despite this ambiguity, as he says himself, he can control it now, so perhaps the exact meaning is of little importance.
9 Some probationers were included in more than one explanation.
10 The alcohol counselling he received was from a partnership agency, who would have continued to see him after his order was over. As such the onus was on him to maintain this contact.
11 A national employment scheme originally aimed at young people.
12 A new 'boyfriend' who appeared to have played a large part in Tracy's offending.

Chapter 11

The factors associated with offending

This chapter focuses upon the offences which probationers were reported to have committed whilst on probation. Its purpose is to report the *types* of offences which probationers committed, the *frequency* with which these were committed and the strength of the *factors associated* with offending.

Virtually every investigation of the impact of supervision has employed further offending, most commonly further convictions, as the main criterion of success or failure. However, there has been a tendency in many of the previous studies to assume that further offences equate to 'failure'. There are good reasons for this assumption – not least of all that continued offending indicates that previous behaviours would appear to have continued. But by accepting uncritically that *any* offending indicates a failure of probation supervision, reductions in the frequency or the seriousness of the offending are overlooked (Mair *et al.* 1997: 41). The previous chapter demonstrated that of the 93 probationers who reported having continuing to offend, 28 (30 per cent) appeared to be in the process of desisting. Similarly, of the 93 probationers reported by their officers to have continued offending, 33 (34 per cent) also appeared to be desisting.

In addition, offending may sometimes lead to more 'positive' outcomes, at least as far as the offender is concerned.[1] For example, one officer [158] reported that the probationer he was supervising was being considered for early revocation on the grounds of good progress. However, almost a year after the original offence (a theft, committed after the probationer had drunk heavily), the probationer committed a very serious assault on a stranger after another very heavy drinking session. Both these offences occurred around the time of the anniversary of the death of the probationer's twin brother, when they were young boys. When interviewed about the second offence, both the officer and probationer explicitly referred to the twin's death. The new offence, taken in the light of some of the probationer's other circumstances (feeling down and drinking heavily at the time of both offences and the probationer's otherwise stable life), brought home to the officer the extent to which the probationer required intensive bereavement counselling as part of his supervision. A further order with this condition was eventually made.[2] In other words, offending on probation allowed the officer to gain a better insight into the factors associated with the probationer's offending.

Similarly, another officer [054] reported how it took several 'crises' to befall the probationer she was supervising before both of them realised that poor life skills lay at the root of many of the probationer's problems:

> I suppose the success we have made is that we are both a lot clearer about what we are dealing with now. She is and I am. This cycle has happened enough times for us to realise what is going on and to focus on things like budgeting, for example. It almost takes quite a few crises for you to suddenly think 'this isn't bad luck, this is the way you are managing – or not managing – your life'.

In some instances, relapses into drug use or offending galvanised the probationer into wanting to desist. One probationer [109] reported having used heroin with an old acquaintance as he 'wanted to have sex with her'. However, they did not have sex and he reported that he 'didn't feel good about having used [heroin]' and 'didn't want to have much to do with her' after this episode. Another probationer also reported how he had used heroin again after several months abstinence: 'the next day I was really pissed off with myself – I'd gained nothing, just five or six hours of pleasure.' He had not used again since. Additionally, those supervising some types of offenders, for example, sex offenders or those who commit acts of domestic violence, may also consider self-reports of 'near-offending' to the officer as indicating an increased awareness of 'risky situations' and a reduction in the denial of harm to others.

These observations are not intended to suggest that offending should be considered in any way as a 'good sign' but, rather, that the issues surrounding offending (and the reporting of offending to officers) must not be thought of as *always* indicating failure. Offending in *some circumstances* can be understood as leading eventually to a positive outcome in that it may increase an offender's desire to desist or – in the case of offending of reduced seriousness – indicate to the supervising officer that progress has been made.

Offending behaviours

Table 11.1 reports the rates of self- and officer-reported offending by motivation. As can be seen, the confidents were *always* those least frequently reported to have offended. Some 44 per cent of the confidents and 54 per cent of optimists admitted to offending, compared to 79 per cent of the pessimists. Officers' reports mirror this trend. How do these rates reported in Table 11.1 compare to other studies of self-reported offending by probationers? Only two other studies are known to have been published – Leibrich (1993) and MacKenzie *et al.* (1999). The current rates are not too dissimilar from those reported in Leibrich's New Zealand study (1993: 31–33). Leibrich found that of the 48 ex-probationers in her sample, 25 (52 per cent) had continued to offend. Leibrich's sample was based on those who had completed probation and not been convicted for three years and, as such, it is difficult to assess whether the offences reported to her took place after the order had been *made* but before it had been completed, after the order had been *completed*, or both.[3] MacKenzie *et al.* (1999: 436–37) in the USA found that of the 107 probationers in their sample, only 22 (21 per cent) reported any offending whilst on probation. Without other similar studies against which to compare these rates, it is hard to assess the typicality of the current sample's rate of offending.

Concordance between officers and probationers

When reports of offending gained from probationers and the officers who were supervising them were compared, very high levels of

Table 11.1: Offending by motivation

| | Probationer-reported offending | | Officer-reported offending | | Total |
	(n)	(%)	(n)	(%)	
Confidents	48	44	41	36	110
Optimists	25	54	24	52	46
Pessimists	33	79	29	63	43
All	106	53	94	47	199

Table 11.2:   Concordance of offending

	Agreeing cases		Disagreeing cases	
	Both 'yes'	Both 'no'	Officer 'yes', Probationer 'no'	Officer 'no', Probationer 'yes'
Offended	70 (35%)	71 (36%)	21 (11%)	37 (19%)

agreement were noted. For example, as the left-hand side of Table 11.2 shows, some 35 per cent of officer–probationer pairs agreed that the probationer had offended. Additionally for 36 per cent of cases both officer and probationer reported that the probationer had not offended. When there was disagreement – see the right-hand side of Table 11.2 – it is interesting to note that this disagreement was most often due to probationers having said they *had* offended, whilst officers reported that they had *not*. This has been interpreted as indicating the probationers' willingness to admit to offences of which their officers were unaware. The offending reported by officers and denied by probationers was reasonably low (11 per cent, see Table 11.2). In addition to the simple 'offended'/'not offended' dichotomies presented in Table 11.2, officers' and probationers' reports of the *number* of offences committed were investigated. These also proved to be positively correlated (Spearman's rho = .364; $p = <.01$). Similarly, high rates of agreement were noted when the *type* of offences reported was investigated. Agreement over violent, property and drug offending was statistically significant at the $p = <.000$ level, whilst for 'other' offences $p = <.010$.

Factors associated with offending during the order

A series of logistic regressions were undertaken to explore some of the possible factors associated with reports of the probationers' offending (see Table A1 in the Appendix). From initial bivariate regression runs, only the most statistically significant and powerful, and theoretically salient variables, were employed in attempts to create multivariate models. Inevitably, some variables were highly correlated with one another and, unless circumstances dictated otherwise, only variables which were *not* correlated with one another were employed in the multivariate analyses. The aim of the multivariate analyses was to produce a model which best accounted for the reported incidents of offending, but which was as uncomplicated as possible.

When probationer's reports of their offending were examined, three variables appeared to be of importance: having had a previous conviction

Table 11.3: Factors associated with offending: final models

	Beta	Df	Sig		Beta	Df	Sig
Probationer				**Officer**			
Theft convictions	.5542	1	.1074	Drug Probs (SWP2)	1.5274	1	.0000
Financial problem (offence)	−1.5095	1	.0000	—			
Drug problem (SWP1)	2.2495	1	.0000	—			
Motivation				*Motivation*			
Confidents		2	.0037	Confidents		2	.0494
Optimists	.4106	1	.3262	Optimists	.3583	1	.3453
Pessimists	1.6227	1	.0008	Pessimists	.9429	1	.0147
Constants	−.1708	1	.5612	Constants	−.7359	1	.0004
Cases correctly predicted	71%				65%		

for theft ($p=<.05$); reporting a drug problem at the time of the first interview ($p=<.000$); and reporting that one did *not* have any financial problems at the time of the offence ($p=<.000$). However, separate analyses (Table 11.1) suggested that motivation was also associated with differing rates of offending. When motivation was entered into the model previous convictions for theft was removed, as shown in Table 11.3.

Thus, whilst previous convictions for theft *initially* appeared to be related to offending this ceased to be the case when motivation was included in the model. The model suggests that those *with* financial problems were less *likely* to have offended during the course of the order, that those *with* drug problems were *more* likely to have offended, and that confidents were no more or less likely to offend than optimists, but that pessimists were much more likely to have offended when compared to confidents. These findings are broadly in line with other investigations into the role of social variables in offending/ reconviction amongst probationers. For example, both Oldfield (1996: 44) and May (1999: 33) reported that those with financial problems were more likely to be reconvicted. Similarly, those with drug problems have been found to be more likely both to reoffend and be reconvicted (May 1999: 33; Oldfield 1996: 44; MacKenzie *et al.* 1999: 439).

When data collected from officers were analysed, a larger number of variables appeared to be related to offending. These included previous convictions for violence; total number of previous convictions; OGRS; the officer's assessment that the probationer had drug, employment and financial problems; and the total number of all problems faced by the probationer.[4] In line with these analyses, both Raynor (1998: 8) and May (1999: 21) found that those probationers with more problems were more likely to be reconvicted. Similarly, Davies (1969: 78), Oldfield (1996: 44) and May (1999:33) found that employment problems were associated with reconviction. However, several of the variables associated with offending from the officers' data set were found to be strongly intercorrelated and the best model which could be fitted contained just one variable: drug problems at the time of the second interview ($p=<.000$). When motivation was introduced into the model, drug problems remained in, but its power was slightly reduced (from a beta of 1.6381 to 1.5274; see Table 11.1).

In keeping with their generally higher rates of offending, the pessimists were the most likely to have reported committing every type of offence. For example, property offences (the emboldened row in the top half of Table 11.4) indicate that whilst 19 per cent of the

Table 11.4: Type of offending by motivation

| | Confidents | | Optimists | | Pessimists | | All probationers |
	(n)	(%)	(n)	(%)	(n)	(%)	(n)
Probationer							
Reported offending	48	44	25	54	34	79	107
Violent/sex[5]	21	19	9	20	15	35	45
Property	**21**	**19**	**14**	**30**	**28**	**65**	**63**
Drugs	28	25	15	33	18	42	61
Other	17	15	6	13	19	44	42
Total	110		46		43		199
Officer							
Reported offending	41	37	24	52	29	67	94
Violent/sex	12	11	10	22	9	21	32
Property	**22**	**20**	**15**	**33**	**21**	**49**	**63**
Drug	16	15	14	30	19	44	53
Other	16	15	14	30	11	26	44
Total	110	100	46	100	43	100	199

confident probationers and 30 per cent of the optimistic probationers reported having committed a property offence, 65 per cent of the pessimists said that they had committed a property offence. The emboldened row in the bottom half of the table (the officers' reports) show a similar trend: 20 per cent of the confidents were reported as having committed a property offence, 33 per cent of the optimists and 49 per cent of the pessimists.

Officers and probationers also asked about the number of times the latter had offended (see Table 11.5). An inspection of Table 11.5 reveals a familiar trend. A smaller proportion of the confident reported they had offended frequently than either the optimists or the pessimists. The emboldened cells in Table 11.5 illustrate this: fewer of the confidents (25 per cent) reported having committed more than four offences than either of the optimists (37 per cent) or the pessimists (54 per cent). This trend is again supported by the officer's reports.

In the course of undertaking bivariate logistic regression runs, several variables presented themselves as possible candidates for inclusion in a multivariate model. The most salient of these are summarised in Table 11.6. Very few studies have investigated social factors and the number of subsequent reconvictions. Oldfield (1996: 47–48), however, found that previous prison sentences, the number of

Table 11.5:   Amount of offending by motivation

	Confidents		Optimists		Pessimists		Total	
	(n)	(%)	(n)	(%)	(n)	(%)	(n)	(%)
Probationer report								
No offending	62	56	21	46	9	21	92	46
One to four offences	20	18	8	18	10	23	38	19
More than four	**25**	**26**	**17**	**37**	**23**	**54**	**65**	**33**
Officer report								
No offending	69	63	22	48	14	33	105	53
One to four offences	26	24	13	28	18	42	57	28
More than four	15	14	11	24	11	26	37	19
Total	110	100	46	100	43	100	199	100

previous convictions and unemployment at the start of the probation order were associated with more frequent reconvictions. Interestingly, and in line with Oldfield (1996) and Murray and Cox (1979, cited in Oldfield), the current data suggest that probation supervision might act to 'suppress' offending. In the current sample those probationers who reported greater levels of general help from their probationers (the Probation Impact Scales,[6] see Table 11.6) committed fewer offences. These scales were, however, significantly related to motivation ($p = <.05$) such that the confidents were the most likely to have reported greater levels of help. However, this relationship was not particularly strong and despite attempts to explore the relationship between motivation, offending and amount of help, it remained unclear as to whether it was the help received or the probationer's motivation which accounted for the reductions in offending. It could, of course, be that whilst the confidents were helped the most, this help was unrelated to their avoidance of further offending.

An inspection of the relationships between these variables suggested that most of the criminal history variables were highly correlated with one another, as was the case with probationers' self-reports of their drug problems and their assessments of the impact of probation supervision. Thus, only three variables were chosen for further use when developing a model of probationers' reports of the amount of crimes they had committed: drug problems at the time of the first interview; Probation Impact (measured at the third sweep); and OGRS (dichotomised as 0–75 and 76–100 per cent). In addition, variables indicating whether the probationer was a confident or a pessimist were employed, only the latter of which entered the final model, shown in Table 11.7.

Table 11.6: Factors associated with the amount of offending: summary

Probationer	Std beta	Sig	Officer	Std beta	Sig
Motivation			*Motivation*		
Confidents	-.247	.000	Confidents	-.179	.011
Optimists	.033	.639	Optimists	.096	.179
Pessimists	.147	.000	Pessimists	.118	.096
Had prison previously	.176	.015	—		
Previous theft conviction	.143	.048	—		
Previous drug conviction	.151	.001	—		
OGRS (76–100%)	.137	.036	—		
Order made for drug offence	.151	.033	Order made for drug offence	.276	.000
Drug problem (at offence)	.211	.003	Drug problem (at offence)	.278	.000
Drug problem (SWP1)	.310	.000	Drug problem (SWP1)	.300	.000
—			Drug problem (SWP2)	.387	.000
—			Friends (SWP2)	.308	.000
—			Drug problem (SWP3)	.348	.000
—			Friends (SWP3)	.194	.006
—			Total problems (at offence)	.147	.039
—			Total problems (SWP1)	.250	.000
—			Total problems (SWP2)	.295	.000
—			Total problems (SWP3)	.205	.004
Probation Impact Scale (SWP2)	-.249	.006	Probation Impact Scale (SWP2)	-.180	.021
Probationm Impact Scale (SWP3)	-.263	.004	—		

Table 11.7: Factors associated with the amount of offending: final models

	Std beta	Sig		Std beta	Sig
Probationer			**Officer**		
Drug problem (SWP1)	.286	.001	Drug problem (SWP2)	.348	.000
Probation impact (SWP3)	−.171	.045	Total problems (SWP3)	.166	.011
OGRS (76–100%)	.120	.152	—		
Pessimists	.277	.001	Confidents	−.095	.156
Constants		.000	Constants		.000
Adjusted R-square		.208			.173

When the officers' data set was analysed, several of the variables were found to be highly correlated with one another. For example, officers' assessments of the probationer's drug problems at each interview were all highly correlated. However, a model including drug problems (at the second interview) and total problems was developed. In this was included a variable indicating whether the probationer had been classified as a confident or not. However, despite being significantly related to the amount of offending during the bivariate runs, this variable did not enter the final multivariate model. As such, the amount of offending was most closely related to drug problems, being a pessimist and the amount of help received from one's officer.

Summarising the variables associated with offending

From this and the preceding chapter, a number of statements relating to desistance and persistence can be made. Motivation appeared to be strongly related to desistance and continued offending. The analyses reported in Chapter 10 (Table 10.2) and the Appendix (Table A1) suggest that motivation was strongly related to desistance, whilst analyses here suggest that motivation was related to both reports of *any* offending by the probationers (Table 11.1) and the amount of offending they were reported to have committed (Table 11.5).

Various of the social circumstances were also related to both reports of offending and desistance. For example, employment and accommodation stability were associated with desistance (Chapter 10 and Table A1). Similarly the number of 'problem' social circumstances was also related to desistance (Chapter 10 and Table A1) and to the amount of offending reported (Tables 11.5 and 11.6). These findings suggest the utility of collecting data which are not solely related to the work undertaken as part of the probation order and which are repeatedly measured. However, as employment and accommodation stability were important factors, so too it must be remembered are changes in the social contexts and the effects of these on solving obstacles (see Figures 7.1, 7.2, 9.1 and 9.2).

Just as with the attempts to account for desistance, social variables and motivation appeared as key influences upon offending by probationers. The social variables were of greater utility and appeared to account for variations in whether the probationer offended, the number of times he or she offended and the types of offences committed. Similarly motivation appeared to be associated with whether the probationer was reported to have offended at all and with the number of times he or she offended. The amount of help provided by officers and the probationer's previous criminal history were of less utility as predictors of reoffending.

The findings relating to the Probation Impact Scales initially suggested that probation supervision had a role in 'suppressing' offending, a finding also noted by Murray and Cox (1979), Oldfield (1996) and MacKenzie et al. (1999: 438). As probationers reported greater levels of help from their officers, so the amounts of crime they reported declined. These scales were, however, significantly related to motivation ($p = <.05$) such that the confidents were the most likely to have reported greater levels of assistance – it remained unclear whether it was the probationer's motivation or the amount of help which he or she received which accounted for the lower number of offences committed.

One of the most surprising results to emerge from the regression analyses undertaken concerns the utility of the criminal history variables. These were not as strongly related to reports of offending as had been anticipated and were on occasion 'forced out' of models by the inclusion of other variables. For example, in Table 11.3 previous theft convictions were forced out of the model of any offending by the introduction of motivation. In fact, OGRS appeared to be weakly associated with most types of offending with the exception of property offending. The explanation for this probably lies in the fact that OGRS was designed to predict future criminal convictions rather than self-reported offending. To this end the comparatively poor performance of OGRS should not be taken as an indication of weakness on the part of the scale itself.

Notes

1 There has been some evidence that this may in some circumstances extend to the victim too – see Sparks *et al.* (1977: 208–209) on reductions of fear following victimisation.
2 When last contacted, some months after the main fieldwork had been completed, the officer reported that the order was progressing smoothly and that the probationer had not offended in the 18 months since the assault.
3 To refresh readers' minds on this topic, the current study is focused upon offending *during* the probation order.
4 In terms of their statistical significance, the criminal history variables were all at the $p = <.050$ level, whilst the social variables ranged from $p = <.050$ (employment and finances) to .000 (drugs and total problems).
5 There was only one sexual offence reported from the respondents in the sample.
6 Probation Impact Scales were developed by summating three questions asked of officers and probationers at sweeps two and three. These asked whether the officer had said or done anything that would be helpful in keeping the probationer out of trouble in the future; probation supervision had helped the probationer stay out of trouble; and whether the probationer had learnt anything whilst on probation. The alpha coefficients for these questions were sufficiently high for them to be summated and used as a scale, and were officers, sweep two: .6324; officers, sweep three: .6158; probationers, sweep two: .7025; probationers, sweep three: .4619. These scales were positively correlated (officer sweep two/probationer sweep two: .289; Spearman's $p = .002$; officer sweep three/probationer sweep three: .211; Spearman's $p = .033$).

Part 4
Conclusions

Chapter 12

Probation, social context and desistance from crime: developing the agenda

Parts 2 and 3 of this book have explored the responses of officers and probationers to the obstacles faced by the probationers, and the continuation or cessation of offending behaviour. This chapter summarises these findings and draws out the lessons from the research.

Resolving obstacles to desistance

When compared to their officers, fewer probationers believed that they faced obstacles to desistance, and those who did frequently identified fewer obstacles than their officers. On the whole, officers and probationers did *not* agree over very many of the obstacles faced. However, both officers and probationers identified a range of obstacles which, to a large extent, mirrored the risk factors identified in the wider literature. Around a half of all obstacles identified and followed up had, according to officers and probationers, been resolved by the end of the order (Tables 6.4 and 6.6, Chapter 6). It would appear both from the obstacles identified and the solutions undertaken to resolve them that only a minority of officers and probationers 'worked together' to tackle these obstacles. The solutions which probationers proposed to employ in overcoming these obstacles were *ad hoc* rather than sustained or focused attempts to deal effectively with the issues at hand (Chapter 5). Officers reported that they intended to rely upon discussions with the probationer in order to tackle the obstacle. The further examination of those officers and probationers who had identified the same obstacles suggested that both officers and probationers expected that the successful tackling of an obstacle would be contingent upon a range of factors – many of which appeared to be outside the direct control of either of them. When the outcome of the work aimed at tackling these obstacles was explored, officers' and probationers' beliefs that such contingencies would play a role in overcoming obstacles appeared to be borne out. The analyses undertaken in Chapter 6 explored the extent to which different interventions were associated with successful obstacle resolutions. Responses from both officers and probationers suggested that no specific probation interventions were associated with successful obstacle resolution. The extent to which officers and probationers 'worked together' was explored and was also found not to be associated with resolving obstacles. A number of possible explanations for this were considered, in particular:

- that the motivation of the probationer may have mediated the outcomes of the attempts to resolve obstacles; and

- that the probationer's social and personal circumstances could also have influenced the outcomes of such efforts.

When – in Chapter 7 – the influence of probationer motivation was considered, it emerged that the optimists and pessimists were the least likely to have successfully resolved their obstacles: 41 per cent of the optimists and 37 per cent of the pessimists said that their obstacle had led to further offending, compared to 21 per cent of the confidents. There was little evidence of extensive 'co-working' between officers and probationers regardless of probationer motivation and very little variation between confidents, optimists and pessimists in terms of the extent to which they were helped by their officers to resolve the obstacles to desistance which they faced.

Chapter 8 continued the investigation into the factors which may have influenced the outcomes of the efforts aimed at overcoming obstacles. The social and personal contexts of the probationers were examined in detail. Both officers' and probationers' descriptions of their responses to the obstacles suggested that the social and personal *contexts* in which these efforts were located were key determinates of the success or otherwise of these efforts. Just as seeds thrown on stony ground will not take root, so efforts to resolve particular obstacles will come to little if the conditions for success are not present, or do not emerge quickly.

Figures 12.1 and 12.2 (previously presented as Figures 7.1 and 9.1, respectively) summarise these findings.[1] In Figure 12.1 the progress of each of the three groups of probationers towards desistance is charted. Fewer of the confidents faced obstacles than either of the other groups

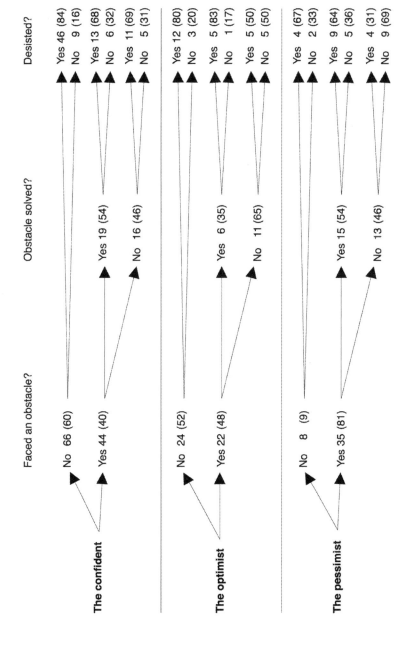

Figure 12.1 Motivation, obstacles and desistance: probationers' reports. All figures are N (%).

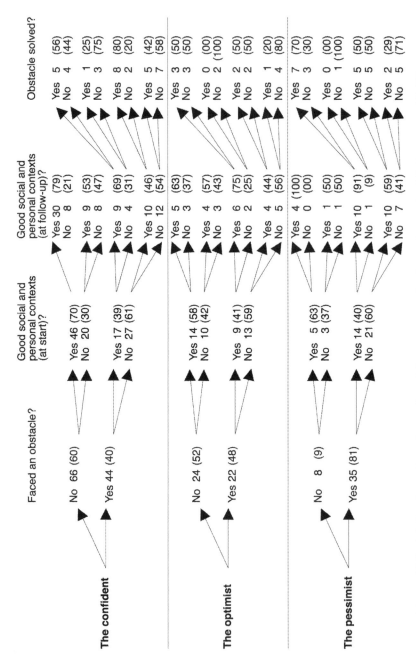

Figure 12.2 Motivation, obstacles and social contexts: probationers' reports. All figures are N (%).

(40 per cent), whilst eight out of ten of the pessimists faced one or more obstacles. Of those pessimists who faced no obstacles, 67 per cent desisted. However, 64 per cent of those pessimists who faced an obstacle but *overcame* it desisted, whilst even fewer – only 31 per cent – of those pessimists who faced an obstacle but did *not* overcome it desisted. For the optimists and pessimists, solving obstacles was particularly strongly related to desistance: of the six optimists who overcame the obstacle they faced, all but one desisted. On the other hand, of the 11 who did not overcome the obstacle they faced, five desisted and five did not (one was lost during the follow-up). Desistance rates were highest amongst those groups that faced no obstacles and lowest (with one exception – the confident) amongst those who faced obstacles and did not overcome them.

Figure 12.2 introduces the issue of social contexts.[2] The figure suggests that social contexts – measured at the start of the probation order and towards the end – were an influence on obstacle resolutions. Consider, for example, the confident who faced obstacles: of those who were living in good social contexts at *both* the start of their orders and the follow-up, 56 per cent overcame their obstacle. Similarly, of those who were not living in good social contexts throughout the duration of their orders, only 42 per cent overcame the obstacles they faced. Changes in social contexts were also important. Of the four confidents who faced obstacles and who started in good contexts which *worsened*, only one overcame the obstacle he was facing. However, of the ten confidents who were initially in poorer social contexts but which *improved*, eight overcame the obstacles they faced. These figures confirm the analyses reported earlier, namely, that motivation and social contexts were important in understanding obstacle resolution rates, and that these co-varied. For example, 57 per cent of confidents were living in good social contexts at the start of their orders; rates for optimists and pessimists were lower, respectively: 50 and 44 per cent.

Chapter 9 explored in greater detail the issue of change in social and personal contexts. Changes in employment status and family formation were observed to be two of the most commonly reported by both officers and probationers. For many probationers, these changes were positive – that is to say, that they gained employment, achieved promotion at work, were reunited with family members or embarked upon new familial relationships. There was evidence also that these positive changes were associated with positive changes in probationers' lifestyles and their offending behaviours.

But what were the roles of probationer motivation and probation supervision in assisting these changes to take place? Because changes in employment and family circumstances had been found to be related to positive changes in lifestyle and offending, the impact of probation supervision on the obstacles related to employment and families was revisited towards the end of Chapter 9. These analyses suggested that most of these obstacles were solved following actions initiated by probationers, rather than by their officers, and, as such, those who were motivated to resolve these obstacles were the most successful in so doing (Table 9.2a). However, the greater the assistance given by the officer, the greater the proportion of cases who successfully tackled their employment and family-related obstacles (Table 9.2b). Thus whilst social and personal contexts were important influences upon the outcomes of the attempts to solve the obstacles faced by probationers (see Chapter 8), there were important interactions between these contexts and motivation – a point confirmed by Figures 12.1 and 12.2.

The process of desisting

Around a half the probationers and almost three quarters of the officers reported offending trajectories which suggested that the probationer was desisting from offending (Table 10.1, Chapter 10). When the factors associated with desistance were examined, it appeared that as the total number of 'problem' social circumstances facing the probationer increased, so desistance became less likely.

A detailed investigation of the experiences of those pessimists who showed signs of desisting confirmed that changes in family and employment circumstances were key factors in accounting for their desistance. For a significant minority of probationers, their officer was key in assisting them to avoid further trouble (e.g. Clive, discussed in Chapter 10). Those pessimists who persisted appeared to do so because of existing addictions to substances or shoplifting, or as a result of the 'lack of change' in their lives. Interestingly, those confidents and optimists who persisted also appeared to do so because of a continued reliance on drugs or alcohol. Others accounted for their persistence by citing a lack of career opportunities and, indeed, it was observed that many were neither employed nor in a stable relationship.

Does this mean probation 'does' or 'does not' work?

The question of whether probation 'works' or not cannot be answered without first addressing what is meant by both 'works' and 'probation'.

Virtually all previous investigations of the outcomes of criminal justice interventions have used 'works' to refer to a reduction from some expected level in the rate of conviction. Further, they have assumed that any such reduction is the direct result of the intervention rather than the result of some other set of factors – i.e. the 'black box' approach. In effect the definition of 'works' employed in the 'What Works?' perspective has been something like the following:

1. A set period of time following the commencement of supervision during which the probationer was not found guilty of further offences.

If it could also be demonstrated for a cohort of probationers that their *actual* rate of reconviction was statistically significantly lower than their *predicted* rate of reconviction (which, thanks to developments like OGRS, it can), then so much the better. However, one has to ask: is this a realistic or appropriate definition of 'works'? A more accurate definition of 'works' would be something like:

2. A positive (or at least, not a negative) impact on the probationer which is wholly or in part attributable to some aspect of the intervention.

This is a more roundabout definition, but one which captures more accurately the problems of undertaking research in an 'open' system (Pawson and Tilley 1997). Such a definition shifts the focus from convictions and, most importantly, by referring to 'some *aspect* of the intervention', alters the way in which we approach such interventions and how these are constituted. It does so by allowing for the possibility that the 'aspects of the intervention' which were of most help in creating the positive impact need *not* be drawn from those originally intended to do so (in this case probation supervision, Worrall 1997: 13). For example, whilst contact with probation officers, drug workers, employment advisers and so on will probably not do any probationer much harm, it need not be these features of their time on probation which ultimately help the probationers overcome the obstacles they faced and avoid offending. The elements which this study has most frequently found to be of most help in assisting probationers overcome obstacles and avoid further offending have *not* come from officers, etc., but from the probationers themselves (their motivation) and from changes in the nature of the social contexts in which they lived. Good motivation, gaining employment, mending damaged relationships, starting new relationships, moving home and so on were key influences on the success or otherwise of many of the attempts to overcome obstacles. In many cases changes in the probationer's social and personal circumstances boosted already existing motivation, provided those with poor motivation or who lacked self-belief with the desire and/or motivation to address the obstacles they faced, and in other cases they better enabled probationers to address such obstacles.

The definition above in (2) opens the possibility of including factors like motivation, employment changes and other life contingencies which have not traditionally been considered to be part of probation supervision by those evaluating the outcomes of criminal justice sanctions. Palmer (1996), in an essay entitled the 'Programmatic and *non-programmatic* aspects of successful interventions' (emphasis added), lists the following as non-programmatic aspects of successful interventions: staff characteristics (for example, whether volunteers or professional); staff–client interactions (the extent and nature of their communications); offender differences (essentially personality differences); and the setting (prison- or probation-based). Palmer (1996: 168) concludes his review with some words of wisdom: 'progress in identifying *key ingredients* of successful programmes has been relatively slow' (emphasis in original). This he attributes to 'the particular analytic framework and the tools that were used'. The solution to this, Palmer (ibid., emphasis added, irony in original) summarised thus: 'To make faster and better progress in identifying key ingredients one needs a *broader* and *more integrated* analytic framework and tool than those used to date to determine whether intervention works and, if so, which types . . . are successful.' It is unclear to what exactly Palmer is referring when he writes of 'a more integrated analytic framework'. However one solution is to conceptualise probation interventions as being aimed at altering some aspects of an individual's social and personal circumstances (for example by assisting the probationer to become a wage-earner rather than a benefit claimant) but which are themselves open to influence by those same circumstances. Thus the probationer's social circumstances and relationships with others are both the *object* of the intervention and the *medium* through which this change can be achieved.

This, of course, means accepting that the social and personal circumstances are, in many respects, integral 'parts' of the programme of probation work. But how plausible is it to accept this? Joan Petersilia (1998: 563, emphasis added), in a recent introduction to probation and parole supervision, has observed that: 'Both [probation and parole] are designed around the concept of offender reintegration, a key element of which is *dealing with the offender's problems in his or her social and community context.*' In other words, probation work is not divorced from community influences, and should not be evaluated as such. Writing from a British perspective, Rex (1998, 1999: 373) has noted that even the architects of cognitive programmes emphasised the requirement that effective supervision should also attend to the social and personal problems faced by probationers (Ross and Ross 1995: 8; cited in Rex 1999: 373). If, as seems reasonable, we accept that social circumstances *are* an integral element of what helps probation supervision to 'work', then 'the community' becomes an integral and constitutive component *of* probation supervision.[3] Giving those found guilty of offending, by way of probation supervision, the chance to address these circumstances is actually a part of what probation 'is' and what sets it apart from other sentences – most notably imprisonment. Therefore, part 'of' probation is allowing probationers to remain in the community and for them to develop techniques for tackling obstacles in a community context. As Haines (1990, cited in Rex 1999) and the current study have demonstrated, probationers and their networks are often more effective than statutory bodies in solving some obstacles, but *this cannot happen if probationers are not in the community.*

Thus it *does* seem reasonable to accept that the influence of social and personal contexts is an element of 'what probation is'. The changes in employment, personal relationships, homes and so on as experienced by the probationers in the current study, as well as being indirect *functions* of probation supervision, would have been much less likely had these people been subject to imprisonment. In many cases, therefore, probation supervision achieved an intended consequence (desistance) through unintended influences: chiefly changes in employment status and family formation.

The answer to the question of whether probation works is a qualified 'yes'. In many cases the work undertaken whilst on probation was of little *direct* help to many of the probationers; however the *indirect* impact of probation (i.e. naturally occurring changes in employment, accommodation and personal relationships) was of greater significance. 'Of greater significance' is unfortunately about as precise an estimation of the impact of social and personal contexts relative to probation work as can be made. It is impossible to quantify more accurately the role of these contexts, as Jock Young (1999: 130) has asserted: 'the social world is a complex interactive entity in which any particular social intervention can have only a limited effect on other social events and where the calculation of this effect is always difficult.'

Encouraging desistance: what does this mean for probation practice?

The foregoing analyses have suggested that motivation and changes in individuals' social circumstances were the main 'motors' which drove desistance. Changes in motivation – when they did occur – appeared to be the result of changes in social and personal circumstances (see Chapter 7). Because the motivation to avoid further trouble either existed from very early on in the life of the order, or was fostered by changes in social and personal circumstances, this section focuses on how such changes in social circumstances can routinely be generated. This discussion is placed within the framework of human and social capital (Coleman 1988, 1990). These terms offer a way of conceptualising how probation practice might intervene in probationers' lives to foster desistance in the light of the observation that desistance was often the result of social processes over which probationers and officers did not have full control.

Human capital refers to the skills and knowledge which individuals possess and which enables them to apply for jobs, hold down work, achieve at work and so on. It '. . . is created by changes in persons that bring about skills and capabilities that make them able to act in new ways' (Coleman 1988: s. 100). Clearly, poor or inadequate human capital will make gaining and keeping employment, for example, all the harder. Social capital, on the other hand:

> . . . is defined by its function. It is not a single entity but a variety of entities, with two elements in common: they all consist of some aspect of social structures, and they facilitate certain actions of actors – whether persons or corporate actors – within the structure. Like other forms of capital, social capital is productive, making possible the achievement of certain ends that in its absence would not be possible (ibid.: s. 98).

The function of such a conceptualisation is to identify the value of 'social capital' to social actors as resources which they can use to achieve their interests (ibid.: s. 101). As such, social capital:

> . . . originates in socially structured relations between individuals, in families and in aggregations of individuals in neighbourhoods, churches, schools and so on. These relations facilitate social action by generating a knowledge and sense of obligation, expectations, trustworthiness, information channels norms and sanctions (Hagan and McCarthy 1997: 229).

Examples of how social capital operated to assist desistance amongst probationers in the current sample are not hard to find. For example, Jamie (case 115, see Chapter 9) found the work which so dramatically altered his life via a family contact. Similarly, case 150 (Chapter 9) was not 'kicked out' of his parents' house after finding work.[4] A further case (163) illustrates how social capital is 'defined by its function'. The probationer, by finding somewhere stable to live, was able to use this resource as a base from which to apply for employment. Officers, when they took direct action to intervene in a probationer's life, often did so by linking probationers to various forms of social capital – families, medical services, the police and housing agencies.

Probation services already try to improve the human capital of the individuals they supervise by referring them to employment partnerships or by running short courses in 'thinking skills', safe drug use and so on. However, as Crow (2000: 121) has noted, studies of employment schemes have frequently been unable to demonstrate an impact on offending, a finding which he suggests is in part due to their being unable to address the wider problem of mass unemployment. In other words, such schemes were ultimately unable to act in such a way as to improve their participants' social capital as they ultimately had little direct control of or influence over wider meso- and macro-level circumstances – in this case employment rates.

Changes in social capital alter the possibilities for various forms of social activity. Coleman (1988: ss. 99–101) cites the example of South Korean student radical activists whose study groups served as the basis for transforming individual discontent into organised rebellion. These study groups constituted a device for organising wider forms of social protest. It follows that variations in other forms of social capital therefore may serve to encourage the avoidance of delinquent acts in some people and the engagement in offending by some others. Employment (or the lack of it) may serve just such a role:

> A key problem is that while for many youth early and sustained employment contacts enhance the prospects of getting a job and subsequent occupational mobility, connections into crime are likely in a converse way to increase the probability of unemployment (Hagan 1997: 299).

> Under [widespread youth unemployment], the peer group takes on a more important and more enduring dimension as the principal (if not only) source of security, status, sense of belonging and identity (Graham and Bowling 1995: 97).

> Inadequate availability of employment is perhaps the biggest obstacle to successfully traversing the gap between a *troubled* adolescent and the entry into a *more stable* adulthood (Hagan 1997: 299, emphasis added).

These quotations suggest that as some forms of social capital are eroded (in this case, employment) so behaviours are altered, and that this frequently has implications for some people's involvement in crime. This process was highlighted during the analyses presented in Chapters 9 and 10, during which employment and employment stability were frequently reported to be associated with desistance. Poor employment prospects encourage engagement in offending which may ultimately serve to block subsequent opportunities for legitimate employment and desistance. Hagan (1997) has argued that western industrialised nations have, during the last quarter of the twentieth century, witnessed an overall slow-down in economic growth. This has been: '. . . characterised by increased unemployment and income inequality, led by the loss and only partial replacement of core sector manufacturing jobs with less stable and poorer paying service sector jobs' (ibid.: 289). Many of the poorest men and women were amongst those who lost most during this period of economic upheaval. These economic changes have resulted in huge social changes. For example, a significant proportion of young people leaving school will either expect *not* to work, will experience economic instability or may become accustomed to periodic unemployment. As well as helping to maintain the concentration of poverty, such changes will create:

> a social context that includes poor schools, inadequate job information networks, and a lack of legitimate employment opportunities [that] not only gives rise to weak labour force attachment, but increases the probability that individuals will be constrained to seek income derived from illegal and deviant activities (Wilson 1991: 10, cited in Hagan 1997: 292).

In other words the economic changes of the last quarter of the twentieth century have resulted in reductions in human and social capital.[5] In less advantaged communities – similar to those in which many of the respondents in the present study were living – individuals, families and 'aggregations of individuals' will be amongst those who have experienced reductions in social capital. Those most likely to be made subject to probation orders are therefore amongst those most likely to have limited legitimate resources both in terms of their human capital (i.e. their own skills) and in terms of the skills and knowledge which permeate the communities in which they live (their social capital).

Given that when they started probation, many of the probationers reported problems with their employment (55 per cent) and finances (53 per cent) and described themselves as having drug and alcohol problems (respectively, 34 per cent and 23 per cent), it is little wonder that about half of them reported offending during the course of their orders, or that officers' efforts to tackle these obstacles appeared to have been so limited. As Moffitt (1993: 415) has noted: 'Interventions with life-course persistent [offenders] have met with dismal results. This is not surprising, considering that most interventions are begun relatively late in the chain of cumulative continuity.' These arguments suggest that the reason why 'traditional' one-to-one probation supervision and more recent innovations such as group programmes have experienced only limited success in helping probationers to desist is because, despite their good intentions, such interventions are unable to get at the heart of the problem facing many of those on probation. Human capital can be relatively easily gained – for example, group programmes can teach employment skills and partnerships can help to develop these – but ultimately if local social and economic circumstances do not encourage employment then no assistance – regardless of intensity, design or commitment of staff – will be of any help. As such the strengthening of *social* capital should become one of the aims of social and criminal justice policy and accordingly the focus of much of the work undertaken by probation services.

How exactly should this proceed? Laub *et al.* (1995), building on Sampson and Laub (1993), outlined two substantive areas in which they felt criminal justice policy could make potentially fruitful interventions: strengthening marriages[6] and increasing attachments to the labour force. Laub *et al.*'s contribution was not aimed specifically at the probation service, but at more general interventions. However, strong ties to marriage partners and employment have both been cited as factors in desistance and, as such, both will be considered here.

Laub *et al.* (1995) were writing from an American perspective and, in this light, it is interesting to note their calls for the greater use of probation and parole as alternatives to custody. They argue that counselling should be available so that:

offenders ... become better spouses and [to] help them through crises in their marriages by making appropriate counselling readily available. Helping offenders repair personal relationships, salvage marriages or improve interpersonal relationships so that permanent relationships are possible will all in the long run, contribute to law-abiding behaviour (ibid.: 100–01).

These sorts of provisions already exist in England and Wales, although their use would not appear to be widespread on the basis of the current study. From Chapters 6 (Table 6.5) and 9 (Table 9.2) it would appear that officers did not readily address the family-related obstacles to desistance which they had reported their probationers were facing. In some respects this is understandable: one hears a lot about probation work being concerned with 'offending-related' factors. However, this is perhaps mistaken. Probation officers should not focus on 'offending-related' factors but, rather, on *'desistance-related'* factors. As Shover and Henderson (1995: 243, emphasis in original) have commented:

> [current repressive crime control policies] ignore entirely the theoretically obvious: Offenders' behaviour can be changed not only by increasing threat but by also increasing *legitimate opportunities*. It is important to make this point if for no other reason than the fact that increased legitimate opportunities extend the choices to offenders . . .

If probation work became desistance-focused rather than offending-related, officers may feel that they had a clearer mandate to help probationers tackle family problems. This may in turn result in a greater involvement of officers in the attempts to tackle such obstacles and greater success in actually resolving them.

Laub *et al.* (1995) suggest that more should be done to increase the job prospects of probationers. They suggest that 'any probationer or parolee who is not working should be required, as a condition . . ., to obtain work or appropriate job training'. This is, perhaps, rather draconian. No one should be forced into work if he or she does not wish to. However, the basic premise is still sound and, as such, raises the question: what can probation services do to alter significantly local economic contexts in such a way as to increase social capital and reduce offending?

One recent development does offer the hope that probation services will be able to alter local contexts. Surrey and Inner London Probation Services have both initiated schemes aimed at developing local employment opportunities which will meet the needs of their caseloads. Interestingly, the project in Surrey aimed to provide 'sheltered employment' in the form of a recycling scheme. Early indications (Sarno *et al.* 1999, 2000) are encouraging, but a final evaluation is still a long way off.

How might such schemes be developed in the future? It is not always easy to find work – and less easy still if one has few skills, a poor or non-existent employment record, a criminal conviction and knows few other people who work. Perhaps, then, probation services should – as well as referring some probationers to employment schemes – attempt to *create jobs locally* for their caseloads. In other words, probation services should provide sheltered employment in the form of schemes like the recycling scheme in Surrey. Probation services could find themselves being in a position to provide employment to suit a range of employment skills and needs. For example, a recycling scheme with its own chain of shops to sell some reclaimed goods and goods made from recycled materials would provide the following types of posts: people to collect the goods for recycling; people to sort them for sale or recycling; people to make new goods from old materials or to refurbish partially damaged goods; people to work in the shops; clerical assistants to process payments (to employees) and supervise revenue from shops; and so on. Clearly, not all these skills could be met by probation caseloads, but a high number of them could be. The aim of such a scheme would be to get people to the first rung of the employment ladder: a job. Employment provides a record of 'employability' in the form of people who can be approached to provide references and, as such, may well provide the basis of further jobs in other occupations.

By offering work with a caring employer (the probation service) which understands the problems facing probationers, such as needing time off to attend court and probation appointments, and which is committed to a notion of social justice, schemes like those sketched above may be able to make a greater contribution to securing 'good' employment for probationers than has previously been the case.[7]

Some may question the innovative nature of such schemes – those working on such schemes will be identified as 'offenders' and may be treated negatively by others. However, Chapman (1995) provides evidence that imaginative schemes aimed at intervening in local community problems can be successfully implemented. Certainly, current criminal justice policies based on 'harshness' may, in the long run, serve only to prolong criminal careers. As Shover (1996: 179) observes:

> In many [US] states, as matters stand today, the heaviest penalties
> fall at the point when many offenders are on the verge of desisting

or shifting to less serious forms of crime. Heavy prison sentences can exact such a toll from offenders that they miss all timetables for achieving success legitimately.

The most recent development in UK probation has been the creation of the National Probation Service. Whilst to be welcomed in that it raises the profile of probation, the programme of work and general orientation towards rehabilitation do not suggest that extra efforts will be aimed at helping probationers to find work or to '. . . become better spouses . . .' (Laub *et al.* 1995). Instead the programme of work appears to differ little from what went before it, namely, 'accredited' programmes on anger management, thinking skills, 'safe' drug use and the such like. Getting people into work (like the Surrey and ILPS schemes) or encouraging people to become better parents and/or partners is *not* on the agenda as current probation thinking is about criminogenic need not desistance-orientated facilitators. This is in direct contradiction with most of the literature on why people stop offending and the findings of the current investigation into desistance following probation supervision and, incidentally, an argument promoted by Bottoms and McWilliams twenty years ago (1979: 175).

What does this imply for the 'what works?' agenda?

The methodology employed and the substantive findings of the study have implications for the 'What Works?' agenda. This body of work has sought to understand which programmes of intervention 'work' best (i.e. which are associated with the lowest rates of subsequent convictions). Many of the reviews undertaken in this field have come to the conclusion that very little can be demonstrated to work with unanimity (see the review in Chapter 1). As also noted in the same chapter, many of those who have researched the outcomes of community sentences have neglected to include the role of the community in their investigations of such outcomes. Palmer's (1996) review of the evidence, discussed above, illustrates this tendency – 'non-programmatic' aspects of interventions were considered only to extend as far as staff characteristics and so forth. By ignoring the role of social contexts, such evaluations ignore what is arguably one of the most important ingredients in probation supervision, and certainly the aspect which sets it apart from imprisonment. In short, future investigations of the outcomes of probation supervision should focus upon the role of the social contexts in assisting probationers to combat risk factors and ultimately to desist. Chiefly amongst these influences, the current study and the literature on desistance would suggest, are personal motivation, gaining employment and changes in family relations.

This will require those interested in the 'what works?' debates to adopt a different approach to the investigation of sentence outcomes. It is not enough to collect data about an individual's employment, accommodation, financial circumstances and so on – what is required is an understanding of how these impacted upon the work implemented under the auspices of probation and how probation influenced these factors. Interests in such bi-directional relationships will require repeated sweeps of data collection to explore these issues and how they change during the course of the period of supervision.

Additionally, good, rigorously collected qualitative data should become part of the methodological toolbox of 'What Works?' evaluation. For too long attempts to evaluate which interventions are associated with better outcomes have relied solely upon quantitative data. Matthews and Pitts (2000: 138) have recently made similar calls in relation to violence-reduction programmes in prison: '. . . evaluation also needs to include more qualitative and "intensive" data gained from discussion with those who have actually participated in the programme'. Such an approach would not just provide information about *whether* a programme works, but *how* it works and how it works in specific *contexts*.

The use of social and personal context variables in evaluation research

Few recent studies have explored the roles of social and personal contexts in mediating the outcomes of probation supervision – or at least those that have, have not done so to the extent which the current project has. Writing towards the end of the report which helped to reinvigorate UK research on the outcomes of sentences, Lloyd *et al.* (1994: 54) called for more research aimed explicitly at exploring the role of social variables in accounting for rates of reconviction following community supervision. May (1999) took up this challenge.

May's investigation into the role of social variables in *predicting* reconviction produced a number of important findings. Some social variables were strongly related to reconviction rates (ibid.: 15–26), and were in fact *so* strongly related that even when age and previous guilty appearances were taken into consideration, social variables were still more strongly associated with reconviction rates than other criminal history variables (ibid.: 28–29). May (ibid.) concluded that, for some groups: 'even when age and previous appearances [in court] are taken into account ... social variables are still linked with differences in reconviction rates and ... this association is stronger than that of other criminal history variables.' Yet despite this, in his attempts at explaining reconviction following a 'community sentence' (the title of May's monograph), he employed criminal history variables ahead of the social variables – that is to say, he attempted to explain reconviction rates using criminal history variables, and then investigated by how much social variables would improve the percentage of correctly predicted cases (ibid.: 27–44). The answer, not surprisingly, was 'not very much' (ibid.: 37). May made various assertions that social variables *could* be used to improve the predictive power of the current (criminal history dominated) models for some groups (e.g. ibid.: xi), but since in aggregate this amounted to only a half a per cent increase in correctly predicted cases and the fifth of a per cent decrease in incorrectly predicted cases (ibid.: 47, Table 6.2), it is hard to imagine that many of those who read May's report would have been convinced of this.

The net result, one fears, is that criminal history variables are likely to remain as the accepted 'best predictors' of future reconviction. This is politically convenient. By repeatedly pointing to (static) criminal history variables as the best predictors of reconviction, those social and economic factors which co-vary with much offending are overlooked. By focusing upon criminal history variables (about which nothing can be 'done') the social origins of offending and recidivism are neatly side-stepped. Cash-strapped local and national government departments need not address the social or economic factors associated with crime, since social variables appear to explain little of the variance. In addition, criminal policy-makers are not forced to promote unpopular, but criminologically sensible policies which might be interpreted as 'rewarding' past offending (Uggen and Piliavin 1998: 1421–22). Target hardening, 'thinking skills' courses, surveillance and longer sentences for repeat offenders are easier to implement than sustained efforts at changing people and communities.[8]

The problem, perhaps, is an interchangeable use of the terms 'explain' and 'predict'. May's study demonstrated that, as far as reconviction data go, social variables *do* account for large variations in rates of reconviction. This held even when other variables were taken into consideration. However, despite their salience, May reverted to the (predictively weaker) criminal history variables and attempted to improve these by using the social variables. What would have happened, one wonders, if he had done the logical thing, and attempted to improve the percentage of cases correctly predicted by the social variables by adding to these the criminal history variables? *Predicting* reconviction is probably better achieved (for the purposes of official bodies such as probation services and the Home Office) by continuing to rely upon OGRS and criminal history variables. *Explaining* reconviction, however, as May's own data suggest, requires the use of social variables – a finding supported by the data collected as part of this study. In short, the current study found that social and personal variables *were* found to account for variations in the extents to which obstacles (i.e. risk factors) were resolved; rates of offending; and rates of desistance. Criminal history variables, were, generally speaking, not as useful. It therefore follows, in line with May, that social variables should form part of our understanding of why probationers reoffend, and therefore should be treated as issues which need to be addressed by social and criminal policy.

A greater use of social and personal variables should certainly be promoted. However, the insights gained from this project also support the assertions made by others (e.g. Haines 1999) concerning an important weakness in current approaches to research on criminal careers. Haines (ibid.: 266) points to one of the most common findings from criminal career research: that unemployment is associated with continued offending. However, as Haines argues, unemployment is not merely a problem for individuals, but is a social problem.[9] By focusing upon the behaviour and attributes of *individuals* (as much quantitative criminal career and What Works research does) this style of research focuses upon *criminals* rather than upon *crime*. This has two outcomes. Obviously there is first and foremost an inbuilt tendency to ignore wider social contexts. Whilst Chapters 8 and 9 suggested that gaining work was associated with reductions in offending, these jobs were the result not simply of an individual 'getting on his or her bike' and looking for work, but also of that work actually *being there* to be found, and an employer being prepared to offer a job to the probationer concerned. For example, would Sandra (discussed in Chapter 9) have been able to find employment so readily if it had not been for an employer deciding to risk employing an individual with little prior work experience and a conviction for stealing thousands of pounds from her previous employer? None of this should be taken as an attempt to discount the role of the probationer in getting employment, but rather to raise the issue that it is not *just* the individual who must be considered when such changes are (or are not) taking place or when these changes are attempted. As Farrall and Bowling (1999: 261, emphasis in original) wrote: '. . . the process of desistance is one that is produced through an *interplay* between individual choices, and a range of wider social forces, institutional and societal practices which are beyond the control of the individual.' It would appear that the *quantitative* research programmes in both the criminal careers and 'What Works?' literatures have yet *fully* to get to grips with the social and personal contexts within which the processes of desistance are embedded – and this is especially the case in the UK. Again this is not to consign these bodies of work to the proverbial waste-bin but, rather, to highlight a current deficiency in order that it may be addressed. As such, the quantitative programme of research in both criminal careers and the 'What Works?' paradigms may be leading us to subtly incorrect conclusions. More research needs to be focused on how probation supervision and individual changes are influenced by local contexts. Whilst this project has investigated the role of social and personal contexts, what is required is a project which locates probation interventions and personal changes in relation to the structure of specific local communities.

Moving the agenda forward

As people who are interested in either helping others to stop offending or evaluating such efforts (or both), we need to develop a new research agenda. The simple focus upon 'what works' has not served us well. It has failed to embark upon a thorough enough investigation of social and personal contexts, become overly reliant upon official data sources and official definitions of 'success' and 'failure', and has had a tendency to analyse data in ways which can only be described as 'static'.

The current research project has attempted to go beyond the rather limited methodologies which have dominated this field of research. In the light of the current project, a programme of research can be identified. Such research should not rely solely upon official data sources, should develop a range of 'outcome' measures which are *not* based on simple reconviction/reoffending data and which is prospective rather than retrospective. On the basis of the findings of this study such a research agenda should focus upon two main areas:

1. what individual officers/the wider probation service can do about addressing not just offending-related factors but also *desistance*-related needs; and

2. how probationers' social capital can be increased in such a way as to foster desistance.

The first of these is perhaps the more straightforward of the two suggestions. Desistance, it is widely becoming accepted, is often the result of attachments to the labour force or to marriage partners or both (see, for example, Sampson and Laub 1993). The current research has found evidence to support these claims. The project also found that officers appeared to be reluctant to work with their probationers to address family and employment obstacles. Yet when officers did assist their probationers, their work appeared to supplement the efforts of the probationers and to be associated with greater rates of success (Table 9.2b, Chapter 9). This reinforces the arguments put forward by Bottoms and McWilliams over twenty years ago (1979: 172–75) when they wrote that '. . . help may be more crime-reducing than treatment' (ibid.: 174). As such, more effort should be focused on how officers can support probationers address either their existing family problems, or attempting to prepare them for events like parenthood. Similarly, more effort should be focused on getting probationers into employment (Bridges 1998). This might entail a shift in the orientation of probation work. One probationer [065], when asked what would prevent him from reoffending, replied:

> Something to do with self-progression. Something to show people what they are capable of doing. I thought that that was what [my officer] should be about. It's finding people's abilities and nourishing and making them work for those things. Not very consistent with going back on what they have done wrong and trying to work out why – 'cause it's all going around on what's *happened* – what you've already been punished for – why not go forward into something . . . For instance, you might be good at writing – push that forward, progress that, rather than saying 'well look, why did you kick that bloke's head in? Do you think we should go back into anger management courses?' when all you want to be is a writer. Does that make any sense to you at all? *Yeah, yeah. To sum it up, you're saying you should look forwards not back.* Yeah. I know that you do have to look back to a certain extent to make sure that you don't end up like that [again]. The whole order seems to be about going back and back and back. There doesn't seem to be much 'forward'.

In other words, probation should assess what people require in their lives to ensure that they stop offending and then attempt to produce these features in their lives in such a way that they do actually stop offending. This might mean, for example, officers assessing whether a probationer's family offers him or her an avenue towards desistance (see Chapter 9). Of course, such efforts should be addressed in the contexts in which the probationer is living.

Increasing individuals' social capital will probably ultimately mean providing them with legitimate employment, which will in turn help to foster the sorts of ties and social contacts which allow for the development of social capital. It is unclear exactly how well probation services will be able to influence local economic conditions. The suggestion made earlier, that probation services develop in some way employment schemes in which they are able to offer probationers work rather than referring them to other agencies, may be only one amongst a number of solutions. Other possible solutions would involve concerted efforts aimed at reinvesting in some of the most deprived and crime-ridden inner-city areas.

These suggestions entail a further point. Namely, a step back from the *exclusive* focus on cognitive behavioural work which has dominated the probation work and 'What Works?' agendas in recent years. As Rex (1999: 373) has correctly noted, even the original architects of such programmes saw them as *complementing* the social and economic problems faced by probationers. This is not to suggest that cognitive behavioural work is to be abandoned but, rather, that whilst it correctly focuses on increasing probationers' human capital, it is unable to address the wider social contexts in which these probationers live and as such is unable to address such social and economic needs. What is required is a research project which attempts to 'fuse' together developments in individual cognitive abilities and changes in their social contexts.

The current project has suggested that probation supervision 'works' indirectly through allowing the probationer's life to develop positively. Ensuring how best to enable those developments to occur and designing working practices which will enable probation officers to intervene more readily should form the next stage of research into probation effectiveness.

Notes

1 Because the trends which emerged from officers' and probationers' reports of the relationships between facing obstacles, overcoming these obstacles and social contexts were very similar (see Figures 7.1, 7.2, 9.1 and 9.2), we concentrate here on the probationers' reports.
2 These measures are summations of the social circumstances which probationers reported were 'problems'. Those with fewer than two problematic

social circumstances were classified as having good social contexts, whilst those with three or more as having poor social contexts.

3 The ultimate test of this is to try to imagine what probation supervision would 'look like' if probationers were not in the community. What would officers attempt to 'do' with those they supervised? What would be discussed during supervisions? What would the goals of such a probation order be? Trying to conceptualise probation as separate from 'the community' is like trying to imagine imprisonment without the loss of liberty.

4 Living with one's parents has been found to act as a protective factor against offending for males – see, for example, Graham and Bowling (1995).

5 These processes should not be thought of as being either irreversible or uniformly distributed.

6 In informal conservations undertaken during the fieldwork for the project, several probation officers expressed their opinions that 'one of the best things we could do to help these young lads is to start a dating agency'. Clearly impractical, but nevertheless interesting to note in the light of the some of the findings reported above.

7 If this sounds familiar to historians of the probation service, this may be because many of the precursors of probation supervision placed an emphasis on providing offenders with suitable employment – see, for example, Bochel (1976: 4).

8 Although, see the New Deal for Communities programme, interestingly a project being run by the Department of the Environment, Transport and the Regions project, rather than the Home Office.

9 Haines' point underlines the earlier comments regarding the development of social capital. Unemployed people living in areas in which unemployment is rife will have fewer chances of gaining work through friends' and neighbours' contacts.

Appendix

Table A1: Variables associated with desistance from logistic regression analyses

	Beta	Df	Sig		Beta	Df	Sig
Probationers				**Officers**			
Had prison previously	−1.1118	1	.0028	—			
Previous violent conviction	−1.0341	1	.0067	—			
Previous theft conviction	−1.4250	1	.0004	—			
Previous other conviction	−.8247	1	.0253	—			
Previous no. of convictions				—			
No previous convictions		2	.0028	—			
1–3 previous convictions	−1.2069	1	.0834	—			
+4 previous convictions	−2.0477	1	.0017	—			
OGRS				—			
OGRS (0–25%)		3	.0177	—			
OGRS (26–50%)	−.7620	1	.3552	—			
OGRS (51–75%)	.2768	1	.7613	—			
OGRS (76–100%)	−1.4182	1	.0891	—			

Variable		df	Sig.
—			
Employment problem (SWP1)	−1.1471	1	.0023
—			
Depressed (SWP1)	−.8589	1	.0175
Accommodation problem (SWP3)	−1.0217	1	.0451
—			
Alcohol problems (SWP3)	−1.3115	1	.0221
—			
Total problems (SWP1)	−.2423	1	.0174
Total problems (SWP2)	−.2079	1	.0250
Total problems (SWP3)	−.3078	1	.0271
—			
Accommodation and employment instability	−.9808	1	.0373
Probation Impact (SWP2)[1]	.5236	1	.0188
Motivation–expectation			
Confidents		2	.0216
Optimists	−.3589	1	.4450
Pessimists	−1.1921	1	.0057

Variable		df	Sig.
—			
—			
Drug problem (at offence)	−.7688	1	.0262
Accommodation problem (SWP1)	−.8472	1	.0190
—			
Drug problem (SWP1)	−.7353	1	.0466
Employment problem (SWP2)	−.8057	1	.0209
Drug problem (SWP2)	−1.1894	1	.0021
Peer group problem (SWP2)	−1.1827	1	.0018
—			
Employment problem (SWP3)	−.9371	1	.0173
Family problem (SWP3)	−1.2199	1	.0028
—			
Drug problems (SWP3)	−1.6441	1	.0008
Peer group problems (SWP3)	−1.0426	1	.0220
Depressed (SWP3)	−.7598	1	.0442
Total problems (SWP1)	−.1935	1	.0260
Total problems (SWP2)	−.2315	1	.0032
Total problems (SWP3)	−.2364	1	.0029
Employment Instability	−.9079	1	.0329
Accommodation Instability	−1.1715	1	.0088
Accommodation and employment instability	−1.6364	1	.0009
—			
Motivation–expectation			
Confidents		2	.0536
Optimists	−.6997	1	.0931
Pessimists	−.9381	1	.0243

Notes

1 Probation Impact Scales were developed by summating three questions asked of officers and probationers at sweeps two and three. These asked whether the officer had said or done anything that would be helpful in keeping the probationer out of trouble in the future; probation supervision had helped the probationer stay out of trouble; and whether the probationer had learnt anything whilst on probation. The alpha coefficients for these questions were sufficiently high for them to be summated and used as a scale, and were officers, sweep two: .6324; officers, sweep three: .6158; probationers, sweep two: .7025; probationers, sweep three: .4619. These scales were positively correlated (officer sweep two/probationer sweep two: .289; Spearman's $p = .002$, officer sweep three/probationer sweep three: .211; Spearman's $p = .033$).

References

Ackerley, E., Soothill, K. and Francis, B. (1998) *When Do Sex Offenders Stop Offending? Research Bulletin* 39. London: Home Office Research and Statistics Directorate, HMSO.

Adams, K. (1997) Developmental aspects of adult crime. In Thornberry, T. (ed.) *Developmental Theories of Crime and Delinquency*. London: Transaction Press.

Andrews, D. (1989) Recidivism is predictable and can be influenced. *Focus on Correctional Research* 1(2): 11–18.

Appleton, C. and Roberts, C. (1999) *Corby Probation Team, Northampton Probation Service Effective Practice Project: A Report of The Findings*. Unpublished PSU report, University of Oxford.

Bailey, R. (1995) Helping offenders as an element of justice. In Ward, D. and Lacey, M. (eds.) *Probation: Working for Justice*. London: Whiting & Brich.

Bank, L., Patterson, G.R. and Reid, J.B. (1987) Delinquency prevention through the training of parents in family management. *The Behaviour Analyst* 10: 75–82.

Barclay, G. (1990) The peak age of known offending by males. *Home Office Research Bulletin* 28: 20–23.

Barnea, A., Rahav, G. and Teichman, M. (1987) The reliability and consistency of self-reports on substance use in a longitudinal study. *British Journal of Addiction* 82: 891–98.

Barr, H. and O'Leary, E. (1966) *Trends and Regional Comparisons in Probation. Home Office Research Unit Report* 8. London: HMSO.

Bean, P. (1976) *Rehabilitation and Deviance*. London: Routledge.

Blaxter, M. (1990) *Health and Lifestyle*. London: Routledge.

Blumstein, A., Cohen, J. and Farrington, D. (1988) Criminal career research: its value for criminology. *Criminology* 26(1): 1–35.

Blumstein, A., Cohen, J., Roth, J.A. and Visher, C.A. (eds.) (1986) *Criminal Careers and 'Career Criminals'*. Washington, DC: National Academy Press (two volumes).

Bochel, D. (1976) *Probation and After-Care*. Edinburgh: Scottish Academic Press.

Boswell, G. (1996) The essential skills of probation work. In May, T. and Vass, A. (eds.) *Working with Offenders*. London: Sage.

Bottoms, A. and McWilliams, W. (1979) A non-treatment paradigm for probation practice. *British Journal of Social Work* 9(2): 159–202.

Bowling, B. (1993) Racial harassment and the process of victimisation. *British Journal of Criminology* 33(2): 231–50.

Bridges, A. (1998) *Increasing the Employability of Offenders. Probation Studies Unit Report* 5.

Brown, I. (1998) Successful probation practice. In Faulkner, D. and Gibbs, A. (eds.) *New Politics, New Probation? Probation Studies Unit Report* 6. Oxford: Centre for Criminological Research, University of Oxford.

Brownlee, I. (1995) Intensive probation with young adult offenders. *British Journal of Criminology* 35(40): 599–612.

Bryman, A. (1984) The debate about quantitative and qualitative research: a question of method or epistemology?. *British Journal of Sociology* 35(1): 75–92.

Burnett, R. (1992) *The Dynamics of Recidivism*. Oxford: Centre for Criminological Research, University of Oxford.

Burnett, R. (1994) The odds of going straight: offenders own predictions. In *Sentencing, Quality and Risk: Proceedings of the 10th Annual Conference on Research and Information in the Probation Service*. University of Loughborough, Midlands Probation Training Consortium, Birmingham.

Burnett, R. (2000) Understanding criminal careers through a series of in-depth interviews. *Offender Programs Report* 4(1).

Bushway, S., Piquero, A., Boidy, L., Cauffman, E. and Mazerolle, P., (1999) An empirical framework for studying desistance as a process desistance. *Criminology* 39(2): 496–515.

Byrne, D. (1998) *Complexity Theory and the Social Sciences*. London: Routledge.

Caddle, D. (1991) *Parenthood Training for Young Offenders: An Evaluation of Courses in Young Offender Institutions. Research and Planning Unit Paper* 63. London: Home Office, HMSO.

Capaldi, D and Patterson, G. (1987) An approach to the problem of recruitment and retention rates in longitudinal research. *Behavioural Assessment* 9: 169–77.

Chapman, T. (1995) Creating a culture of change: a case study of a car crime project in Belfast. In McGuire, J. (ed.) *What Works: Reducing Reoffending*. Chichester: Wiley.

Chylicki, P. (1992) To cease with crime: pathways out of criminal careers. Unpublished PhD. thesis, Department of Sociology, Lund University, Sweden.

Coleman, J.S. (1988) Social capital in the creation of human capital. *American Journal of Sociology* 94 (Suppl): s95–s120.

Coleman, J.S. (1990) *Foundations of Social Theory*. London: Belknap Press.

Cordray, S. and Polk, K. (1983) The implications of respondent loss in panel studies of deviant behaviour. *Journal of Research in Crime and Delinquency* 20: 214–42.

Cromwell, P.F., Olson, J.N. and Avary, D.W. (1991) *Breaking and Entering*. London: Sage.

Crow, I. (1996) Employment, training and offending. In Drakeford, M. and Vanstone, M. (eds.) *Beyond Offending Behaviour*. Aldershot: Ashgate.

Crow, I. (2000) Evaluating initiatives in the community. In Jupp, V. *et al.* (eds.) *Doing Criminological Research*. London: Sage.

Cusson, M. and Pinsonneault, P. (1986) The decision to give up crime. In Cornish, D.B. and Clarke, R.V. (eds.) *The Reasoning Criminal*. Springer-Verlag: New York.

Dale, M.W. (1976) Barriers to the rehabilitation of ex-offenders. *Crime and Delinquency* 22(3): 322–37.

Davies, M. (1969) *Probationers in Their Social Environment. Home Office Research Unit Report* 2. London: HMSO.

Ditton, J. (1977) *Part-time Crime: An Ethnography of Fiddling and Pilferage*. London: Macmillan.

Elder, G.H. (1985) Perspectives on the life-course. In Elder, G.H. (ed.) *Life-Course Dynamics*. Ithaca, NY: Cornell University Press.

Elliott, D. (1989) Improving self-reported measures of delinquency. In Klein, M.W. (ed.) *Cross-National Research in Self-Reported Crime and Delinquency*. Dordrecht: Kluwer Academic.

Elliott, D. (1994) Serious violent offenders: onset, developmental course and termination – American Society of Criminology 1993 Presidential Address. *Criminology* 32: 1–22.

Elliott, D. and Menard, S. (1996) Delinquent friends and delinquent behaviour: temporal and developmental patterns. In Hawkins, J.D. (ed.) *Delinquency and Crime: Current Theories*. Cambridge: Cambridge University Press.

Fagan, J. (1989) Cessation of family violence: deterrence and dissuasion. In Ohlin, L. and Tonry, M. (eds.) *Crime and Justice: An Annual Review of Research. Vol. 11*.

Farrall, S. (2000) Introduction. In Farrall, S. (ed.) *The Termination of Criminal Careers*. Aldershot: Ashgate.

Farrall, S. (2002) Long-term absences from probation: officers' and probationers' accounts. *Howard Journal of Criminal Justice* 41(3): 263–78.

Farrall, S. (n.d.) Self, officer and officially recorded offending on probation: (how) are they related?. Unpublished paper.

Farrall, S. and Bowling, B. (1999) Structuration, human development and desistance from crime. *British Journal of Criminology* 39(2): 252–67.

Farrington, D.P. (1977) The effects of public labelling. *British Journal of Criminology* 17(2): 112–25.

Farrington, D.P. (1989) Self-reported and official offending from adolescence to adulthood. In Klein, M.W. (ed.) *Cross-National Research in Self-Reported Crime and Delinquency*. Dordrecht: Kluwer Academic.

Farrington, D.P. (1992a) Criminal career research in the UK. *British Journal of Criminology* 32(4): 521–36.

Farrington, D.P. (1992b) Juvenile delinquency. In Coleman, J. (ed.) *The School Years*. London: Routledge.

Farrington, D.P. (1997) Human development and criminal careers. In Maguire, M. *et al.* (eds.) *The Oxford Handbook of Criminology* (2nd edn). Oxford: Clarendon Press.

Farrington, D.P., Gallagher, B., Morley, L., St Ledger, R.J. and West, D.J. (1986) Unemployment, school leaving and crime. *British Journal of Criminology* 26(4): 335–56.

Farrington, D. and Hawkins, J.D. (1991) Predicting participation, early onset and later persistence in officially recorded offending. *Criminal Behaviour and Mental Health* 1(1): 1–33.

Farrington, D.P., Osborn, S.G. and West, D. (1978) The persistence of labelling effects. *British Journal of Criminology* 18(3): 277–84.

Feld, S.L. and Straus, M.A. (1989) Escalation and desistance of wife assault. *Criminology* 27: 141–61.

Feld, S.L. and Straus, M.A. (1990) Escalation and desistance of wife assault. In Straus, M.A. and Gelles, R.J. (eds.) *Physical Violence in American Families: Risk Factors and Adaptations to Violence in 8,145 Families*. New Brunswick, NJ: Transaction Publishers.

Flood-Page, C., Campbell, S., Harrington, V. and Miller, J. (2000) *Youth Crime: Findings From the 1998/99 Youth Lifestyles Survey. Home Office Research Study.* 209. London: HMSO.

Folkard, S. Fowles, A.J., McWilliams, B.C., McWilliams, W., Smith, D.D., Smith, D.E. and Walmsley, G. (1974) *IMPACT: Intensive Matched Probation and After-Care Treatment. Home Office Research Study* 24. London: HMSO.

Folkard, S., Lyon, K., Carver, M.M. and O'Leary, E. (1966) *Probation Research: A Preliminary Report. Home Office Research Unit Report* 7. London: HMSO.

Folkard, S., Smith, D.E., Smith, D.D. and Walmsley, G. (1976) *IMPACT: Intensive Matched Probation and After-Care Treatment, Volume II: The Results of the Experiment. Home Office Research Study* 36. London: HMSO.

Gendreau, P. (1996) The principles of effective intervention with offenders. In Harland, A. (ed.) *Choosing Correctional Options that Work*. London: Sage.

Giele, J.Z. and Elder, G.H. (eds.) (1998) *Methods of Life Course Research*. London: Sage.

Gottfredson, M. and Hirschi, T. (1986) The true value of lambda would appear to be zero: an essay on career criminals, criminal careers, selective incapacitation, cohort studies and related topics. *Criminology* 24(2): 213–34.

Gottfredson, M. and Hirschi, T. (1990) *A General Theory of Crime*. Stanford, CA: Stanford University Press.

Gottfredson, S.D. and Taylor, R.B. (1988) Community contexts and criminal offenders. In Hope, T. and Shaw, M. (eds.) *Communities and Crime Reduction*. London: HMSO.

Graham, J. and Bowling, B. (1995) *Young People and Crime. Home Office, HORS* 145. London: HMSO.

Guidry, L.S. (1975) Use of a covert punishment contingency in compulsive stealing. *Journal of Behaviour Therapy and Experimental Psychiatry* 6: 169.

Hagan, J. (1994) *Crime and Disrepute.* London: Pine Forge Press.

Hagan, J. (1997) Crime and capitalization: toward a developmental theory of street crime in America. In Thornberry, T. (ed.) *Developmental Theories of Crime and Delinquency.* New Brunswick, NJ: Transaction Press.

Hagan, J. and McCarthy, B. (1997) *Mean Streets.* Cambridge: Cambridge University Press.

Haines, K. (1990) *After-Care for Released Offenders: A Review of the Literature.* Cambridge: Institute of Criminology, Cambridge University.

Haines, K. (1999) Crime is a social problem. *European Journal on Criminal Policy and Research* 7: 263–75.

Harland, A. (ed.) (1995) *Choosing Correctional Options that Work.* London: Sage.

Haslewood-Pocsik, I. and Roberts, C. (1999a) Humberside Probation Service Effective Practice Project: a report of the findings. Unpublished PSU Report, University of Oxford.

Haslewood-Pocsik, I. and Roberts, C. (1999b) Northumbria Probation Service Effective Practice Project: a report of the findings. Unpublished PSU Report, University of Oxford.

Haslewood-Pocsik, I. and Roberts, C. (1999c) The West Midlands Probation Service and Probation Studies Unit Demonstration Project: using the ACE system. Unpublished PSU Report, University of Oxford.

Hazaleus, S.L. and Deffenbacher, J.L. (1986) Relaxation and cognitive treatments of anger. *Journal of Consulting and Clinical Psychology* 54: 222–26.

Hedderman, C. (1998) A critical assessment of probation research. *Research Bulletin* 39: 1–7.

Henry, S. (1978) *The Hidden Economy: The Context and Control of Borderline Crime.* Oxford: Martin Robertson.

Hirschi, T. and Gottfredson, M. (1995) Control theory and the life-course perspective. *Studies on Crime And Crime Prevention* 4(2): 131–42.

Hogan, D.P. and Astone, N.M. (1986) The transition to adulthood. *Annual Review of Sociology* 12: 109–30.

Home Office (1995) *The Criminal Careers of those Born Between 1953 and 1973. Home Office Bulletin* 14/95. London: Home Office.

Home Office (1996) *Guidance for the Probation Service on the Offender Group Reconviction Scale (OGRS). Home Office Circular* 63/1996. London: Home Office.

Home Office (1999) *Digest Four.* London: Home Office.

Hood, R. (1963/1967) Research on the effectiveness of punishments and treatments. In *Collected Studies in Criminological Research. Vol. 1.* Council of Europe.

Hood, R. and Sparks, R. (1970) *Key Issues in Criminology.* London: Wiedenfeld & Nicolson.

Horney, J., Osgood, D.W. and Haen Marshall, I. (1995) Criminal careers in the short term: intra-individual variability in crime and its relation to local life circumstances. *American Sociological Review* 60: 655–73.

Hughes, M. (1997) An exploratory study of young adult black and latino males and the factors facilitating their decisions to make positive behavioural changes. *Smith College Studies in Social Work* 67(3): 401–14.

Hughes, M. (1998) Turning points in the lives of young inner-city men forgoing destructive criminal behaviours: a qualitative study. *Social Work Research* 22: 143–51.

Irwin, J. (1970) *The Felon*. Englewood Cliffs, NJ: Prentice-Hall.

Jamieson, J., McIvor, G. and Murray, C. (1999) *Understanding Offending among Young People*. Edinburgh: HMSO.

Johnson, J.E. (1979) *Juvenile Delinquency and its Origins*. Cambridge: Cambridge University Press.

Jones, P. (1996) Risk prediction in criminal justice. In Harland, A. (ed.) *Choosing Correctional Options that Work*. London: Sage.

Knight, B.J., Osborn, S.G. and West, D.J. (1977) Early marriage and criminal tendency in males. *British Journal of Criminology* 17(4): 348–60.

Knight, B.J. and West, D.J. (1975) Temporary and continuing delinquency. *British Journal of Criminology* 15(1): 43–50.

Kratzer, L. and Hodgins, S. (1999) A typology of offenders: a test of Moffitt's theory among males and females from childhood to age thirty. *Criminal Behaviour and Mental Health* 9: 57–73.

Laub, J., Nagin, D. and Sampson, R. (1998) Trajectories of change in criminal offending: good marriages and the desistance process. *American Sociological Review* 63: 225–38.

Laub, J.H. and Sampson, R.J. (1993) Turning points in the life course: why change matters to the study of crime. *Criminology* 31(3): 301–25.

Laub, J.H. and Sampson, R.J. (2001) Understanding desistance from crime. In Tonry, M. (ed.) *Crime and Justice: An Annual Review of Research. Vol. 26.*

Laub, J., Sampson, R., Corbett, R. and Smith, J. (1995) The public policy implications of a life-course perspective on crime. In Barlow, H. (ed.) *Crime and Public Policy*. Oxford: Westview.

Lawson, L.S. (1983) Alcoholism. In Hersen, M. (ed.) *Outpatient Behaviour Therapy: A Clinical Guide*. New York: Grune & Stratton.

Leibrich, J. (1993) *Straight to the Point: Angles on Giving up Crime*. Otago, New Zealand: University of Otago Press.

Leibrich, J. (1996) The role of shame in going straight: a study of former offenders. In Galaway, B. and Hudson, J. (eds.) *Restorative Justice*. Monsey, NJ: Criminal Justice Press.

Lipsey, M. (1995) What do we learn from 400 research studies on the effectiveness of treatment with juvenile delinquents? In McGuire, J. (ed.) *What Works: Reducing Reoffending.* Chichester: Wiley.

Lloyd, C., Mair, G. and Hough, M. (1994) *Explaining Reconviction Rates: A Critical Analysis. Home Office Research and Planning Unit Report* 136. London: HMSO.

Loeber, R. and LeBlanc, M. (1990) Toward a developmental criminology. In Tonry, M. and Morris, N. (eds.) *Crime and Justice. Vol. 12.* Chicago, IL: University of Chicago Press.

Loeber, R., Stouthamer-Loeber, M., Van Kammen, W. and Farrington, D.P. (1991) Initiation, escalation and desistance in juvenile offending and their correlates. *Journal of Criminal Law and Criminology* 82(1): 36–82.

Lösel, F. (1995) The efficacy of correctional treatment: a review and synthesis of meta-evaluations. In McGuire, J. (ed.) *What Works: Reducing Reoffending.* Chichester: Wiley.

MacKenzie, D.L., Browning, K., Skroban, S.B., and Smith, D.A. (1999) The impact of probation on the criminal activities of offenders. *Journal of Research in Crime and Delinquency* 36(4): 423–53.

Mair, G., Lloyd, C. and Hough, M. (1997) The limitations of reconviction rates. In Mair, G. (ed.) *Evaluating the effectiveness of community penalties.* Aldershot: Avebury.

Mair, G., Lloyd, C., Nee, C. and Sibbitt, R. (1994) *Intensive Probation in England and Wales: An Evaluation. Home Office Research Study* 133. London: HMSO.

Mair, G. and May, C. (1997) *Offenders on Probation. Home Office Research Study* 167. London: HMSO.

Mair, G. and Nee, C. (1992) Day centre reconviction rates. *British Journal of Criminology* 32(3): 329–39.

Manchester City Council (1998) *Crime and Disorder: An Audit of Problems and Priorities for Manchester.* Manchester: Community Safety Team, Manchester City Council.

Martinson, R. (1974) What works? Questions and answers about prison reform. *The Public Interest* 35: 22–54.

Maruna, S. (1997) Going straight: desistance from crime and life narratives of reform. *The Narrative Study of Lives* 5: 59–93.

Maruna, S. (2000a) Desistance from crime and offender rehabilitation: a tale of two research literatures. *Offender Programs Report* 4(1).

Maruna, S. (2000b) Criminology, desistance and the psychology of the stranger. In Canter, D. and Alison, L.J. (eds.) *Beyond Profiling: Developments in Investigative Psychology.* Aldershot: Dartmouth Books.

Matthews, R. and Pitts, J. (2000) Rehabilitation, recidivism and realism: evaluating violence reduction programmes in prison. In Jupp, V. *et al.* (eds.) *Doing Criminological Research.* London: Sage.

May, C. (1999) *Explaining Reconviction Following a Community Sentence: The Role of Social Factors. Home Office Research Study* 192. London: HMSO.

McConville, M., Sanders, A. and Leng, R. (1991) *The Case for the Prosecution*. London: Routledge.

McDougall, C., Barnett, R.M., Ashurst, B. and Willis, B. (1987) Cognitive control of anger. In McGurk, B.J. *et al.* (eds.) *Applying Psychology to Imprisonment: Theory and Practice*. London: HMSO.

McGuire, J. (ed.) (1995) *What Works: Reducing Reoffending*. Chichester: Wiley.

McGuire, J. and Priestly, P. (1995) Reviewing 'what works': past, present and future. In McGuire, J. (ed.) *What Works: Reducing Reoffending*. Chichester: Wiley.

Meisenhelder, T. (1977) An exploratory study of exiting from criminal careers. *Criminology* 15(3): 319–34.

Meisenhelder, T. (1982) Becoming normal: certification as a stage in exiting from crime. *Deviant Behaviour* 3: 137–53.

Mischkowitz, R. (1994) Desistance from a delinquent way of life? In Weitekamp, E.G.M. and Kerner, H.J. (eds.) *Cross-National Longitudinal Research on Human Development and Criminal Behaviour*. Dordrecht: Kluwer Academic.

Moffitt, T. (1993) 'Life-course persistent' and 'adolescent-limited' antisocial behaviour: a developmental taxonomy. *Psychological Review* 100: 674–701.

Moffitt, T.E. (1997) Adolescence-limited and life-course persistent offending: a complementary pair of developmental theories. In Thornberry, T. (ed.) *Developmental Theories of Crime and Delinquency*. London: Transaction Press.

Mulvey, E.P. and Aber, M. (1988) Growing out of delinquency: development and desistance. In Jenkins, R.L. and Brown, W.K. (eds.) *The Abandonment of Delinquent Behaviour: Promoting the Turnaround*. New York: Praeger.

Mulvey, E.P. and La Rosa, J.F. (1986) Delinquency cessation and adolescent development: preliminary data. *American Journal of Orthopsychiatry* 56(2): 212–24.

Murray, C. and Cox, L. (1979) *Beyond Probation: Juvenile Corrections and the Chronic Delinquent*. London: Sage.

National Standards (1995) London: Home Office.

Newburn, T. (1997) Youth, crime and justice. In Maguire, M. *et al.* (eds.) *The Oxford Handbook of Criminology* (2nd edn). Oxford: Clarendon Press.

O'Donnell, C.R., Lydgate, T. and Fo, W.S.O. (1979) The buddy system: review and follow-up. *Child Behaviour Therapy* 1: 161–69.

O'Donnell, I. and Edgar, K. (1996) *The Extent and Dynamics of Victimisation in Prisons*. Oxford: Centre for Criminological Research, University of Oxford.

Oldfield, M. (1996) *The Kent Reconviction Survey*. Kent Probation Service.

Osborn, S.G. (1980) Moving home, leaving London and delinquent trends. *British Journal of Criminology* 20(1): 54–61.

Osborn, S.G. and West, D.J. (1979) Marriage and delinquency: a postscript. *British Journal of Criminology* 18(3): 254–56.

Osler, A. (1995) *Introduction to the Probation Service*. Winchester: Waterside Press.

Ouimet, M. and Le Blanc, M. (1996) The role of life experiences in the continuation of the adult criminal career. *Criminal Behaviour and Mental Health* 6: 73–97.

Palmer, T. (1996) Programmatic and non-programmatic aspects of successful interventions. In Harland, A. (ed.) *Choosing Correctional Options that Work*. London: Sage.

Parker, H. (1976) Boys will be men: brief adolescence in a down-town neighbourhood. In Mungham, G. and Pearson, G. (eds.) *Working Class Youth Culture*. London: Routledge.

Pawson, R. (1997) Evaluation methodology: back to basics. In Mair, G. (ed.) *Evaluating the Effectiveness of Community Penalties*. Aldershot: Avebury.

Pawson, R. and Tilley, N. (1994) What works in evaluation research? *British Journal of Criminology* 34(3): 291–306.

Pawson, R. and Tilley, N. (1996) What's crucial in evaluation research: a reply to Bennett. *British Journal of Criminology* 36(4): 574–78.

Pawson, R. and Tilley, N. (1997) *Realistic Evaluation*. London: Sage.

Petersilia, J. (1998) Probation and parole. In Tonry, M. (ed.) *The Handbook of Crime and Punishment*. Oxford: Oxford University Press.

Pezzin, L.E. (1995) Earning prospects, matching effects and the decision to terminate a criminal career. *Journal of Quantitative Criminology* 11(1): 29–50.

Phillpotts, G. and Lancucki, L. (1979) *Previous Convictions, Sentence and Reconviction. Home Office Research Study* 53. London: HMSO.

Priestly, P., McGuire, M., Flegg, J., Hemsley, M., Welham, D. and Barnitt, R. (1984) *Social Skills in Prisons and the Community: Problem Solving for Offenders*. London: Routledge.

Quigley, B.M. and Leonard, K.E. (1996) Desistance of husband aggression in the early years of marriage. *Violence and Victims* 11: 355–70.

Radzinowicz, L. (ed.) (1958) *The Results of Probation*. London: Macmillan.

Rand, A. (1987) Transitional life events and desistance from delinquency and crime. In Wolfgang, M.E. *et al.* (eds.) *From Boy to Man, from Delinquency to Crime*. Chicago, IL: University of Chicago Press.

Raynor, R. (1998) Attitudes, social problems and reconvictions in the 'STOP' probation experiment. *Howard Journal of Criminal Justice* 37(1): 1–15.

Raynor, P. and Vanstone, M. (1997) *Straight Thinking on Probation (STOP). Probation Studies Unit Report* 4. Oxford: University of Oxford, Centre for Criminological Research.

Rex, S. (1998) Promoting effective supervisory relationships. In Faulkner, D. and Gibbs, A. (eds.) *New Politics, New Probation? Probation Studies Unit Report* 6. Oxford: Centre for Criminological Research, University of Oxford.

Rex, S. (1999) Desistance from offending: experiences of probation. *Howard Journal of Criminal Justice*.

Ross, M.W., Stowe, A., Wodak, A. and Gold, J. (1995) Reliability of interview responses of injecting drug users. *Journal of Addictive Diseases* 14(2): 1–12.

Ross, R.R. and Ross, R.D. (1995) *Thinking Straight*. Ottowa: Air Training and Publications.

Sampson, R.J. and Laub, J.H. (1990) Crime and deviance over the life-course: the salience of adult social bonds. *American Sociological Review* 55: 609–27.

Sampson, R.J. and Laub, J.H. (1993) *Crime in the Making: Pathways and Turning Points through Life*. London: Harvard University Press.

Sampson, R.J. and Laub, J.H. (1995) Understanding variability in lives through time: contributions of life-course criminology. *Studies on Crime And Crime Prevention* 4(2): 143–58.

Sampson, R.J. and Laub, J.H. (1997) A life-course theory of cumulative disadvantage and the stability of delinquency. In Thornberry, T. (ed.) *Developmental Theories of Crime and Delinquency*. London: Transaction.

Sarno, C., Hearden, I., Hedderman, C., Hough, M., Nee, C. and Herrington, V. (2000) *Working their Way out of offending. Home Office Research Study* 218. London: Home Office.

Sarno, C., Hough, M., Nee, C. and Herrington, V. (1999) *Probation Employment Schemes in Inner London and Surrey – An Evaluation. Home Office. Research Findings* 89. London: Home Office.

Shover, N. (1983) The later stages of ordinary property offender careers. *Social Problems* 31(2): 208–18.

Shover, N. (1985) *Aging Criminals*. Beverley Hills, CA: Sage.

Shover, N. (1996) *Great Petenders: Pursuits and Careers of Persistent Thieves*. Oxford: Westview.

Shover, N. and Henderson, B. (1995) Repressive crime control and male persistent thieves. In Barlow, H. (ed.) *Crime and Public Policy*. Oxford: Westview.

Shover, N. and Thompson, C. (1992) Age, differential expectations and crime desistance. *Criminology* 30(1): 89–104.

Simon, F. (1971) *Prediction Methods in Criminology. Home Office Research Unit Report* 7. London: HMSO.

Smith, D.A., Visher, C.A. and Jarjoura, G.R. (1991) Dimensions of delinquency. *Journal of Research on Crime and Delinquency* 28(1): 6–32.

Sommers, I., Baskin, D.R. and Fagan, J. (1994) Getting out of the life: crime desistance by female street offenders. *Deviant Behaviour* 15(2): 125–49.

Sparks, R., Bottoms, A. and Hay, W. (1996) *Prisons and the Problem of Order*. Oxford: Clarendon Press.

Sparks, R., Genn, H. and Dodd, D. (1977) *Surveying Victims*. Chichester: Wiley.

Stewart, J., Smith, D. and Stewart, G. (1994) *Understanding Offending Behaviour*. Harlow: Longman.

Stone, N. (1998) *A Companion Guide to Enforcement*. Ilkley: Owen Wells.

Tarling, R. (1993) *Analysing Offending*. London: HMSO.

Thornberry, T. (1987) Toward an interactional theory of delinquency. *Criminology* 25: 863–91.

Thornberry, T. (1997) Introduction: some advantages of developmental and life-course perspectives for the study of crime and delinquency. In Thornberry, T. (ed.) *Developmental Theories of Crime and Delinquency*. London: Transaction Press.

Thorogood, M., Arscott, A., Walls, P., Dunn, N.R. and Mann, R.D. (forthcoming) Matched controls in a case-control study: does matching by doctors' list mean matching by relative deprivation? *International Journal of Social Research Methodology*.

Tilley, N. (2000) Doing realistic evaluation of criminal justice. In Jupp, V. *et al.* (eds.) *Doing Criminological Research*. London: Sage.

Tolman, R.M., Edleson, J.L. and Fendrich, M. (1996) The applicability of the theory of planned behavior to abusive men's cessation of violent behavior. *Violence and Victims* 119(4): 341–54.

Trasler, G. (1979) Delinquency, recidivism and desistance. *British Journal of Criminology* 19(4): 314–22.

Tunnell, K.D. (1992) *Choosing Crime*. Chicago, IL: Nelson-Hall Publishers.

Uggen, C. (2000) Work as a turning point in the life course of criminals: a duration model of age, employment and recidivism. *American Sociological Review* 67: 529–46.

Uggen, C. and Kruttschnitt, K. (1998) Crime in the breaking: gender differences in desistance. *Law and Society Review* 32(2): 339–66.

Uggen, C. and Piliavim, I. (1998) Asymmetrical causation and criminal desistance. *Journal of Criminal Law and Criminology* 88(4): 1399–422.

Ulmer, J.T. and Spencer, J.W. (1999) The contributions of an interactionist approach to research and theory on criminal careers. *Theoretical Criminology* 3(1): 95–124.

United Nations (1951) *Probation and Related Measures*. Document E/CN.5/230. New York: United Nations.

Wallace, C. (1986) From girls and boys to women and men: the social reproduction of gender roles in the transition from school to (un)employment. In Walker, S. and Barton, L. (eds.) *Youth, Unemployment and Schooling*. Milton Keynes: Open University Press.

Wallace, C. (1987) *For Richer, for Poorer: Growing up in and out of Work*. London: Tavistock.

Warr, M. (1998) Life-course transitions and desistance from crime. *Criminology* 36(2): 183–215.

Weis, J. (1986) Issues in the measurement of criminal careers. In Blumstein, A. *et al.* (eds.) *Criminal Careers and 'Career Criminals'*. Washington, DC: National Academy Press, Volume Two.

West, D.J. (1982) *Delinquency: It's Roots, Careers and Prospects*. London: Heinemann.

West, G.W. (1978) The short term careers of serious thieves. *Canadian Journal of Criminology* 20: 169–90.

Whitfield, D. (1998) *Introduction to the Probation Service*. Winchester: Waterside Press.

Wilkinson, J. (1997) The impact of Ilderton Motor Project on motor vehicle crime and offending. *British Journal of Criminology* 37(4): 568–81.

Williams, M. and May, T. (1996) *Introduction to the Philosophy of Social Research*. London: UCL Press.

Willis, A. (1986) Help and control in probation: an assessment of probation practice. In Pointing, J. (ed.) *Alternatives to Custody*. Oxford: Blackwell.

Wilson, W.J. (1991) Studying inner-city social dislocations: the challenge of public agenda research. *American Sociological Review* 56: 1–14.

Wolfgang, M.E., Figlio, R.M. and Sellin, T. (1972) *Delinquency in a Birth Cohort*. London: University of Chicago Press.

Worrall, A. (1997) *Punishment in the Community*. London: Longman.

Young, J. (1999) *The Exclusive Society*. London: Sage.

Index

Case index

This index allows the reader to follow the progress of specific probationers through the course of the book, and hence their time on probation. Where a case has been given a name, this too has been recorded.